D1603641

COGNITION, CONVENTION, AND COMMUNICATION

COGNITION, CONVENTION, AND COMMUNICATION,

Mark H. Bickhard

PRAEGER

PRAEGER SPECIAL STUDIES • PRAEGER SCIENTIFIC

Library of Congress Cataloging in Publication Data

Bickhard, Mark H
    Cognition, convention, and communication.

    Bibliography: p.
    Includes index.
    1. Interpersonal communication.
2. Psycholinguistics. 3. Cognition. 4. Social
systems. I. Title.
BF637.C45B52   153.6   80-20799 ✓
ISBN 0-03-056098-5

Published in 1980 by Praeger Publishers
CBS Educational and Professional Publishing
A Division of CBS, Inc.
521 Fifth Avenue, New York, New York 10017 U.S.A.

© 1980 by Praeger Publishers

0123456789   038   987654321

Printed in the United States of America

Dedicated to
Jack L. Bickhard and Ruby E. Bickhard

PREFACE

This book was first intended as a chapter in a book on basic psychological processes but soon grew into the major section of a second volume of that book. I decided to write an article outlining the major points of that language section, but there seemed to be no place to stop, and it ended up being far too long for an article. Finally I accepted the inevitable and expanded and revised that "article" into the present book.

This growth and momentum was due in part to my struggle with the general metatheoretical issues, in their myriad specific guises, discussed in the second chapter of this book. In particular, I was working within a strictly interactive conception of knowledge, which was my major focus at the time, and was trying to say a few words about language from that perspective. This led me into frequent and ever deepening confrontations with standard basic assumptions about language that would not fit the underlying interactive model of knowledge I was working with. Eventually, over several years, this yielded a different conceptualization of language, the one presented here. Only in retrospect did the metatheoretical necessities that forced that rather long and perplexing theoretical evolution become clear.

The book begins with a presentation of the metatheoretical understandings that were a primary fruit of its development. The substantive chapters of the book that follow trace the internal logic of the development of a model of language on an interactive knowing base. Thus, the organization of the presentation of the model reflects not only its internal conceptual dependencies but also something of the steps through which it was originally developed, hopefully with most of the missteps removed.

Being an exploration and development of its own internal logic, the model and its presentation tend to be somewhat self-contained. Connections with other literature are made primarily in the footnotes and discussion chapters at the ends of the major sections. The topics for these discussions were chosen partly by a careful and thoughtful selection process and partly by a pseudo-random haphazardness imposed by constraints on time and space. I would like to have included many more. Furthermore, the discussions are necessarily brief. Most have more the nature of short comments rather than thorough analyses and arguments, even though many could become books on their own. Nevertheless, they should help considerably in understanding the model's relationships to and consequences for other approaches and areas of study.

Undoubtedly, the model presented here is wrong (as are all models), though at this moment I do not know where or I would do something about it. Certainly it is incomplete; that I know all too well. But I am convinced that its basic direction is correct. At a mimimum, it is different in fundamental ways and, correspondingly, deserves attention. May its destruction, both critical and empirical, prove fruitful.

ACKNOWLEDGMENTS

In a long project it becomes impossible to do justice to the innumerable friends, colleagues, and acquaintances who contribute, directly and indirectly, to its progress and ultimate completion. To those I may overlook, I apologize; it is not from lack of appreciation. My gratitude and acknowledgments are due most especially to Robert G. Cooper for aid across the range of the physical, conceptual, and spiritual. Members of my department, both individually and collectively, have provided immeasurable and absolutely critical personal and political support. I would particularly like to mention Frank Richardson, Guy Manaster, Ollie Bown, Jack Reid, Gordon Anderson, Carl Hereford, Earl Jennings, Paul Kelley, Phil Powell, and Claire Weinstein. I have benefited greatly from discussions with members of the Center for Psychosocial Studies in Chicago: Ben Lee, Jim Wertsch, Barney Weissbourd, Maya Hickman, and Addison Stone. Other critical support has come from J. McVicker Hunt, Chet Lieb, Gene Gendlin, and Victor Yngve, and critical help from Tom Hoeffner, Amy Willis, Robert Campbell, Mike Richie, Jan Ford, Lee Ford, Catherine Cooper, and Ann van Kleeck. The development of the model has been partially supported by two University Research Institute (URI) small grants from The University of Texas at Austin. The foundational model out of which this model evolved has its own debts, some of which extend to the present. I would like to mention David Wiley, G. David McNeill, Carol Feldman, Wilbur Hass, Marlene Dixon, Sebastian Grossman, Jack Butler, Dan Freedman, Bob Marvin, Joseph Goguen, Starkey Duncan, Robert Levine, Karl Pribram, Joe Cobb, Barbara Kopp, Richard Kopp, Debby Salisbury, and, especially, Margaret Iwanage. Marian Morse has been the indefatigable wizard who has translated my drafts covered with insertions, deletions, and arrows into readable copy.

CONTENTS

COGNITION, CONVENTION, AND COMMUNICATION

1
PRELIMINARIES

PURPOSES

One of the primary purposes of this book is to present a
metatheoretical perspective for the study of mental phenomena.
Another is to present a specific model of communication within that
perspective. The metatheoretical perspective is a departure from
the approaches to mind that have been dominant in Western culture
since the pre-Socratic Greeks. The major historical precursors for
this departure extend back no more than a few centuries (for example,
Kant) and, in the case of language, no more than a few decades (for
example, J. L. Austin). I will argue that the classical approaches
are intrinsically untenable and that they form asymptotically limiting
cases of the favored perspective.

The model to be presented is primarily a model of communication and language. Communication is simultaneously a sociological
and a psychological phenomenon. It forms, in fact, the boundary of
emergence of the one from the other. The model presented is an
analysis of the nature of that emergence and of some of its consequences. Toward that end, critical foundations in both psychology
and sociology are also developed. These psychological and sociological models are also of potential interest independent of their foundational role for the communication model.

APPROACHES

Mode of Development

The development of this model proceeds by way of conceptual
analysis and explication. It is not a report of empirical findings nor

of empirical generalizations; instead, it is an examination of the conceptual framework within which such empirical studies and generalizations take place. In its method, then, the model is at the interface between psychology and sociology, on the one hand, and philosophy, on the other. It is an analysis of conceptual foundations.

Foundational studies have not been common in psychology for some time now, and, although that situation is changing, often they are still not appreciated or understood. In particular, it is commonly thought, under the influence of a degenerate logical positivism, that conceptual studies have no empirical content and, thus, are not relevant to science. This orientation, however, is in error in both of its major premises. First, a study with no empirical content can be relevant to science. If it could, then the philosophy of science in general would not be relevant to science, and, in particular, the logical positivism that gives rise to such premises would be self-contradictory. Second, and much more important for current purposes, foundational studies are always conceptual in nature and may, nevertheless, have quite impressive empirical and scientific content. This point is perhaps made most strongly with the example of the Theories of Relativity: their grounding in strictly conceptual analyses is well known, and, in the case of the General Theory, even the motivation was strictly conceptual; and their scientific relevance and empirical content are hardly to be denied. Far from being irrelevant, I would contend that good conceptual foundation studies are what psychology currently needs most.

Conceptual Ground

A conceptual analysis requires some system of concepts to be taken as primitive or given: a conceptual analysis must be in terms of other concepts, and the process must halt somewhere. Such conceptual grounds ideally have the virtues of precision and coherence and, when formalized, constitute an area of mathematics. Thus, for example, we have analysis as a formal system regarding quantity, algebra regarding discrete structure, and topology regarding continuous structure. The relevant conceptual area for this work is systems that engage in interactive processes; the relevant mathematics is abstract machine theory. Abstract machine theory is that part of mathematics devoted to interactive systems. Correspondingly, abstract machine theory forms the conceptual ground for the model to be presented.

The linkages that lead to that ground form a progression from action systems to control structures to machine theory. First, psychological communication systems are to be analyzed and differentiated within the category of general psychological action systems. Second, action systems are considered from within a mentalistic perspective, that is, action system conceptualizations are developed in terms of the mental structures and processes that constitute those systems. Third, mental structures are taken to be explicable as control structures, and mental processes as executions of those structures. Fourth and last, control structures and processes are taken to be explicable in terms of abstract machine theory. Thus, communicative action systems are analyzed within a control structure-based mentalism through conceptualizations that are explicable in terms of the mathematics of abstract machines.

An Issue of Ontology

The study of communication encounters an important issue concerning the nature of the subject matter. This issue arises because the study of communication has been dominated by the study of the primary means of communication, language, and the study of language has been restricted by a serious conceptual difficulty: a reification of language which has sundered it from its psychosocial framework. The subject matter has tended to be an idealization of language with seriously problematic relationships to the real world.

Linguistics has its historical origin in two millennia of pre-scriptivist approaches to language. [1] Classically, the prescriptive concern has been with what language ought to be and what ought to be said rather than with what language is and what is said. The concern, in fact, has often been one of preserving "good" language against the "degeneracies" of language change. Intrinsic to prescriptivism is an idealistic reification, around which the prescriptivist rules can be constructed; that which ought to be involves a timeless abstraction and idealization away from the actual variations and processes of that which is. My suggestion is that linguistics has dropped the prescriptivism but has not yet lost the idealistic reification. It has exchanged prescriptivism for descriptivism, but the focus of analysis is still a timeless idealization: the ideal speaker-hearer (Chomsky 1965).

The flaw in this focus is that to describe an idealization is to describe that which is created by the descriptions, for idealizations have no other existence. Thus, linguistics is the descriptive science of language, and language is that which linguistics describes: a pernicious circularity. There is, of course, an intuitive and traditional sense at least of the ability to recognize language, if not understand it, that informs and constrains those descriptions—language is a conceptual natural kind in any folk psychology—but the exploration of its nature has been prevented by the distraction of the idealization away from language as a manifestation of the actual psychosocial world.

For example, language cannot be usefully conceptualized independently of meaning. Meaning, in turn, can be conceptualized as an entity or property of psychosocial interaction, in which case linguistics properly becomes a part of the social psychology, and the circular idealization is eliminated. Or meaning can be conceptualized as an entity or property of language, in which case the circularity of the idealization is maintained.

The perniciousness of this circularity is that the subject so defined loses all but the most narrow connections to the actual world. The subject is only what it is taken to be, and any troublesome logical or empirical considerations can be accommodated simply by ruling them irrelevent, not part of the subject matter, not part of the idealized competence. Such judgments of relevance are not purely ad hoc, of course—they are strongly constrained by tradition— but neither are they strictly matters of empirical hypothesis testing and logical criticism as they would be in a legitimate science. The point, then, is that the definitional boundaries of a subject contain just as much empirical and falsifiable content as any theory constructed within those boundaries and that circular ideal definitions of those boundaries make that content empirically and logically immune. [2]

The deficiencies of this approach have visited themselves upon the broader study of communication through a general acceptance of linguistics as foundational to the study of communication. This acceptance not only incorporates the reification of linguistics itself but it compounds the problem since it has the proper foundational relationship reversed: speech is a form of communication, not the other way around, and thus language should be studied within the framework of a broader theory of communication, not the other way around. It is difficult to trace the difficulties that such errors cause back to their source. Nevertheless, it has become evident that new conceptual orientations and empirical methodologies are needed (for example, Derwing 1973; Gumperz and Hymes 1972).

A critical question in the pursuit of such new conceptual orientations, and the one to be pursued in this discussion, is the nature of communication and language, not as traditional idealizations but as psychological capabilities and sociological institutions. The dominant idealizations have removed themselves from the real phenomena of communication thereby blocking our understanding of its nature. The critical question, then, is what are communication and language— what is their psychosocial ontology?

STRUCTURE OF THE BOOK

There are five chapters in this book. The first presents the metatheoretical perspective within which the model of communication is developed. The next four present the model. At the end of each chapter there is a discussion relating the contents of that section to selected relevant literature. There are also four appendixes presenting the rudiments of some relevant background to the model.

The metatheoretical perspective is presented primarily in terms of approaches to knowledge and communication. These are not only two of the most important aspects of mind, they are the two that are most salient to the model developed in the remainder of the book. The classical and dominant approaches are called picture models of knowledge and transmission models of communication. The core assumptions involved are that knowledge in its essence is a structural encoding of what is known and that communication is a signal encoding of knowledge structures. I argue that these basic encoding assumptions are fundamentally untenable. The alternative approaches are called interactive models of knowledge and transformational models of communication. The core assumptions are that the essence of knowledge is task capability and that communication is the transformation of a special social reality. Potential objections to and some consequences of these alternatives are discussed.

The first section of the model focuses on its psychological foundations, especially its cognitive and interactive constituents. Two primary concepts developed are the situation image and the world image. These are representational aspects of the overall action system and correspond, roughly, to one's knowledge about the current environmental situation; and about the potentialities of the world in general. Some of the issues examined are the intimate relationship between situation image and world image, the processes of apperceptively updating the situation image in accordance with the flow of experience, and some of the characteristics of major representational types, such as for objects. The discussion proceeds within a strictly interactive perspective, with no picture model encoding assumptions about the nature of knowledge.

The second model section presents the sociological foundations, and the primary concept developed is that of a situation convention. A situation convention is essentially a socially common understanding of a social situation among the various participants in that situation. It is developed as a special kind of congruence among the situation images of those participants. Formally, the development of the concept is an extension of Lewis' (1969) analysis of conventions. Situation conventions serve as a broader category within which common conventions, the symbolic interactionists' social definitions of the situation, and Goffman's frames can all be understood; situation conventions also capture a number of the basic properties of social encounter that are of concern to ethnomethodologists. The concept of a situation convention is the core concept of the model. It constitutes the emergence of social reality out of psychological reality.

The third model section begins the communication model proper and consists of a sequence of definitions, primary among which is that of a meaningful communication, and an examination of a few properties of those definitions. The basic concept of a meaningful communication is any interaction that transforms a situation convention. The meaning of such a communication is that transformation of the situation convention. Language is defined as a special kind of conventional system for the generation of meaningful communications.

The fourth, last, and longest model section analyzes a large number of the consequences of the preceding explications. The major part of the discussion is concerned with an analysis of communicational action systems. This discussion is structured by a sequence of differentiations of increasingly specialized and powerful communicational action systems, beginning within the broad category of general goal-directed action systems and proceeding to linguistic systems. The nature of the differentiations, the relationships among the resultant levels, and the special properties arising at each new level are the primary focuses of discussion.

The discussion of the model, then, is in four basic parts: (1) a mentalistic, machine-theoretic explication of action systems and some of their corresponding cognitive aspects, with particular emphasis on situation and world images; (2) an explication of the emergence of the level of social reality out of that of psychological reality, primarily in terms of situation conventions; (3) a definitional system for types of communicational acts, with meaning constituting the core concept; and (4) an application of these conceptualizations to the problem of communicational action systems, yielding a progressive differentiation of levels of communicational systems beginning with general action systems and ending with linguistic systems.

2
A METATHEORETICAL PERSPECTIVE

ON MODELS OF KNOWLEDGE AND COMMUNICATION

Assumptions regarding the study of mind have tended to be fragmented among the various aspects of mind, cognition, motivation, learning, and so forth. I suggest that there is an underlying unity to the classical and dominant approaches to these multiple aspects of mind that has been obscured by the lack of an alternative perspective on mind from which to make the necessary comparisons. Roughly speaking, classical approaches to mind have been dominated by metaphors and properties drawn from our most familiar world of physical structures. In what way could a physical structure constitute a representation of something? It could be a picture or sculptural model of it, hence the dominant metaphor of structural encoding in the approach to knowledge. In what way could a physical structure move? Only by the application of some motive force, hence the dominant metaphor of overcoming passivity in the approach to motivation. And so on.

The historical movement away from such substance-and-structure intuitions in psychology parallels similar movements in other sciences. For example, at one time heat, fire, magnetism, and life were all thought to be substances (fluids, usually) but are now recognized to be processes and relationships of various sorts. This movement, moreover, has involved fundamental shifts in the ontologies, not just the details, of the models involved. Fire is a certain chemical process, for example, and not just a substance released by a process. Life is a certain open system process and not just a vital substance dependent on food and air exchanges. It has not generally been easy to recognize that the essence of something is constituted as some kind of process rather than a substance or structure that may participate in some process.

The move away from substance-and-structure intuitions in psychology has involved at least the recognition of mind as active, mind as an open system, and, I would claim, mind as a special sort of control structure process. The conclusions about the proper ontology for the conceptualization of mind are far from settled, but I suggest that mind as control structure process is a necessary aspect of it and, furthermore, that it encompasses a number of other necessary aspects. Thus, mind as control structure process is necessarily also active and in open exchange with the environment. Other necessary characteristics of the ontology of mind, I claim, are constraints that apply only within the general category of control structure processes, such as that mind is goal-directed (knowing), self-organizing (learning), self-monitoring (emotions), and self-knowing (consciousness). (See Bickhard, in press, for further developments of these concepts.) Insofar as this holds, then the move from substance-and-structure intuitions to control structure conceptualizations is a first necessary ontological step toward the understanding of mind. Just as fire is a certain kind of chemical process and life is a certain kind of open system process, so also is mind a certain kind of control structure process.

The basic intuition of the concept of control is that any process that influences or determines the course of another process is said to control that second process. That second process may, in turn, serve to control still other processes. The organization of potential such control influences in a system is said to be the control structure in that system. Note that the concept of a control process is emergent from the concept of a physical process in the sense that any particular control structure organization can in principle be realized in an indefinite number of different possible physical systems; it is the functional organization of the control influences that counts, not their physical instantiation. The notion of control is potentially recursive and quite complex, such as when the nature of the control relationship between one process and another is itself controlled by a third process or when the processes that control one another are themselves constituted as control processes rather than directly as particular physical processes. Also, the concept of information is subsidiary to that of control in the sense that any signal or structure contains information relative to a particular system only insofar as it is capable of exerting control on that system. Mathematical information is a measure of the degree of potential control. The formal languages of abstract machine theory provide a means for keeping these complexities clear and, thus, serve as a conceptual ground for exploring mind as a control structure process.

The basic contrast that I wish to draw, then, is between the approach to mind in terms of substance-and-structure intuitions and the approach to mind in terms of interactive control processes. I will not be exploring these alternative approaches to mind in their full ramifications throughout the various aspects of mind, however, but rather in terms of two particular aspects of mind—knowledge and communication. I choose only two aspects primarily from space and time limitations, and I choose these particular two aspects for two reasons. First, they are core aspects. Knowledge is a foundational characteristic of mind, and communication is one of its most advanced and most revealing manifestations. Second, these two aspects are the most salient to the model presented in the rest of the book. Certain other aspects are touched upon in passing, such as motivation, but a full examination of these contrasting approaches is a separate task.

For the last two milennia, models of knowledge and communication in Western culture have been dominated by two particular types of models, two particular approaches to model building, which I wish to call, respectively, picture models of knowledge and transmission models of communication. I will contrast these with two alternative approaches to the modeling of human processes which I will call interactive models of knowledge and transformational models of communication.

Basically, I will be arguing that picture models of knowledge and transmission models of communication are intrinsically and fundamentally untenable and, therefore, that we must focus on the construction of interactive models of knowledge and transformational models of communication. The discussion proceeds first with brief considerations of the nature and history of each model type. A clear conclusion is that interactive and transformational models are very recent compared with picture and transmission models. Next, there is an examination of some of the relationships among the model types, followed by a critique of each type. The principal conclusion of the examination of relationships among the model types is that the classical approaches to knowledge and communication have a basic conceptual unity, as do the alternative approaches which I will be favoring. The critiques show the untenability of picture and transmission models, and demonstrate the at least programmatic viability of interactive and transformational models. The discussion ends with illustrative considerations of some of the consequences of the shift to interactive and transformational model perspectives.

PICTURE MODELS OF KNOWLEDGE

The basic metaphor of picture models is the assumption that knowledge of something must somehow constitute a picture of it.

This can be conceptualized in terms of an image, a model, a form, an imprint, and so on. The formal commonality among them is the assumption of some kind of a structural isomorphism between knowledge and that which is known. In fact, the relationship of representation between knowledge and known is taken precisely to be that of such an isomorphism: to represent is to re-present, to "capture" the structure or form of that which is represented. Representative art, such as painting, sculpting, or photography, is taken as the basic metaphor for knowledge.

This assimilation of knowledge to structural representation has been a powerful theme in Western thought at least since the pre-Socratic Stoics (Copleston 1962), reaching an almost untainted development with the British Empiricists. British Empiricism, as the foundation of associationism, has been the dominant influence on American psychology.

A variant on the theme has been the attempt to assimilate knowledge to language: knowledge about the world somehow consists of sentences (propositions) about the world. In fact, however, this only removes the problem by one step to how a sentence can constitute knowledge. At this point, knowledge is again assimilated to structural representation, and we get some theory about how sentences can re-present structures in the world. The pinnacle of this development was Wittgenstein's Tractatus Logico-Philosophicus (1961), in which we find the meanings of propositions explicated in terms of their constituting an isomorphic picture or model of the structure of atomic facts "in" the world. The Tractatus, itself a variant of British Empiricism, was the keystone for logical positivism. Logical positivism, in turn, was the ground upon which the pseudo-philosophy of modern psychology was constructed, for example, behaviorism and operational definitionalism. Picture model assumptions of knowledge, thus, have been powerfully injected into modern psychology through both the associationists and the logical positivists.

TRANSMISSION MODELS OF COMMUNICATION

The core assumption of transmission models of communication is that communication consists fundamentally of the transmission of the encodings of underlying knowledge. The form of such models is the classic sender-transmission channel-receiver structure. The focus of such models is on the encoding and decoding rules in the sender and receiver, respectively. Thus, the sender encodes some knowledge using some coding rules and transmits the resultant signal along the channel, where the receiver decodes the signal according to appropriate decoding rules, thereby acquiring a "copy" of the knowledge structure that was encoded to begin with. Computer to computer "communication" is almost the perfect realization of such a model.

As with picture models of knowledge, transmission models of communication have been around at least since the Stoics (Graeser 1978; Yngve 1974, 1975), and have been dominant ever since. Correspondingly, the dominant focus has always been on the obvious problem within the transmission model, the encoding and decoding rules. Thus, the concern has been with the relationships between the structure and the content of the signal, on the one hand, and the meaning of the signal (the structure and content of the information or knowledge underlying it), on the other.

Current efforts in linguistics proceed within these same basic assumptions. The issues are concerned with the specifics of the relationships between the semantic base and the well-formed signal (sentence). The meta-issues are concerned with the best ways to formally describe such relationships. Transmission models have become immensely sophisticated, but they are still transmission models.

INTERACTIVE MODELS OF KNOWLEDGE

Interactive models of knowledge assume that knowledge consists of the ability to successfully interact with the environment. Such interactive competence presumably resides in some kind of control structure that carries out the relevant interactions. Such control structures can be wired in, as in the case of a thermostatic system that interacts with the temperature in a room, or flexibly variable, as with a program in a computer. The distinction between successful and unsuccessful interactions must be made in terms of some sort of goal for the interaction. Thus, knowledge consists of the ability to transform situations in the environment in accordance with goal criteria, and that ability is constituted within goal-directed and goal-competent control structures.

The first major step away from picture models of knowledge toward interactive models of knowledge was Kant's (1965) realization that the knowing mind brings structures to the world instead of just passively (pictorially) receiving them from the world. Kant's conceptual structures, however, were not interactions. Their static structural character, in fact, would seem to be a residual from picture models.

A century later, C. S. Pierce (for example, Scheffler 1974), the founder of pragmatism, recognized that knowledge was fundamentally involved with action and expectation, but he had no adequate way to conceptualize the relationships among or the constitutions of such actions and expectations. In effect, he had nothing to play the conceptual role of the control structure. Thus he, too, had ultimate recourse to "picturelike" elements and constructions.

Piaget (Piaget and Inhelder 1969) presents an explicitly action-based model of the construction of knowledge. The nature of knowledge, however, is again structural, "pictorial," though at a very abstract level. Piaget's schemes and structures, in fact, have tantalizingly ambiguous characteristics as action determining control structures, on the one hand, and Kantian "pictorial" categories on the other. Clearly, the pictorial abstract structural aspect of Piaget's model is the most thoroughly developed, though, equally clearly, the power of the model depends critically on the interactive control structure aspect. The unexplicated relationship between these two aspects constitutes one of the greatest (and, in my opinion, a fatal) flaw in Piaget's model.

Other areas in psychology in which interactive model characteristics are developing include artificial intelligence, where the proceduralist (interactionist) versus declarative (linguistically pictorial) controversy is explicit (for example, Winograd 1975), and cognition, in which at least some of the interactive characteristics of knowledge and perception are being recognized (for example, Gibson 1966; Miller, Galanter, and Pribram 1960; Neisser 1967, 1976). Realizations of the fundamentalness of interaction are also occurring in philosophy (for example, Bernstein 1971; Heidegger 1962), but in neither case has a strictly interactionist model with reasonable programmatic claims to adequacy been presented.

TRANSFORMATION MODELS OF COMMUNICATION

Transformation models of communication view communication as a form of interactive transformation. Just as walking transforms position, manipulations transform materials, updating transforms data structures, and functions transform numbers, so also is communication an interactive transformational process. The focus is on interaction and manipulation rather than on passive encoding, transmission, and decoding.

The historical development of transformational realizations in the study of communication has lagged far behind the development of interactive models of knowledge. The first significant steps toward action-based transformational conceptualizations of communication were by the later Wittgenstein (1958) and J. L. Austin (1968). Wittgenstein's discussions of language as a rule-governed game and Austin's analyses of speech as action set the stage for transformational communication models. But, though in both cases acknowledgment is made of action and transformational characteristics of communication, in neither is there a developed focus on what is being transformed or on how such transformations are possible, or on how they are carried out. In effect, they are models of communication as action, but the acts are acts of transmission of an encoded signal (propositions, or "proposition-radicals") and, in that sense, constitute critical steps away from pure transmission models but not yet examples of true transformation models.

This hybrid focus on acts of encoded transmission has been retained in subsequent models. Searle (1969, 1971, 1972), for example, analyzes speech acts in terms of illocutionary acts and propositional contents of those acts, but both illocutionary and propositional aspects of speech are encoded elements-to-be-transmitted rather than transformations-to-be-undertaken. His analyses of "happiness conditions" for successful speech acts, correspondingly, are in terms of successful transmission rather than successful interactive transformations. The basic Gricean program for the explication of meaning (Bennett 1976; Grice 1967, 1969; Schiffer 1972) has similarly considered speech-as-action (utterance) but, also similarly, as action that transmits something, in this case, that transmits a signal decodable into various structures of recognitions of intentions regarding propositions. Again, there is no focus on the object of transformation or on the transformational process.

Another kind of seeming transformational communication model has occurred in artificial intelligence research. Winograd's (1972, 1973) model has a strong flavor of transformationalism, but this derives primarily from its underlying interactive model of knowledge and its ability to engage in simple conversational interactions. The conceptualization of a particular communication still does not go beyond the encode-transmit-decode framework. The model of Miller and Johnson-Laird (1976) has, for the purposes of my current comparisons, essentially the same features. In fact, both models illustrate a current tendency to attempt an interactive explication of semantics wedded to a transmission model of communication. Such attempts to join interactive with transmission models can also be found in other areas of psychology and philosophy. For example, as mentioned earlier, Heidegger (1962) has a basically interactive conceptualization of knowlege, but his view of communication has a distinct encoding flavor. I will argue that such weddings of interactive with transmission models are intrinsically incompatible and, thus, doomed to failure.

Perhaps the most consistently transformational models of communication are to be found within phenomenological sociology (for example, Cicourel 1974; Turner 1974). In these models, communication is recognized to be an activity, and an object of transformation is sometimes indicated (generally something to do with the social situation), but the process of transformation is still left to the transmission models.

Another area of striking movement toward transformational models is developmental psycholinguistics, in which the growing recognition of pragmatics as the foundation for language learning is forcing development of increasingly transformational models of what language and communication are (for example, Bates 1976; Ervin-Tripp and Mitchell-Kernan 1977; Lewis and Rosenblum 1977). Again, however, though recognition of the active and interactive character of communication is strong, and objects of transformation are sometimes loosely acknowledged, the process of transformation does not go beyond the act-that-transmits.

Transformational model insights concerning communication, then, are late on the historical scene, and still are not at all well developed. As with interactive models, however, and even though they are a much more recent phenomenon, such insights appear to be growing rapidly.

THE UNITIES AMONG THE MODELS

The thesis to be developed in this section is that the picture model of knowledge and transmission model of communication together constitute a basic conceptual unity, as do the interactive and transformation models. The argument for this thesis is in two parts. First, each separate pair of approaches shares a core assumption, and the shared assumption for the classical approaches is different from that for the more recent alternative approaches. Second, there is a fundamental incompatibility between interactive models of knowledge and transmission models of communication such that the interactive approach to knowledge entails the transformational approach to communication and, conversely, the transmission approach entails the picture approach. [3]

I will consider first the various compatibilities among the model types and then the critical incompatibility. Transmission models of communication and picture models of knowledge have been linked implicitly in the preceding discussion. The compatibility underlying this linkage is rather easily understood once it is grasped that they share their core assumptions. In particular, they both assimilate knowledge to representation, and representation to some sort of encoding of that which is represented. In picture models, such knowledge encodings tend to be static, relatively permanent, and available for multiple access (as in cognition). In transmission models, the encodings tend to be mobile, transient, and restrictedly accessible (as in messages). Written language, of course, tends to combine the two sets of characteristics, being both storable and transmittable. This is perhaps one of the reasons why sentences are often taken as the ground for pictorial models of knowledge. Transmission and picture models, then, are compatible by virtue of their common assumptions of knowledge as representational encoding. Transmitted encodings, of course, are generally indirect: a transmitted signal is an encoding of a picture knowledge encoding.

The compatibility between interactive models of knowledge and transformational models of communication is similar: that is, they share their core assumptions. In this case, the core assumption is that of the interactive character of mental phenomena. Interactive models consider knowing as successful interacting and knowledge as the capability for knowing. Transformational models view communication essentially as the interaction with, the knowing of, a special social object of interaction. Communication is a special kind of interactive knowing, differentiated by its special object of knowing. Transformation models, then, are a particularization of interactive models, just as transmission models are of picture models.

There is also a compatibility between picture models and transformation models. It is not an especially pretty compatibility, not one of shared assumptions, aesthetic particularizations, or any kind of special affinity for one another. It is, rather, the crude fact that the two kinds of models can be grafted together without direct logical contradiction. The basic point is that pictures, too, can be the objects of transformation. They can be updated, revised, created, destroyed, and so on. Thus, pictorial knowledge structures, in some form or another, can in principle be taken as the interactive objects of transformational communication. Picture models, then, are at least technically compatible with either kind of communication model, and transformation models with either kind of knowledge model. The deep affinities, however, are clearly more restricted.

We now turn to the incompatibility between interactive models of knowledge and transmission models of communication. Very simply, transmission models require representational knowledge structures to be coded as representational message structures, which interactive models do not have. Picture models provide basic picture elements and principles of construction to be coded, but knowledge in interactive models is the ability to interact with the environment, and such abilities do not provide common foundations for encoding and decoding message forms between individuals. Thus, they do not provide grounds for transmission models.

It might be contended that the control structures of interactive models provide such grounds. Control structures might seem to involve basic elements and construction principles that could be structurally encoded just like picture elements and constructions. There are two problems with this contention. First, there are an infinite number of potential alternative sets of basic control structure elements and construction principles, and these could in principle vary widely from individual to individual. Second, even if the basic elements and principles are fixed, any interactive ability, or structure of abilities, still can be manifested by an infinitude of different control structure organizations constructed out of those basic elements. Thus, the structure to be encoded would vary unpredictably from individual to individual for a fixed "chunk" of interactive knowledge. Thus, there could be no interindividual message form that could structurally encode such variable underlying structures. Therefore, again there is no common ground for encoding and decoding message forms between individuals and, correspondingly, no ground for transmission models.

There is rather a subtle reason why picture models do not encounter similar problems as grounds for transmission models. It might seem that picture constructions could be just as variable from individual to individual as control structures and, thus, provide the same difficulties for interindividual encodings and decodings. First of all, most picture models of knowledge tend to posit the basic elements and construction principles as being universal, either genetically or somehow implicitly in the nature of what is being represented. For a given structural representation, this assumption ensures a basic commonality between individuals and, thus, equivalent grounds for encodings and decodings. That is, most picture models do not allow the seemingly troublesome variations among individuals.

More fundamentally, however, even if the basic elements and principles are not held constant across individuals, the compatibility with transmission models still follows. The core of the picture models is the view of knowledge as consisting of a structural isomorphism between a representation and that which is represented. An isomorphism is essentially a structural equivalence, by some rule of equivalence, and such rules of isomorphic equivalence can be of indeterminate complexity and abstractness just as long as the original structural information is preserved. Furthermore, the relationship of isomorphism is transitive and symmetric: that is, if A is isomorphic to B, and B is isomorphic to C, then it follows that A is isomorphic to C; and if A is isomorphic to B, then B is isomorphic to A. Thus, even though the particular representations of a fixed "chunk" of knowledge may vary from individual to individual, those representations will all be isomorphic to what they represent in common, and thus they will nevertheless all be isomorphic to each other. Similarly, transmitted communications will share in the isomorphism with what is represented. Therefore, even though the particular representations and thus the particular encoding and decoding rules may vary from individual to individual, the message forms will constitute interindividual representational forms which will be isomorphic to each individual's personal representations of the same things. The picture model ground for transmission models, then, is not necessarily a commonality of representational structures (though it usually is in particular models) but is, rather, a more subtle commonality of representational isomorphism.

Picture models are structural in nature: what makes a structure a representation is its structural relationship to what is being represented. Therefore they provide grounds for the structural coding of transmission models. Interactive models are functional in nature: what makes a structure a representation is its interactive functional relationship to what is being represented. Functional relationships impose very loose constraints on the structural relationships underlying them and therefore provide no socially common grounds for the structural coding of transmission models. Thus, interactive and transmission models are incompatible, and therefore transmission models entail picture models and interactive models entail transformation models. In particular, any evidence or argument for interactive models of knowledge over picture models of knowledge is thereby also evidence or argument for transformation models of communication over transmission models of communication.

CRITIQUE OF PICTURE MODELS

I contend that picture models and, thus, transmission models, are untenable. This contention is in two parts: what they claim to do is not adequate as a model of knowing, and they cannot do what they claim to do. These two basic objections correspond to the two basic components of the picture model assumption: knowledge can be assimilated to representation, and representation can be assimilated to structural isomorphism. Thus picture models assume that structural representation constitutes the essence of knowledge, and I will argue that that assumption is false. Picture models attempt to model the essence of representation as some form of structural isomorphism, and I will argue that that attempt is impossible.

First, consider the issue of representation as isomorphism. An isomorphic representation must be built out of some set of basic elements according to some principles of construction that accomplish the isomorphism. The fundamental task of a picture model is to provide those basic elements and principles of construction and to show how they accomplish such isomorphisms. The elements may be such things as points, features, or propositional facts. The principles of construction may be such things as juxtaposition, associations, linkages, or logical connectives. There are two synergistically fatal problems for this task: how to provide sufficient elements and principles to account for the required representations, and how to account for the origins of these elements and principles.

The provision of elements and principles does not seem unduly difficult in paradigmatic cases, such as templates for visual scenes or notations of simple facts. It increases dramatically in difficulty as less paradigmatic cases are considered. Thus, a representation of an object, as opposed to a scene, must be simultaneously from a very large number of possible perspectives. General categories, such as "chair" or "triangle," cannot be managed by any number of scenes and generally induce a move to features as basic elements. Abstract conceptualizations, such as number or economy, have no particular perceptual content at all and tend to induce moves either to correspondingly abstract features or to propositions. (Once propositional-based models are considered, they may then be applied even to scenes.) Value-laden concepts, such as democracy, justice, and honesty, cannot be handled adequately by any combination of features and propositions unless the values themselves become introduced as basic elements. [4]

Clearly, the problem here is an ad hoc proliferation of basic elements and corresponding construction principles. The number of elements and of basic types of elements increases with each new problem considered to the point that very little parsimony of explanation is achieved. Furthermore, some of the new elements, such as those involving propositions or values, are in at least as much need of explanation as what they are supposed to explain: in such cases, the elements simply become names for ignorance.

Actual picture models tend to avoid this problem by restricting themselves to some narrow range of application, suggesting some potential economy of representation within that range (usually itself a false sense of economy yielded by a few examples, for example, Katz and Fodor 1971), and then either explicitly suggesting or implicitly assuming that the small-scale model presented supports the general programmatic promise of the broader approach. In fact, however, the problem of proliferation can be dealt with only as a whole; it is an issue of possibility in principle, not one of little forays into the wilderness. Such a possibility in principle can never be proven, but it can be addressed. Picture models either avoid it or founder on it.

The problem of the ad hoc proliferation of elements and principles is compounded immensely by the necessity of accounting for the
origins of such elements and principles. To posit them as innate
founders on two problems: it compounds the ad hod-ness; and it
becomes essentially impossible to explain new forms of conceptualization that are clearly cultural inventions, for example, new forms
of mathematical investigation and reasoning (such as category
theory or the theory of abstract machines). To posit them as being
products of development yields its own fatal problem: if a new element
or principle is developed, then it must have been constructed or
learned; if constructed or learned, it must have been so from the
prior available elements and principles; if constructed from prior
elements and principles, then it is not itself basic, and must be
modelable in terms of those prior resources. Thus, a proliferation
cannot be accounted for from either an innatist or a developmentalist
view. The only alternative is to avoid the proliferation itself, and
the feasibility of that has been undermined by every failure to do so
for the last two thousand years. [5]

Thus, the assimilation of the essence of representation to
structural isomorphism is best judged impossible. It assumes that
the nature of things to be represented is necessarily structural,
when in fact structural aspects capture only a part of all but the most
paradigmatic cases. It also assumes that all possible structures of
all possible kinds can be captured with a relatively small set of
elements and principles of construction. The proliferation of types
of elements comes from the necessity of new types to "account" for
new nonstructural characteristics. The proliferation of elements
within any given type attests to the multiplicity of kinds of structures.
Such ad hoc proliferation is inadmissable on its own terms and,
besides, makes it impossible to explain the origins of elements and
principles. Attempts to model representation as some form of
structural isomorphism must be considered misguided.

Having rejected the assimilation of representation to structural
isomorphism, I now wish to consider the assimilation of knowledge
to representation. Actually, the issue is the assimilation of knowledge to structural representation, for the assimilation of knowledge
to interactive representation is, at least in some readings, the basic
step of interactive models. There are two related problems with
structural representation as the essence of knowledge: the need for
an interpreter of the structure, and the need for an account of nonstructural forms of knowledge.

Knowledge is manifested in action. Picture models assume
that knowledge is constituted as structural representation, but they
cannot deny that it is manifested by action. It immediately follows,
however, that picture models must assume implicitly or explicitly

an active interpreter of those representations. Some active process must make use of the knowledge in those representations in order for that knowledge to be manifested. Some active process must compute the encoding rules. Often that active element is simply an implicit homunculus in picture models—either not mentioned at all or assumed to be a necessary adjunct but not directly relevant to the basic task of understanding knowledge. In fact, however, the necessity for such an active interpreter eliminates the essential assimilation of knowledge to structural representation upon which picture models are based. Once an active rule-following agent is allowed as an interpreter of structure, the picture structure itself becomes logically superfluous. The dynamic organization of the agent can serve every function that the structural representation was assumed to serve. It can incorporate exactly the same information in functional rather than structural form, but, when that possibility is fully realized, we have an interactive model of knowledge, not a picture model. Thus, structural representation cannot capture the essence of knowledge: it is not even a necessary component of it.

It should be noted that the argument here is not against the possibility or the actuality of structural representation, or against such representation constituting knowledge. The argument, rather, is that: (1) structural representation is a limited, though sometimes useful, form of representation and knowledge; (2) structural representation exists only relative to and subsidiary to an interpretive interactive agent; (3) such structural representation is logically superfluous relative to such an interactive agent; and (4) structural representation therefore cannot constitute the essence of either representation or knowledge. Structural representations plus interpreters may well be present in interactive models, but, if so, it is for such reasons as simplicity and efficiency and not out of necessity.

Thus, picture models must assume an active agent as interpreter of structure, and that assumption is contradictory to the fundamental assumption of picture models. Allied to the need for an agent as interpreter is the necessity for an agent as knower in ways that are simply not structural at all. Knowing entities not only know such things as what their living room looks like, which has a structural "feel" to it, but also such things as how to walk, or drive a car, or catch a ball, or enlist cooperation, or comfort a friend, which can only ludicrously be considered essentially structural. The point, then, is that not only do picture models require interactive agents as interpreters of structure, they also require them for knowledge that cannot even be construed as structural. In both cases, the full acknowledgment of the necessity of such an agent destroys the basic picture model assumption and forces a move to an interactive model perspective.

The historical move from picture models toward interactive models seems to have been following exactly this path of the progressive recognition of the necessity of an agent. It seems sufficiently clear by now that the move is necessary and must be complete: the basic assumption of picture models is simply not tenable in any of its components or guises. Neither the assimilation of representation to isomorphism nor the assimilation of knowledge to representation can be upheld. Doubly, then, attempts to construct still another picture model must be considered as misguided.

CRITIQUE OF TRANSMISSION MODELS

In this section, transmission models will be examined. The conclusion is the same as that for picture models: they are untenable. First, it should be noted that, insofar as transmission models require underlying picture models, their viability has already been undermined by the preceding discussion. Furthermore, insofar as transmission models make the same knowledge-as-isomorphic-coding assumption as picture models, the preceding arguments not only undermine transmission models but apply with equal force directly to transmission models. In addition, however, transmission models have a basic flaw all their own.

The problem involves the encoding and decoding rules that are the heart of any transmission model. In particular, it involves the origin of those coding rules. The coding relationships between message and message form in a transmission model are infinitely arbitrary. That is, no finite amount of data or experience will be sufficient to specify any particular set of coding rules. Thus, the rules cannot be primarily a product of learning. But, if not learned, where do they come from? The problem of infinite arbitrariness is usually either ignored with an assumption that the rules can somehow be learned, or it is "solved" with the ad hoc postulation of innate grounds for language learning (for example, Chomsky 1965). In addition to the basic inadmissibility of such an ad hoc turn, it encounters still further problems even if it is allowed. Specifically, since such innate grounds for language coding rules would be both necessary and specific to language, it is difficult to conceive of any selection pressures that could have brought about the evolution of such grounds. The relevant selection pressures presumably would derive from the survival value of learning a language, but languages could not exist to exert such selection pressures until such innate grounds for language learning had already been established. [6]

The only way out of the infinite arbitrariness dilemma for transmission models is to postulate some initial nontransmissional, presumably transformational, form of communication within which the transmission coding rules can be implicitly or explicitly defined. The clearest examples of strictly transmissional communication, for example, computer to computer communication, all have exactly such an origin. But such a necessary grounding of transmission on transformational communication, of course, eliminates any claim of transmission models to capture the essence of communication. As with picture models relative to interactive models, transmissional forms of communication can be constructed as subsidiary to transformational forms of communication for reasons, perhaps, of efficiency, but transmission models cannot stand alone and are not even a logically necessary component of a communications model. Thus, again as with picture models relative to interactive models, transmission models cannot capture the essence of communication, and any attempts based on such an assumption must be considered misguided.

CRITIQUE OF INTERACTIVE MODELS

Clearly, I do not anticipate reaching a conclusion in this section that interactive models are untenable. My intention, instead, is to explore potential difficulties with interactive models and to indicate programmatic directions of solution. Thus, while the difficulties with picture models seem ultimately fatal, the difficulties with interactive models seem ultimately solvable. Furthermore, the solutions are not simply ad hoc "fixes" but constitute interesting directions of investigation in their own right.

Interactive models can be construed as involving a two-part assumption similar to that of picture models: knowledge is assimilated to interactive representation, and interactive representation is assimilated to control structures. The issues associated with the two components of the assumption, however, are quite different.

To begin with, the assimilation of interactive representation to control structures offers virtually no problems at all. Interactive representation is a property of the interactive organization of a system, and "control structure" is simply a name for that interactive dynamic organization. Control structure is a dynamic functional concept, not a material concept. That is, it refers to the functional organization among processes and not to the material substrates for those processes. Thus, it imposes no additional and potentially troublesome constraints beyond that of interactive representation itself. It simply acknowledges that interactive representational ability must somehow reside in the dynamic organization of the system.

The focus of potential difficulties, then, is on the assimilation of knowledge to interactive representation. First, it should be noted that, unlike picture models, interactive representations do not require an interpreter. A control structure interprets itself in its own functioning, in its own execution. This self-interpretive characteristic of control structures is one of the sources of the great power of interactive models. Through such self-interpretive characteristics, interactive representations have both static and dynamic, structural and interactive properties simultaneously.

Second, it should be noted that interactive models can easily accommodate structurally isomorphic representations by differentiating a static structural component from the dynamic interpreter of that component. Thus, just as picture models require interpreters, control structures can be interpreters. Third, it is clear that such interactive skills as walking or catching a ball offer no problems in principle, however complex in fact, to an interactive model.

Interactive models, then, are easily invulnerable to the three basic criticisms that were directed against the assimilation of knowledge to structural representation in picture models. Interactive models, however, have their own apparent difficulties. Primary among these are two related challenges to the very foundations of interactive models: how can an interactive control structure be considered to represent anything at all, and how can it be considered to represent something about something else, such that it can be considered to be true or false in that representation? For picture models, the representation is in the sense of structural isomorphism, and the truth or falsity is in terms of whether or not that isomorphism does in fact hold. These seem fairly clear for picture models (though the "aboutness" can give further problems), but the corresponding senses for interactive models are, at least within this cultural heritage, less directly intuitive.

First, consider the question of how an interactive control structure can represent anything at all. The basic idea derives from the fact that the course of an interaction is determined not only by the corresponding control structure being executed but also by the object or environment with which the interaction takes place. Thus, for a given control structure, different objects (environments) of interaction will yield different outcomes of the interaction, and those differing outcomes of interaction serve as the bases for differentiating among classes or categories of those objects of interaction. A control structure, then, can represent a category of objects in the sense that it can detect an instance of it. A control structure can represent a single entity in the sense that it can represent a category that has only one instance. In effect, control structure representations act as interactive, implicit definitions: they implicitly define, and thus represent, the category of all those things which will fit into a certain pattern of interactions so as to yield a particular outcome.

How can interactive representations be true or false? We have just seen how control structures can represent, but it might seem that, as representations, they either apply or not, but that they could not apply falsely (and, therefore, not truly, either). That is, how can they apply and be false at the same time? The answer derives from a distinction between representations, on the one hand, and connections among representations, on the other. With this distinction, it can be seen that representations may apply or not, but a connection among representations constitutes a connection among the categories that they represent and, thus, constitutes an expectation of a connection among the instances of those categories. The detection of an instance of one category yields an expectation of instances of other categories. That expectation may be falsified by particular instances. Thus, interactive representations may be true or false.

It must be recognized, of course, that any representation is constituted by the organization of functional connections within it and that these connections internal to representations are not different in kind from the connections between representations. With this realization, however, it would seem possible to expand the boundary of what we considered to be a single representation to include all of the prior representations plus the connections among them. This move would seem to eliminate the connections between differing representations, thus to eliminate the expectations between categories, and, thus, to eliminate the potentiality for truth or falsity and return to applicability or lack of applicability. So it does, yet it is equally clear that the move, and its reverse, are arbitrary shifts of perspective on the part of the observers who are considering or analyzing the control structure. But the arbitrariness of that move entails that the distinction between applicability and truth or falsity is one of analytic perspective on a common underlying control structure, not a difference in kind of control structure or control structure connection. A single functional connection has characteristics of both applicability and expectation. Truth, then, is related to the potentiality for successful applicability.

Thus, the characteristics of applicability and truth value hold intrinsically for all interactive control structures. Correspondingly, the challenges against the potentiality for interactive models to represent and to be true or false are defeated.

The capability of an interactive model to represent something has, thus, been established, but it is still possible to challenge the adequacy in principle of interactive models to account for various particular kinds of representation and knowledge. Correspondingly, I will consider the various kinds of representations mentioned in the discussion of picture models, providing programmatic suggestions of how each kind might be dealt with within an interactive model. That is, I will consider scenes, objects, general categories, abstract categories, and values as they might be approached within an interactive perspective.

Scenes and general categories, such as "chair," offer the least difficulty in principle to interactive models. As discussed earlier, interactive representations are readily interpreted as representing general categories in the sense of constituting detectors for their instances. Scenes, on the other hand, can be construed as patterns of outcomes of potential visual scanning and sampling interactions. In either case, the complexities are great, but the possibility of approach within an interactive perspective is clear.

Objects require somewhat more consideration. A primary barrier to accounting for objects within an interactive perspective is a tendency to confuse ontology with epistemology. In particular, we tend to think of objects, to understand what objects ontologically are, in terms of structures of molecules, atoms, and so forth. Correspondingly, we tend to require that any representation (knowledge) of an object somehow account for (be isomorphic to) such an ontological structure. But it is clear upon a moment's reflection that molecules and the like are cultural and theoretical elaborations about objects which are built on much more basic object representations, sufficiently basic as to be developed by roughly age two. In general accord with Piaget, this fundamental epistemological essence of objects, as differentiated from our ontological conjectures about objects, is something like an invariance of a pattern of interactive properties (for example, in the case of a physical object, an invariance of the potentialities for various manipulations and handlings) with respect to a class of interactive transformations (for example, with respect to physical displacements). Epistemologically, then, objects are invariant patterns of interactive potentialities. Again, the complexities in fact are clearly great, but the possibility in principle of accounting for objects within an interactive perspective is also clear.

Abstract conceptualizations, such as those of mathematics or logic, would at first appear to be a fatal challenge to interactive models of knowledge. An interactive knowing system clearly interacts with an environment and, insofar as it knows anything at all, it knows about that interactive environment. But where in that environment are there numbers and vector spaces and axiomatic systems to be known? It would seem that interactive models could only know about the physical world.

The requirement is for an interactively accessible realm of greater abstraction than the physical world. I suggest, again in general accord with Piaget, that the properties of the interaction patterns themselves provide the needed realms of abstraction. In particular, control structures in a system will constitute knowledge about the external world, but the control structures themselves have properties that may be worth knowing. Such higher-level properties could be known by a higher, second-level control structure which interacts with the first-level control structure. This second-level control structure would, in turn, have properties that could be known by a third level, and so on. Clearly, we have an unbounded hierarchy of levels of abstraction of knowledge. The adequacy of such a hierarchy of levels of knowing can only be demonstrated for any particular abstract objects of knowledge by the construction of an interactive, hierarchical model appropriate to that object. Clearly, however, far from being fatally embarrassed by abstract knowledge, interactive models provide a rich approach to it.

Value-oriented knowledge poses the general problem of motivational directedness to the interactive perspective. Goal-directedness, emotional valences, and conscious intentionality are some of the phenomena that fall under this general motivational heading, along with value orientations. The issues posed by such motivational phenomena relate to the interactive perspective in at least two interesting questions: what do motivational phenomena have to do with models of knowledge in the first place, and, assuming that there is some appropriate connection, how do interactive models handle such motivational phenomena? The first question leads to an extremely important characteristic of interactive models. The second question ultimately can be answered only by specific interactive models for the various phenomena and will be correspondingly dealt with somewhat more cursorily.

The first answer to the question of what motivational phenomena have to do with models of knowledge is simply that some conceptualizations, for example, honesty or justice, intrinsically involve motivational or value orientations. Thus, as with picture models, the ultimate adequacy of interactive models depends upon their being able to account for such orientations.

There is, however, a much more fundamental answer from the interactive perspective. Basically, the answer is that motivation and knowledge are not two separate components of human processes or capacities, they are not two separate things. Rather, they are two different aspects of the same thing. In particular, motivation and knowledge are two differentiable aspects of interactive systems.

To see this, however, first requires understanding the problem of motivation differently than in its historical version. Historically, the basic problem of motivation has been viewed as explaining why behavior rather than no behavior occurs. The picture knowledge structures are intrinsically static, and the interpretive agent interacts with the world only when moved to do so by some external force or energy, some drive or instinct (for example, Freud 1963). The problem of motivation, thus, has been construed as being concerned with what makes the system active rather than quiescent.

From an interactive perspective, however, if the system is functioning at all, it is engaged in interaction, in behavior. The fact of interaction is intrinsic to the nature of the system and requires no independent explanation. What does require explanation and what constitutes the actual problem of motivation is why one particular interaction occurs rather than another. That is, motivation has to do not with the fact of interaction but, rather, with the selection of the course of interaction (for example, Atkinson and Birch 1970).

But the selection among alternative paths of interaction is precisely what the organization of a control structure is all about. The organization of a control structure is precisely an organization of such selections. Thus, the motivational property of interaction selection is intrinsic to the dynamic organization of interactive systems.

Accordingly, we now have both knowledge and motivation as aspects of the same underlying interactive systems. Knowledge is concerned with the issues of the successful applicability of interactive control structures, and motivation is concerned with the flow of selections concerning which control structures to attempt to apply. Thus, knowledge and motivation ultimately cannot be separated within an interactive perspective. [7] One aspect may be developed more than another in particular interactive models, but both are intrinsically present. Interactive models, in other words, cannot be just models of knowledge: they are intrinsically models of the broader scope of psychological reality.

The interactive perspective, then, provides not only an approach to motivational phenomena, but an approach that is intrinsic to the interactive perspective itself and not a separate set of assumptions about motivation arbitrarily tacked onto the basic interactive knowledge assumption. It is still questionable, however, whether that approach is sufficient for various phenomena at issue, whether it is sufficient, for example, to goal orientation, drives (such as hunger), emotions, or intentionality. Goal direction per se clearly gives no problems in principle to an interactive control structure perspective; similarly with drives, once they are recognized as biologically given set points within their own goal-directed subsystems. However, such phenomena as emotions and intentionality, however much they involve motivational issues, are certainly much more than that. Such phenomena require models of massive proportions in their own right. The question is whether these models can be constructed within the interactive perspective.

That question forms part of the frontier for the interactive perspective. It is certainly conceivable that phenomena like emotions and intentionality will require basic changes in the interactive perspective rather than elaborations and model constructions within it. [8] At this point, however, there seems to be no indication of such an inadequacy in the perspective, and it is difficult to imagine what such basic changes would consist of. As it must be, then, the interactive perspective remains subject to potential falsification, to the potential for fatal challenges, but it has withstood a number of serious challenges and has not yet been falsified.

In particular, it handles easily the need to account for interpretive and agentive knowledge; it meets the challenge to its ability to account for representation at all; and it provides intrinsically interesting and productive approaches to general categories, objects, abstract conceptualizations, and motivational phenomena. The interactive perspective, then, appears to be alive, well, and increasingly powerful.

CRITIQUE OF TRANSFORMATION MODELS

As argued before, the criticisms of picture models and the strengths of interactive models are also points in favor of the viability of transformation models over transmission models. Furthermore, transmission models have their own fatal problem of the infinite arbitrariness of the coding rules for transmission message forms. The indirect evidence, then, is highly in favor of transformation models of communication.

Transformation models, however, are subject to their own challenges. The challenges, moreover, are formidable and, in an implicit form, seem at least partly responsible for the late and difficult emergence of transformational perspectives in the understanding of communication. An overpowering reason for the historical dominance of transmission models, of course, is simply the corresponding dominance of picture models. It is only recently with the progressive emergence of interactive models that interactive-transformational realizations concerning communication have begun to develop. With growing recognition of the necessity of interactive models, however, it is the direct challenges to transformation models that remain. In this section I will consider those challenges, both historically and logically.

A major reason for the historical difficulty in moving from transmission models to transformation models has been that communication is most easily conceptualized, and has historically been conceptualized, in terms of the social institution of language, with sentences as abstract objects within that institution. Communication, then, comes quite naturally to be viewed as the transmission of (tokens of) sentence-objects from a sender to a receiver. To escape fully such a transmissional perspective, then, requires the equivalent escape from a social-institutional perspective into a psychological-interaction perspective. But that move, in turn, requires that the "obvious" institutional characteristics of language somehow be explicated beginning from within a psychological-interaction framework. That is, that move requires that the institutional be explicated in terms of the psychological, but this problem of the emergence of the social from the psychological has not yet been solved in the general case, let alone in the specific case of language.

Thus, the development of true transformation models of communication has encountered the difficulty of an implicit requirement that they account for both the social-institutional and the psychological-interactive characterisitics of communication. This requirement has invariably been dealt with by simply importing some part of an available institutional analysis (for example, a grammar) without explicating it in terms of the underlying interactive perspective, and, thereby, importing an implicit transmission model, an act-that-transmits-the-institutional-sentence-object model, of communication. It is interesting to note that institutional analyses of language and communication are not usually asked to account for the psychological characteristics of communication, whereas psychological models are usually required to account for, or "take into account," the institutional characteristics. I suggest that the problem can be dealt with only in terms of the emergence of the social from the psychological and not the other way around as people have been futilely attempting for so long. Whatever the approach, it is precisely this issue of the relationship of the psychological to the social that poses the greatest challenges to transformation models.

There have always been two basic problematic components of the relationship between the social and the psychological aspects of transformational communication: how can we account for conventionalized (institutionalized) communication, and what is the object of transformation? In order to indicate the basic programmatic feasibility of transformational communication models, I would like to sketch the approaches to each of these two problems.

The classically insurmountable problem of how to account for conventionalized communication derives from the fact that conventions are most easily conceived of as being established by agreement among the parties to the convention. This conceptualization worked well for such conventions as driving on the right side of the road or church ritual, but it made the consideration of language as conventional untenable. The problem was simply that language could not have been established by agreement since, prior to establishment of language, there was no way that agreement could be reached—there was no language within which the agreement process for language could have taken place. Correspondingly, there was no known way to account for the emergence of institutionalized language within a psychological interactive framework, and people continued to conceive of communication as some sort of transmission of abstract institutionalized sentence objects. As long as the emergence of institutions from individual activity wasn't explicable, the out has been to reify institutional patterns into things and then treat them as given objects upon which further model construction can be based.

Fortunately, this particular barrier to transformational communication models has recently been eliminated. Lewis (1969) showed how conventions could be established as patterns of activity strictly by precedent and habitualization, without any necessary agreement process, and even without any explicit awareness of the fact of a convention being established. Lewis' insights are already being incorporated into language and communication models (for example, Bennett 1976). The problem of the object of transformation, however, remains.

The obvious candidate for the object of transformational communication is the mind (or minds) of the audience or at least their knowledge structures. That is, the obvious candidate for the object of transformation is the same as the supposed receiver in transmission models. Clearly, communication affects knowledge in some sense, but, it turns out, there are grave difficulties in positing minds (or knowledge structures) as the proximate objects of transformation.

In particular, if mind is the proximate transformational object of communication, then the success or failure of a communication action will depend on the success or failure in effecting the desired transformation of the audience's mind(s). That is, if the nature of an act of communication is to transform the audience's mind, then to fail to accomplish such a transformation is to fail to successfully carry out an act of communication. But this would suggest, for example, that one could not successfully utter a command unless it were believed. Yet, clearly it is quite possible to engage successfully in such communicative activities without their necessarily having the desired consequences. Thus, mind cannot in any simple sense be the proximate transformational object of meaningful communication.

Furthermore, the object of communication, whatever it is, must in some sense be symmetrically available to all parties to the communication, audience and communicator alike. For if I successfully utter a (token of a) sentence, then everyone involved understands the sentence, and understands it in the same way—the understandings are symmetrical or equivalent. Now, the meaning of the sentence may not be symmetrically or equivalently <u>relevant</u> to all parties, (it might be about you or about me or about someone or something else, for example), but, nevertheless, all parties will symmetrically and equivalently <u>understand</u> it to be about you or me or someone or something else. Such symmetry is a further constraint on the object of communication and another reason that mind cannot be that object: mind is not symmetrically available to the parties to a communication. [9]

At this point I will not develop in any detail a candidate object of communication but will suggest a general area of potentiality. Specifically, I suggest that the object of communication is itself a social entity. I suggest that it is a commonality of understanding among the participants in a social situation; it is a social definition of the situation (Goffman 1959; McHugh 1968; Thomas 1967). Such a social definition of the situation can, in principle, be transformed successfully without necessarily having the desired ensuing consequences, for example, a command can be understood to have been uttered without its necessarily being obeyed, and such a social definition of the situation is symmetrically accessible to all participants by virtue of their symmetrical roles in constituting such a commonality of understanding. Clearly, this suggestion is programmatic and requires explication, but it does indicate what I consider to be a viable approach to the problem of the object of transformational communication.

Thus, neither the problem of conventional communication nor that of the object of transformation is fatal to transformational models. In fact, as with the interactive perspective in general, responses to those challenges seem to require and yield creative explorations of independently interesting and fruitful areas, the emergence of the social from the psychological in this case, rather than ad hoc patch-ups. Thus, although the movement from transmission to transformation models is still quite young and still in a stage of ugly and ultimately untenable hybridization, the transformation perspective on communication appears to be highly promising and, thus, another indicator of the power of the general interactive perspective.

CONSEQUENCES OF THE INTERACTIVE PERSPECTIVE

The assumptions of picture and transmission models are based on powerfully obvious and appealing analogies, and those assumptions and analogies have dominated Western culture for several thousand years. Correspondingly, they are deeply embedded in our ways of thinking. It is, in fact, quite a difficult and long process to uncover and replace the myriad implicit picture and transmission assumptions that permeate our approaches to psychology. They are pervasive, subtle, and insidious. In these last sections, I would like to indicate some of the perspective shifts that are logically required, though not generally psychologically very easy, by the move toward interactive and transformational models.

Virtually every area of psychology looks different from an interactive perspective than from a picture perspective. Even when we have grasped the basic interactive assumption, however, its consequences come into focus only slowly and with effort: the perspective shift required is not immediate or all at once. For example, with respect to the challenges to the interactive perspective that have been discussed, we find further not immediately obvious consequences of every one of the interactive perspective responses.

Consider for a moment the focus on interactive epistemology suggested in the discussion of objects. If we accept that our cognitions function as interactive implicit definitions, always of general categories, then it follows that intrinsically cognition must be a matter of differentiation from the more general interactive patterns to the more specific rather than an accretion from the specific to the general as with picture models. That would imply, for example, as Piaget has recognized, that the cognitions of space, time, objects, and causality exist only in differentiation from and with respect to each other. None of them can be defined alone. More generally, it implies that there are no fixed points for cognition, no anchors tying cognition immutably to some part of the world. Cognition and cognitive development are matters of differentiation and exploration within patterns of potential interaction, all of which patterns connect to the world only by the implicit definition of successful interactive application.

The hierarchy of levels of abstraction that was discovered in response to the challenge of abstract knowledge leads to its own consequences. In particular, it leads to developmental stages and other developmental phenomena as logically necessary consequences of the interactive nature of knowing (Bickhard 1978). Further, it leads to the conclusion that there are an infinite number of potential developmental stages and to a noticeably different conceptualization of what those stages are.

The reasoning, briefly, is as follows. Potential knowing is organized as an unbounded hierarchy of levels of abstraction of what can be known. Each potential level of knowing corresponds to a knowing system interacting with the system at the next lower level, except for the lowest level, which interactively knows the environment. Any developing system, therefore, must ascend those levels one at a time and without skipping any level. To skip one would require a knowing system at some level with nothing below it to be known. But this imposes precisely an invariant sequence of stages on the development of any knowing system.

The fact that, from the interactive perspective, knowledge and motivation are differing aspects of the same underlying interactive control structure has consequences such as that motivation has nothing to do with pushes, pulls, energies, forces, or any of the rest of the common conceptual paraphernalia for thinking about motivation. None of those things exists. Further, the tie between knowledge and motivation implies that motivation and cognition develop together, as aspects of the same thing, in children. Questions such as whether or not some particular change is a result of cognition or motivation are fundamentally misstated. Still further, that tie implies that the concept of knowledge as objective, to which we then attach values, purposes, goals, and so forth, is mistaken. Objective knowledge is a myth. All knowledge is motivationally structured. The closest we can get to objective knowledge is to differentiate partially, at a higher level of abstraction, the knowledge aspect of lower-level interactive patterns. In its turn, however, such a differentiation is only partial and is itself motivationally structured.

I have briefly considered some consequences of a focus on interactive epistemology, of the hierarchy of abstractions, and of the intrinsic connection between knowledge and motivation. An area of major change in the interactive perspective, however, has not yet been mentioned: learning. In particular, the interactive perspective yields the conclusion that learning cannot be by induction, that it must be by hypothesis testing.

The basic point is fairly simple. The underlying metaphor for induction is the external stamping in of some sort of structural representation on a passive, static mind. Clearly this passivity is intrinsically associated with the picture model perspective. It is impossible, however, to passively stamp in an interactive control structure. In the first place, no general passive operation from the environment will succeed in creating any kind of control structure and, in the second, the structure of whatever might be considered to be doing the stamping imposes only the loosest constraints on the control structures that represent it. Control structures must be internally constructed and then tried out to see if they successfully apply, to see if the implicit hypotheses are falsified; and that is hypothesis testing, not induction.

This is in addition to Popper's (1965) demonstration that induction is logically impossible even on its own terms. Popper points out that the paradigmatic form for induction is to notice multiple instances of some pattern and then generalize that pattern beyond those instances. But to notice the multiple instances of the pattern

in the first place is to have tried out that pattern and to have found
that it applies to those instances, and that is hypothesis testing, not
induction. Thus, the argument from control structures and Popper's
argument reinforce each other. The point is also another fundamental
failure for picture models in that the necessity for a hypothesis generation and testing mechanism in a picture model is simply one
more entree for an interactive rule-governed agent.

One reason that the myth of induction is so difficult to give up
is that the nature of hypothesis generation and testing is usually
poorly understood. In particular, hypothesis testing is usually thought
of in terms of something like having a major premise, a minor
premise, and a conclusion, which conclusion then counts as the
hypothesis to be tested, thereby (perhaps) indirectly testing the minor
and major premises. Undoubtedly this form does occur. Far more
common, however, is the case in which something like a major
premise (theory, viewpoint, assumption) exists, and an empirical
pattern has been noted to apply (by its own hypothesis-testing process),
and the problem is to find a minor premise (hypothesis) that will
connect the major premise to the empirical pattern (conclusion).
For example, Newton's laws and the tide tables were both around
for some centuries before the complexities of how gravitational forces
yielded the tides were worked out. This kind of data-guided hypothesis
testing seems to be what people want to persist in calling induction.
But, it is not passive, it is not isomorphic or structural, it is not
consistent with picture models, and it is not induction. It is hypothesis
testing, and it underlies all learning and development.

Thus, we have noted some changes that the interactive perspective yields in cognitive psychology, developmental psychology, motivation, and learning. There are others, and each one mentioned has
its own ramifications. The basic point, however—that the interactive
perspective is a different perspective and that things look different
within it—has, I think, been made. It also seems clear that the
progressive shift from picture models to interactive models, the
shift to that different perspective, is taking place and, perhaps more
importantly, that it must take place.

CONSEQUENCES OF THE TRANSFORMATION PERSPECTIVE

The consequences of the transformation perspective for the
study of communication are also manifold. I will briefly mention
one or two illustrative examples each from the philosophy of language,
linguistics, psycholinguistics, and developmental psycholinguistics.
One of the more interesting consequences of the transformational
perspective for the philosophy of language is that sentences and

utterances cannot be said to have any direct truth value. From the transmission perspective, sentences are simply differently coded versions of the structural isomorphisms that constitute knowledge. Thus, sentences should be equally as true or false as the underlying knowledge structures. Even within the transmission perspective, of course, this has yielded fantastic contortions in trying to deal with nondeclarative sentences, and the strain is obvious even for the paradigmatic case of declaratives (for example, Evans and McDowell 1976). Nevertheless, truth value semantics is still very much around.

From a transformation perspective, however, the objects of communicative interaction may constitute representations, and thus have truth values, but the communicative interactions themselves are operators on, functions on, such representations. They are not representations themselves and, thus, have no truth values themselves.

The situation is analogous to that of functions operating on integers: the integers may be prime or not, or odd or even, but to apply such concepts to the functions is to commit a category error. Similarly, to speak of the truth value of sentences is to commit a category error. Of course, if we focus largely on constant functions, those which always have the same value no matter what the arguments, we may become tempted to falsely assimilate the function to its value and then try to consider the function's primeness. In effect, this is what has been done with language. The closest to constant functions that language offers are proper nouns, and the idealized naming relationship of proper nouns has been taken as paradigmatic for all of language. This, of course, is like trying to assimilate all functions to constant functions and thence to the values of those functions: it doesn't work. The appeal of the idealized naming relationship derives from the fact that pure name-to-named connections fit ideally into the one-to-one isomorphism conceptualizations of the picture and transmission models. Nevertheless, it still doesn't work. The assimilation of language to the naming relationship is false, even if the underlying picture assumptions of knowledge are ignored. Utterances are transformational operations, and sentences are operator forms, neither of which have truth value.

The point concerning sentences' lack of truth value is related to a consequence of the transformation perspective in linguistics: all utterances are context-dependent. In other words, the resultant transformational object of communications is dependent not only on the transformational utterance but also on the object upon which the transformation was performed, the context within which it was uttered. [10] Similarly, the value of any function is dependent on its argument. This point, of course, applies least to constant-function-like proper nouns, but even proper nouns minimally require an appropriate context of conventional understanding to have their desired effect, and for many, such as "John" or "Mary, " that context and those resultant understandings can vary widely. Deicticness, indexicality, and other variations of context dependency have been being discovered throughout language. The transformational perspective yields the conclusion that context dependency is intrinsic to the nature of language.

Another consequence of adopting the transformational perspective is that the standard distinction between semantics and pragmatics becomes incoherent. Within the transmission sentences-as-institutional-objects perspective, the rules of well-formedness for such objects constitute the subject matter for syntax; the coding relationships between such sentence-objects and underlying knowledge structures are the subject matter for semantics; and the (interactive) uses to which such sentence-objects can be put are the subject matter for pragmatics. Clearly, even a focus on pragmatics within this perspective yields at best an act-that-transmits conceptualization of communication. Within an interactive-transformational perspective, however, a conventionalized sentence form has a correspondingly conventionalized transformation-on-object-of-communication, that is, a correspondingly conventionalized function. The sentence form is uttered in a particular context for the sake of its conventionalized transformation of that context which, in turn, is for the sake of the resultant context. There are only two potential subject matters here: the conventionalized transformations and the contextual objects of transformation. If we identify semantics with the transformations and pragmatics with the contextual objects, then the semantics of an utterance has no truth value, while the pragmatic point of the utterance does. On the other hand, if we identify semantics with the objects of communication and pragmatics with the conventionalized transformations, then semantics becomes the study of the point for which utterances are made their uses and has no specific connection to particular sentences, while pragmatics becomes the study of that which provides those uses (conventionalized transformations) as properties of specific sentences. Either way, pragmatics and semantics as currently conceived become incoherent.

The transformational perspective also has consequences for lexical semantics, concerned with the meaning of words, including semantic memory and organization as studied in psycholinguistics. Lexical semantics is generally considered from a transmission perspective in which word meanings are taken to be codings of the elements and construction principles of structural representations. From a transformational perspective, however, word meanings must in some sense be contributions to the specifications of communicative transformations. Thus, lexical semantics must be the study of the composition and decomposition of communicative transformations and not of structural representations. At some level of abstraction, then, it should be similar to the study of the compositional organization of noncommunicative transformational skills, such as manipulating an object or building a house.

To the extent that transformational organizations are sensitive to the structures they operate on, the organization of sentence forms should be similarly sensitive to the representations upon which they operate. Those representational objects of transformational communication, in turn, should be sensitive to the organization of the cognitive representations out of which they are formed. Thus, sentence organizations will be at least partially sensitive to the organization of cognitions in terms of objects, actions, space, time, and so on. It is such indirect sensitivities of organization that provide the semblance of plausibility to transmission model coding approaches. That sensitivity, however, is no more a coding relationship than is the twist of a steering wheel a coding of the curve of a road, or a work organization plan the coding of the building to be constructed. In all such cases there are organizational sensitivities to be studied, but there are no transmission model coding relationships.

The organization of a transformation on the world will not only be sensitive to the objects of transformation, but it will also be constrained by the nature of what a transformation is. One fundamental case of such a constraint is that a transformation must somehow select its specific object of transformation out of the available potentialities as well as perform its particular interactions with that object. This, of course, applies to communicative transformations as much as to any other kind. Thus, a communication must perform two related tasks: it must select within the relevant context a focus of transformation, and it must transform that focus in some way.

Furthermore, it must perform both of those tasks without the use of classical ideal naming relationships: such ideal name-to-named connections do not exist. Both tasks, then, must be performed through differentiations within the field of available potentialities: selection of focus through differentiation and selection of operation through differentiation.

The general nature of such differentiation processes and the sensitivities that they manifest to the contextual objects of communication should form a major part of the subject matter of linguistics and psycholinguistics as viewed from a transformational perspective. But these issues cannot even be defined within a classical encoding-transmission perspective, and, correspondingly, they are not to be found within these classically dominated areas of study.

A consequence of the transformational perspective for developmental psycholinguistics is that language learning must be preceded by the establishment of communicative conventions through precedent and habitualization, generally between infant and mother. Only within such an established framework of communication can the institutionalized resources of language be incorporated.

The argument for this consequence depends on two other consequences of the transformational perspective which, therefore, must be considered in preparation. First, there is the consequence that, among other things, language learning must proceed by differentiations within whole communicative acts. Thus, a holophrastic period must exist. Within a transmission perspective it would seem to make sense to learn single bits and pieces of isomorphic relations one at a time, and, therefore, a holophrastic period, though not necessarily ruled out, is not required. Within a transformation perspective, a communication is such only insofar as it succeeds in a communicative transformation, and a piece of communication, such as a word, is such only insofar as it compositionally contributes to the specification of such a transformation. That is, there is nothing for words to be except compositional contributors to utterances, but such contributions can only exist and, thus, be learned within the framework of complete transformational utterances. That is, they must develop through differentiation within whole communicative acts.

The second relevant consequence is that the transformational perspective requires no special principles of learning. The interactive-transformational perspective, in fact, is restricted to hypothesis testing by the same reasoning as within the interactive perspective per se, [11] contrary to the infinite arbitrariness problems and inductive assumptions of transmission approaches.

With language development by differentiation within whole communications and language development by hypothesis testing both established, the necessity for an initial phase of precedent-and-habitualization conventional communication can be approached in two related ways. The first, simply, is that there must be conventionalized communicative acts already established within which linguistic differentiations can begin, and the only possible origin of such prelinguistic communicative forms is precedent and habitualization. The second is that the testing of hypotheses about communicative differentiations itself requires communication which, initially, can only be of the precedent-and-habitualization form. Thus, the transformational perspective yields three illustrative constraints on language development: development of word meanings must be by some process of differentiation within whole communicative transformations; language development must proceed by hypothesis testing; and language development must be preceded by a period of precedent-and-habitualization conventional communication.

The transformational perspective, then, has significant consequences within philosophy, linguistics, psycholinguistics, and developmental psycholinguistics; within, in fact, the entire area of language studies. The shift from transmission to transformational perspectives, correspondingly, is far-reaching and nontrivial. It is a shift that uproots a deeply embedded and pervasive assumption.

The core encoding assumption of the transmission perspective has seemed so intuitively obvious that it has virtually never been questioned. But so also was it once intuitively obvious that the earth was flat. Part of the reason that the encoding assumption has seemed so obvious is that it has not been recognized that there were any alternatives to it. The transformational perspective would now seem to provide such an alternative. I have made and do make the strong claim that the shift from transmission to transformational model is necessary. A minimal claim, however, would be that the transformational approach is a genuine alternative to the classical approach and that it deserves consideration.

A PERSPECTIVE SHIFT

I have argued for a massive shift in approaches to the modeling of human processes, a shift from picture-transmissional perspectives to interactive-transformational perspectives. Furthermore, I have argued that such a shift is ultimately necessary and inevitable. The move from picture to interactive models is some centuries old and well under way. The move from transmission to transformational models is very recent and barely begun. In both cases, the consequences of the shift are complexly and densely ramified throughout the areas of concern: it requires a great deal of exploration to sort out even a small region of those consequences. It is hoped, however, that if the necessity for the perspective shift is understood, and something of its nature is elucidated, then that shift can proceed much more rapidly.

DISCUSSION: A METATHEORETICAL PERSPECTIVE

Piaget

Piaget's strong emphasis on epistemological interactivism and constructivism (for example, Piaget 1971) has had a major influence on my own thinking. Nevertheless, there remain significant differences which I would like to indicate briefly.

My core difference with Piaget is that he has retained picture model assumptions throughout an otherwise strongly interactive model. One instance of this is Piaget's postulation of both figurative (or configurational) and operative knowledge as distinct, though inter-dependent, forms of knowledge (Piaget 1969; Piaget and Inhelder 1969). Operative knowledge is essentially interactive; figurative knowledge is essentially picture knowledge. Piaget has tried to con-struct a hybrid of the two which, in my opinion, has not and could not succeed. The concern with figurative knowledge is most prominent with respect to perception (Piaget 1969) and imagery (Piaget and Inhelder 1971), which has the peculiar character of being derived from action, on the one hand, and being figurative, on the other.

A major instance of Piaget's attempted hybridization of picture and interactive conceptual approaches is his concept of cognitive structures. On the one hand, these structures are supposed to underlie and explain interactive task capabilities in much the same way as a control structure does. On the other hand, they cannot serve that function because they are static algebraic structures, such as groups and lattices, and they have much more the character of descriptive logical task analyses than of explanatory control struc-tures. The assumption that the ground for the explanation of a capa-bility has a structural relationship to the logical structure of the capability to be explained is a basic picture model axiom. Although Piaget no longer writes of these structures as being the unitary and unifying structures-of-the-whole that define his stages, he still uses them as purported grounds and explanations for interactive capabilities (Piaget 1976, 1978).

A second major difference between Piaget's model and my own concerns the stages of development. The stages that derive from the progressive development through the levels of knowing differ from the classical Piagetian stages in a number of characteristics (Bickhard 1978). Among these are that the levels-of-knowing stages are not necessarily characterized by any particular structure, that the general age boundaries seem to differ, and that there is no level-of-knowing stage corresponding strictly to the sensory-motor period. In part, these differences stem from Piaget's focus on logical task analysis structures in that, from the perspective of the knowing level stage model, Piaget has taken the attainment of the major task capa-bilities within a knowing level (for example, object permanence within level one, or conservation within level two) as demarcating a stage boundary rather than as being a major accomplishment within a stage. Thus, Piaget's stage boundaries are half a cycle off, and the sensory-motor period is the extra half-cycle. Piaget's more recent writings (1976, 1978) have moved much closer to the levels-of-knowing model, but much is left unclear, and he still relies on his structures as explanations, even if no longer unitary.

Wittgenstein

The claim that the later Wittgenstein presents a hybrid position between transmission and transformation models would probably be disputed by some. The disagreement would most likely rest on two assertions. First, Wittgenstein in his later works repudiated the picture model of his Tractatus (1961); and, second, Wittgenstein, especially in the Philosophical Investigations (1958), explicitly focuses on the instrumental, that is, the transformation, nature of language. In view of this, I would like to expand my position a little.

The short versions of my responses to these two claims are as follows. First, Wittgenstein repudiated most of the details of the logical atomism of the Tractatus, but he never repudiated, never developed an alternative to, and strongly seems to have retained, a basic transmission-encoding conceptualization of the thought-expressive function of language. Second, Wittgenstein explicitly focused on the multiple instrumental functions of language as a contrast with and correction to the single language function of thought expression considered in the Tractatus, but thought expression through encoding remained one of his basic and central functions of language, and his conceptualization of instrumental functions was not transformational. In particular, he focused on the multiple uses of language, which might include transformations, but he did not place interactive transformations in any central position and certainly did not provide any object of transformation for language.

That Wittgenstein repudiated much of the logical atomism of the Tractatus is clear. That he did not repudiate its basic picture model foundations is less clear; obviously, he never took an explicit stand on the issue. It could not even be posed without a strict transformational conceptualization for contrast, but, nevertheless, the conclusion seems to me inescapable. First, it is clear that the expression of thought is still one of the functions of language. He even explicitly warns that we must "make a radical break with the idea that language always functions in one way, always serves the same purpose: to convey thoughts" (1958, para. 304). Second, he writes of the usages of propositions (1958, para. 278) and explicitly compares propositions to pictures (1958, p. 11). Essentially, Wittgenstein seems to be suggesting "that the picture theory needs supplementing, rather than that it is false; that the theory of meaning as use is a complement rather than a rival to the picture theory" (Kenny 1973, p. 226). The model that emerges, in fact, is in these general respects inclusive of the Austin (1968) and Searle (1969) model of the various uses to which knowledge-encoding propositions can be put.

Wittgenstein focuses explicitly and extensively on the instrumental nature of language. He likens language to a tool kit (1958, para. 11). His concern with this instrumental nature, however, is an aspect of his concern with "meaning as use," and it is in this context that it becomes clear that it is not essentially transformational. Meaning as use refers to the use of sentences and words in various rule-governed language games; it is from these uses that the full meaning of "dead" signs is derived. Use in this sense has two basic aspects: the rule-governed usage of the sign in the language game per se and the instrumental utility for which we engage in some of the language games (not all language games necessarily have an instrumental utility, for example, riddles). Neither use as rule-governed usage nor use as instrumental utility is necessarily transformational, and certainly neither suggests an object of transformation. These aspects of Wittgenstein's theory are compatible with a model of language as a conventional means for transforming social reality, in which the rule-governed usages are the manners in which we engage in such transformations and the instrumental utilities are the reasons for which we engage in (some of) those transformations, but he does not develop such a model himself. Instead, Wittgenstein's primary focus is on the multiplicity and diversity of language games (for example, 1958, para. 23) and on some of the consequences of that variation in language games, such as for the proper understanding of certain psychological terms; he does not focus on the processes by which those usages are engaged in or by which those utilities are attained.

Wittgenstein is so impressed by the multiplicity of language games, in fact, and by their open-endedness to new invention, that he concludes, "Language as a whole is not an instrument for a particular purpose specifiable outside language, and it is in this sense that its rules are arbitrary" (Kenny 1973, p. 177): arbitrary in the sense of not being constrained by any such outside purpose. In this respect, as well as in his retention of a picture model version of thought-expressive language, Wittgenstein is directly incompatible with the transformational perspective. In the transformational perspective, language is explicitly a conventional tool for the manipulation of social definitions of the situation, sometimes for its own sake, sometimes for the indirect sake of other instrumental purposes, and the rules of language (games) are definitely constrained by the nature of that social object of interaction.

Wittgenstein, then does not construct a transformational model; he retains a transmission picture-encoding model of thought-expressive languages; and he denies any general unifying function for language. In at least these respects, he does not have and is incompatible with a transformational perspective. His core concern with meaning as use, however, both as usage and as utility, is quite compatible with a transformational model.

3
INTERACTION, COGNITION, AND SITUATION

THE INTERACTIVE PERSPECTIVE

In this section, a model of cognitive representational structures will be presented which will serve as the conceptual foundation for the later discussions of psychosocial structures and processes. In particular, the basic distinction between situation images and world images is developed, and various structures within and relationships between them are discussed.

The perspective within which this model is constructed is strictly interactional. From an interactive perspective, to know something is to interact successfully with it. A successful interaction is one that maintains the interactive capacity of the system, that maintains its stability, its adaptability (Bickhard in press). Thus, the capacity for interactive knowing is an extension of biological stability and adaptability (Piaget 1971).

A system can gain knowledge about its environment only through interactions with that environment. Most importantly, the only sense in which a system can have knowledge about its environment is to know the actual and potential interactions within that environment. The world is constituted as a structured field of potential interactions. It is that field that is experientially explored and cognitively modeled (Rescher 1973).

It is clear that, according to the perspective of interactive knowing, what is being known is the environment, but it is not so readily clear what it is about the environment that is to be known. That is, from an interactive perspective, what are the structures, the units, of knowing? Common sense tells us that objects, events, properties, and so on are the units of knowing, but if we contact only a field of potential interactions, how are such structures and units constituted? How can a model of interactive knowing account for the reality of such structures and units?

If the only things a system can know about its environment are the potential interactions that constitute that environment, then the structures and units of knowing are precisely the structures and units of the field of potential interactions. It seems odd to think of the everyday structure of our world—objects and persons in space-time—as a structure of potential interactions, and it is clear that such a claim writes a rather large promissory note for the reinterpretation of our normal world in such interactive terms. Making good on that reinterpretation, however, has been under way at least since Kant (1965) and by many people since then (for example, Peirce 1972, Piaget 1954, Rescher 1973). The interactive perspective I am adopting stems from this broad tradition. [12]

If knowing in the immediate active sense is constituted by successfully interacting, then what constitutes knowledge? There are several senses of knowledge that might be considered, for example, "knowledge of how to do something" or "knowledge that something is the case," but I take the most fundamental sense of having knowledge of something as being equivalent to having the capacity of actively knowing that something. Knowledge in this sense is potential knowing, potential successful interacting.

In taking such a version of "knowledge how" as fundamental, I assume that other senses, such as "knowledge that," can be reduced to it. The constructive defense of that assumption is part of the task of the general tradition of interactive knowing, and one intention of the sections that follow is to contribute to that task. The basic point is that any declarative knowledge ("knowledge that") must ultimately be given some sort of interactive interpretation(s) in order to participate in the activities of the system at all, in order to have any status as real for the system.

The structured field of potential interactions constitutes the object of knowing. There are two senses in which a system can have knowledge of such an interactive field: (1) a general knowledge of the organizational structure of interactive potentialities, for example, that the occurrence of some particular type of interaction generally indicates the potentiality of (accessibility of) some other particular type of interaction; and (2) a specific knowledge of the immediate interactive potentialities of the current situation, for example, that a particular type of interaction is possible right now. The organization of the interactive potentialities of "right now," of the current situation, must be consonant with the organization of interactive potentialities in general. What is possible in the current situation is simply a special case of what is possible in the world in general, and, therefore, the structures of those potentialities must be in accord. The current situation, in fact, is simply a location in the overall web of interactive potentialities that constitutes the world. These two senses of knowledge of the potential interactive field, the general world knowledge of its structure, and the specific situational knowledge of the system's current location in that structure form the foundations of the world and situation images, respectively, developed in the following sections.

The intent of the following sections in this chapter is to present and develop some of the structures and processes of an interactive knowing model, particularly those relating to the situation and world image distinction. These explications and analyses are presented within the mathematical framework of abstract machine theory. The discussion begins with machine theoretic explications of the concepts of knowing and knowledge, within which the distinction is made between the two kinds of knowledge constituted by the situation and world images. The focus then shifts to a consideration of the processes by which the situation image is constructed and kept up to date in ongoing interactions with the environment. Such situation image maintenance processes are called apperceptive processes. Lastly, the situation image structures that are constructed by apperceptions are examined, as are the relationships of those structures to the world image. Special emphasis in this discussion is placed on the concept of a scheme as a representational unit and on the special role that representations of objects play in the organization of the situation image.

KNOWING AND KNOWLEDGE

In an interaction between a system and an environment, the system's actions in that environment will be determined in general by the internal conditions or state of the system. That internal state, in turn, will be determined jointly by the prior state of the system together with the inputs from the environment. [13] In such an interaction, a system will be said to be <u>knowing</u> (some characteristic of) that environment insofar as the interaction does not yield a condition in the system for which the system's actions are not defined, that is, insofar as the course of the interaction is well defined from the system's perspective. [14] This is the automata theoretic version of a successful interaction. Such interactions will generally be organized within (structures of) goal-seeking servomechanisms: thus, knowing, in this sense, will be constituted by successful goal seeking, successful task accomplishment.

If <u>knowledge</u> is defined as the capability of knowing, then knowledge is constituted by the structure of possible conditions or states that could determine the system's participation in the interaction. That is, knowledge is constituted by the control structure of the system.

THE SITUATION IMAGE

Knowledge thus defined, however, is of a rather special nature. A particular control structure determines a set of potential inter- actions which can become actual only if that control structure is in fact executed, and it will be executed only if the interactive processes in the remainder of the system's control structures are such that the flow of control, the state transition path, leads up to the given struc- ture. Thus, a particular control structure determines a set of interactive rules, constitutes an interactive procedure, and its em- bedding in the overall structure determines the conditions under which those rules are to be applied: If such-and-such particular prior conditions are met (if particular outcomes[15] of prior interactions occur), then proceed in accordance with the given set of rules. Knowl- edge as constituted by control structures is, therefore, always hypothetical; it is knowledge about what to do or what might be done if some (complex) condition is in fact the case. It is knowledge about how the world might be.

The execution of any particular control structure, and therefore any actual interaction, thus depends on the fulfillment of that control structure's embedding conditions, and the fulfillment of those conditions constitutes knowledge about the current condition of the world. Thus, the initiation of a particular interaction depends on the current actualization of the antecedent of a hypothetical conditional. This knowledge about the current interactive status of the situation is generated by the outcomes of prior interactions, and those outcomes, in turn, are constituted by the states in which the system is left at the ends of those interactions. Knowledge of the current situation, therefore, is constituted by the total state of the system at a particular time.

Structures of knowledge about the potential interactive world can be defined in terms of structures of procedure or control, but there is at this point no way to define structures of knowledge about the present actual situation in the world: this knowledge is constituted by the current state of the system, which is a nonstructured unitary concept. I propose to give this concept appropriate structure and to recognize the information-generating function of interaction outcomes by considering that an interaction outcome sets an indicator or index in an appropriate register for such indices and by defining the state of a system to be the set of all its contemporary indices. An index (indicator) as constructed by such an outcome thus indexes (indicates) whatever it was about the environment that yielded that particular outcome to an interaction rather than some other outcome. Processes within the system now amount to changes in register contents, and control structures correspond to rules for changing register contents, together with rules for outputs. [16] Most importantly, structures of knowledge about the current situation in the world now correspond to structures of indices.

I propose to refer to the knowledge inherent in a system's control structure as that system's image of the world, or world image, and to the knowledge inherent in a system's index structure as that system's image of its current situation, or situation image. [17]

APPERCEPTION

A particular set of indices will in general imply a great number of things about the environment, or, more specifically, will have a great number of potential implications about the course of potential interactions. If one of these potential interactions should be initiated, the relevant implication(s) of the given set of indices may have to be actually computed by a subsidiary procedure before the primary control structure can make use of those implications in the determination of the course of the interaction. The reason for this is simply that the implications of a set of indices will in general be large in number and individually complex and thus not always susceptible to simple and immediate recognition: the implications must be recognized and computed in their own right. The interactive implications of a visual scan of a room, for example, go far beyond the direct outcomes of the scanning interactions themselves. Such a richness of implications from directly constructed indices about the environment simply reflects the complex redundancy of reality. [18]

The currently constructed indices in a system will be called the system's explicit situation image, while the structure of interactive implications that may be constructed from a particular, already constructed explicit image (by the procedures in the given system) will be called the implicit situation image of the system. The logical relationship of a system's explicit image to its implicit image, as well as the processes of constructing the one out of the other, will be referred to as the system's apperception. [19]

INTERACTION AND KNOWLEDGE CONSTRUCTION

Corresponding to the distinction between world image and situation image, there will be two forms of knowledge acquisition. An interaction that successfully proceeds to one of the control structure's available outcomes thereby constructs (or changes) one or more indices and thus contributes to the system's knowledge of its situation. Such constructions of situation knowledge have two aspects:

(1) the interaction that constructed the index will have required that certain characteristics be true of the environment in order for the interaction to have reached the particular outcome that it did—implications based on such characteristics will be called perceptual; and (2) the interaction that constructed the index will have changed some characteristics of the environment—implications based on these changes will be called transformational. [20,21] Both perceptual and transformational aspects of the implicit image form parts of the situation image.

The situation image is thus constructed by successful interactions—interactions that reach an outcome of the relevant control structure. The world image, on the other hand, is constructed in response to unsuccessful interactions. Only when an interaction has failed, for example, by reaching an undefined condition or an infinite loop in the control structure, is there reason to modify—and try to improve—the control structure. Only a failure indicates a need to modify it; otherwise, modifications might destroy valid knowledge. [22] Constructions of the world image will be called learning. [23]

SITUATION TRAJECTORIES

The apperceptive construction of the situation image has two primary aspects corresponding to two fundamental forms of redundancy in the environment: instantaneous redundancy and temporal redundancy. Instantaneous redundancy refers to the fact that the outcomes of quite limited interactions with the environment suffice to predict the outcomes of multitudes of other potential interactions that might occur. The standard example of this form of apperception is that of the physical object in which initial limited interactions (say, a visual scan) suffice to imply the general outcomes of potential interactions of many forms and modalities and from multiple perspectives. As Piaget (1954) has shown, the development of the ability to compute these apperceptive implications occupies a major portion of our early lives. [24] It is important to note that what we mean by a physical object is in fact constituted by a particular structure of apperceptive implications concerning particular classes of interactions with which we might engage the world, the structure of interactive implications is the closest we can get to the "thing in itself." [25]

Temporal redundancy leads to a more complex and more pervasive form of apperception. Its pervasiveness derives from the fact that we are frequently unable to reconfirm at will the explicit situation image from which our instantaneous redundancies are computed and therefore must assume fundamental temporal continuities in the environment as we base our interactions on the outcomes of past interactions. Its complexity derives from the fact that the continuities involved are seldom simple identities through time but are rather networks of implications through time, networks whose complexity of structure may become awesome. Thus, to take a "trivial" example, the interactive implications of a visual scan of a nearby object are not the same once we have taken a step, say, to the side but must be recomputed taking that step into account.

Even this relatively simple example illustrates two major points. First, we normally would not recompute the implications of the first visual scan after taking the step but would instead redo the scan from our new position (we would "look again"), that is, reconstruct the explicit image. [26] This ability to reconstruct and reconfirm the explicit image is so powerful in the visual field, and vision so dominates our epistemological theories and metaphors, that it is easily not noticed that such an ability is vastly more limited to immediate visual space. [27] In all but our most immediate circumstances, we must rely on temporal structures of implications.

The second point illustrated by the example is that the temporal implications from an original explicit image are not a unitary path determined solely by that original set of indices. In the example, the implications of the first scan depend on the ensuing step to the side as well as the scan itself and would be different for a different intervening interaction, for example, a step in a different direction. Thus, an initial explicit image component (and its instantaneous apperceptive implications) does not determine a fixed temporal apperceptive path but rather fixes a point in a network of possible trajectories of transformations of the situation (and thus of the situation image). The actual trajectory taken within the network will depend on intervening events.

Correspondingly, the system's knowledge of that trajectory (assuming it cannot simply generate appropriate new explicit images) will depend on, among other things, its information about those intervening events and on its world image knowledge of how to take those events into account. The events may be external or may be activities of the system itself, but in either case (and as with all else about its environment) the system can only know about them through the index register outcomes of its interactions. Thus the initial explicit image, from which an instantaneous apperceptive image may be derived, is supplemented by the explicit register outcomes of subsequent interactions, from which the apperceptive temporal trajectory of transformations of that image may be derived. In both cases, the instantaneous and the temporal, there is an explicit skeleton filled out by apperceptive implications. Apperception is not a process of the repetitive replacement of old situation images by new ones; it is a process of the continuous enriching and updating of old situation images into new ones.

Two points need to be made concerning the computation of such transformational trajectories. First, it is possible that in some cases the initial explicit image will be quite incomplete or even ambiguous in its implications and that ensuing interactions will serve both to complete and to disambiguate the full situation image as well as to represent its trajectory of transformations, for example, an initially uninterpretable sound whose significance is clarified by later events. Second, the trajectory implications of intervening interactions can themselves range from clear to ambiguous and from straightforward (context-independent) to highly context-dependent.

The apperceptive computation of a trajectory will depend (in general) on both perceptual and transformational implications of ensuing interactions, that is, the system can both notice and affect the course of the situation transformations. Extreme examples of the two cases might be, in the case of perceptual implications, keeping track of the relative position of an object through a sequence of hidden external motions, as in Piagetian object permanency, [28] and, in the case of transformational implications, the similar computation of relative position through a sequence of system self-locomotions. [29] The system (in general) participates in the construction of the trajectory as well as in the construction of its image of the trajectory.

PRINCIPLES OF REPRESENTATIONAL ORGANIZATION

Indices are constructed by the executions of procedures in the world image. These executions are in the form of either direct environmental interactions or of internal apperceptive processes. Indices are also referenced by the executions of procedures in the world image, either as apperceptive processes or as further environmental interactions. The functional existence of an index is completely captured by these two points. Therefore, any functional properties of indices in the situation image must be aspects of, or derivable from, these two points—including, in particular, representational properties of indices. In this chapter, the discussion will turn to an examination of those representational properties, to an examination of the principles of representational organization of the situation image within the world image.

Indices indicate, on the one hand, something about the course or outcome of the interactions that set them. On the other hand, they indicate various choices or selections to be made in the course of relevant ensuing interactions. Indices carry information from past interactions of potential relevance to the flow of future interactions.

Future interactions, however, will set future indices. Thus, current indices carry information concerning the potentiality of future indices. An index is functional only insofar as it might be referenced, only insofar as it is relevant to some potential execution, and, thus, only insofar as it is relevant to some potential future indices. There is, then, a network of relevancy relationships, of indications relevant to potential construction, extending throughout the space of potential indices. Such indications of potentiality, such relevancy relationships, are the foundation of representational organization.

The indications of a particular index considered alone might conceivably be unambiguous. In general, however, the indicative relevancies of an index will depend upon other indices. These other indices may in turn have their own context-sensitive relevancies. Such structures of context sensitivity among indices will be of the form of some indices differentiating, or further specifying, the indicative content of other indices, such as the specification of an object in a room or of the orientation or color of that object. Another form of such specification would be the specification of the consequences of particular interactions in particular contexts, such as the consequences of turning the key or the steering wheel in an automobile.

Relationships of context sensitivity are the inverses of relationships of indicative relevance. That is, a context sensitivity relationship is a relationship of potentiality indication looked at from the opposite end. For an index (or index structure) to specify an object in a room, for example, is the inverse of the indices for the room indicating the potentialities for objects in the room. The filling out of such relevancies and sensitivities is the task of apperception, and the organization of such relationships is the representational organization of the situation image, both explicit and implicit.

THE SITUATION IMAGE IN THE WORLD IMAGE

Any interaction changes the situation image, changes some of its constituent indices, moves it along one of its potential trajectories. Conversely, any change in the situation image implies and corresponds to the interaction that yielded that change; any movement along a situation image trajectory corresponds to the execution flow through the control structures that produced that movement. Thus, any situation image indicates an interlocking web of potential trajectories of future situation images, and that web of potential trajectories corresponds exactly to the web of potential interactions that could proceed from the current situation.

The world image is the organization of control structures within which any interaction must take place (ignoring learning). The overall web of potential interactions, of potential control flows, therefore, is determined by the world image. The web of potential interactions, however, is simply the dual perspective on the overall web of potential situation image trajectories. Thus, the full organization of potential situation image trajectories is given by the world image.

A particular situation image will constitute a point in that overall organization of potential situation images, a point in the overall web of potential trajectories. The potentialities that are indicated by the indices and index structures of a particular situation image are of the various trajectories and groups of trajectories that proceed from that point in the overall web. A situation image specifies a current point in a web of potential interactions, and the representational content of that situation image is given by the access it provides to those potential interactions. Knowledge is potential interaction, and the situation image fixes the current relevancy organization within the web of knowledge in the world image.

MOTIVATIONAL SELECTIONS

Potential situation image trajectories correspond to potential paths of interaction. Potential future situation images located along those trajectories, and potential index structures in those situation images, correspond to potential outcomes of interactions. But such potential outcomes of interactions encompass precisely the potential transformational accomplishments and the potential perceptual detections of those interactions. Such potential accomplishments are the potential goals of interactions, and the potential detections are of events and conditions which may be relevant to reaching those goals. In specifying the current accessibility of potential trajectories, then, the situation image also specifies the currently available potential goals of interaction and the potential paths of interaction toward those goals.

Selections among available potential paths of interaction will be made by the world image with respect to, and in the service of, the current goals of interaction. These goals will themselves be index structures set by prior interactions as directives to further interactions. Selections among available potential goals of interaction will be made by the world image with respect to, and in the service of, current higher-order goals. Such a hierarchicalization of goals corresponds to a hierarchicalization of servomechanisms. The highest-level goal in such an organization will, in general, correspond to the stability and adaptability of the overall system in its environment.

The availabilities of interaction paths and subordinate goals are represented at a given time by the situation image within the world image. Those availabilities are ongoingly constrained and elaborated during the course of an interaction by the environment and the world image jointly. The constraints and elaborations, in turn, are incorporated into the apperceptive updating of the situation image, into the computation of the trajectory of the situation image. New path and goal selections may be made as part of that updating.

Thus, a potential interaction path may be initiated depending on whether it is relevant to current goals. Conversely, a potential goal is approachable only if there is a currently available path leading to it. A visual scan of a chair, for example, may indicate the potentiality of sitting down (with all of its resultant indices), but it is not likely to be actualized if the current goal structure is to walk out the door on the way to a movie. Conversely, a goal of sitting down is moot if there is nothing in the current situation to sit on. In general, the situation image represents the structure of current potentialities, and the goal-directed selections among those potentialities constitute the process of motivation. [30]

FORMS OF REPRESENTATIONAL STRUCTURE

Functional organization among potential indices has been discussed thus far primarily in terms of indicative relevancies between single indices. It is of fundamental importance to note that functional relationships within situation images can and will occur with respect to higher levels of organizational units, in particular, with respect to types of structures of indicative relevancies as well as particular single relevancies. That is, instances of types of relevancy structures among indices may be indicated, constructed, and recognized without those type instances being fully specified in all their single index detail. A situation image, for example, might indicate the general structure of interactive potentialities of a physical object without indicating every detail of those potentialities, say, with respect to the back side of the object. This possibility of general types of indicative relevancy structures constituting units of relevancy structures is a consequence of two facts, one about environments and one about systems. On the one hand, the redundancy-based environmental implications of a particular index are not necessarily about other particular potential indices but rather can be about such general structural or organizational characteristics of sets of potential indices. On the other hand, it is possible to constitute, or represent, such general structural-level relevancies in the world image via procedures whose computations are precisely appropriate to those general structural levels, without regard for variations at more detailed levels of specificity. The specifics of interactions with regard to such within-type details may, for example, be relegated to appropriate subprocedures. Thus, environmental redundancies exist at levels of structural types, and procedures of appropriate generality are capable of representing them and, thus, of constituting knowledge of them. The world image and situation image, therefore, will be structured in terms of them.

One fundamental distinction to be made among relevancy structures is between those in which the potentiality indications are reciprocal or reversible and those in which they are not. [31] A structure of reversible relevancies is one in which each potentiality indication is reciprocated, in which each potential path of execution has at least one return or reverse path. In such a structure, each element will suffice to indicate though not necessarily to specify completely the whole structure as an interactive potentiality. Thus, any one of many possible visual scans of an object would suffice to indicate the whole of a rich structure of potential interactions with that object (and, thus, to indicate a correspondingly rich structure of potential goals). Furthermore, each of the elements of (most of) that structure, for example, the visual aspects of the object produced by various manipulations, will indicate simultaneously the potentiality of all of the others. That rich structure, however, may structurally delimit but, nevertheless, not fully specify potential interactions involving the back of the object. Such reversible structural types will be called frames. [32]

Structures of irreversible relevancies are those in which the indicative relationships of possible index constructions (task accomplishments) are not reciprocal and, therefore, impose an irreversible functional ordering among the potentialities. In particular, an index may indicate the potentiality of some other (characteristics of) indices, through the execution of appropriate procedures but do so irreversibly, in the sense that construction of the indicated indices through the corresponding procedure(s) may eliminate the potentiality of the original index. [33] Thus, elements of structures of irreversible relevancies do not necessarily indicate the whole structure: they may indicate but not be reciprocally indicated. A visual scan of a match, for example, might indicate the potentiality of striking it but will do so irreversibly. Structures of irreversible relevancies will be called networks.

Structures of relevancies, both frames and networks, can be indexed (indicated) in a situation image as being potential or accessible within that situation. Being subject to such general structural-level indexing entails that types of relevancy structures are themselves subject to further higher-level structuring: structuring and categorizing[34] are recursive, and structures (and instances of types of structures) can be elements of other structures. Thus, frames can be elements of frames, in a strictly hierarchical fashion, as in the case of frames for various objects being parts of the frame for a room, and networks can be elements of networks, in the sense that one network of potentialities may indicate the possibility of (the irreversible transformation into) another network. Thus, within the network of potentialities constituting the interactive representation of a glass bottle will be (the asymmetric potentiality of) a network of potentialities constituting the representation of a broken glass bottle. Frames can also be elements of networks, insofar as frames can indicate the irreversible constructive potentiality of other frames—the glass bottle example clearly involves frames (of physical objects) within networks (of irreversible transformations); and networks can be elements of frames, insofar as networks and network categories can reciprocally indicate potentiality.[35] Thus, a kind of object (a glass bottle) might be capable of two differing irreversible transformational networks (breaking or melting) such that the potentiality of either one of those networks would reciprocally indicate the potentiality of the other. The generic term for such structures of interactive relevancies, including such hybrid forms, and, thus, for such structures of potential goal (task) definitions, will be <u>scheme</u>.[36] The scheme for a glass bottle, thus, would include the frame of the reversible potentialities of various manipulations of it together with the networks of irreversible potentialities of breaking or melting it.

The basis for the distinction between frames and networks has been the reversibility, or lack thereof, of the potentiality indications within a relevancy structure. Many other principles of organization, both functional and logical, are possible within sets of potential indices. One, for example, would focus on the sequencing patterns of potentiality indications, of which the subpattern of reversibility is but an instance. Another example would be relationships of compatibility or mutual exclusivity of potential simultaneous existence within sets of potential indices. The primary concept desired from this discussion, however, is that of a scheme, and, therefore, such further refinements of situation image structuring (and scheme structuring) will not be pursued at this time.

The conceptualization of a scheme has been discussed primarily in terms of potentiality indication organizations among potential indices. As in an earlier discussion, there is a control structure or procedural perspective that is dual to the potential index perspective. In particular, potential paths of index construction correspond to potential paths of control structure execution which, in turn, correspond to potential paths through the state-transition organization of the system. Similarly, potential index structures correspond to potential interaction outcomes. The structures among potential indices mirror the structures among potential states. Schemes, then, have their reality in the organization of the world image as well as in the potentialities of the situation image. Frames, networks,

and their embeddings in one another are structures of potential interaction selections within the control structure of the world image.

Some of those interaction selections will yield a filling out of
apperceptive expectations, such as visually scanning for greater
detail concerning the objects in a room. Others will yield an attainment of a transformational possibility, such as the rotation of an
object so that a new aspect is visible. In other words, some potential
index structures correspond to potential perceptual detections, while
others may also constitute potential transformational goal definitions.
Potential goal definitions will form a subset of potential interaction
outcomes, since any potential goal must be a potential interaction
outcome, and a proper subset, since not all potential interaction
outcomes can be taken as goals.

Schemes may be organized around structures of potential indices
in either the potential perceptual detection sense or the potential goal
sense. A goal-directed scheme associated with its structured set of
potential goals is a servomechanism. A scheme with both perceptual
and goal-directed organizations around the same organization of
potential index structures will be called cofunctional. A cofunctional
scheme, then, can produce whatever situational transformations or
states of affairs that it can recognize. Cofunctional schemes are
particularly powerful components of servomechanism hierarchies
because apperceptive potentialities will generally be broader than
goal potentialities. That is, a knowing system will generally be able
to recognize states of affairs that it cannot construct. Thus, not all
schemes will be cofunctional.

SOME PARTICULAR STRUCTURES
AND CONSTRAINTS

The schemes (both frame and network components) in a situation
image will, in general, be embedded as general structural potentialities with many undefined specifics. For example, in the case of the
object scheme with its frames and networks of potential manipulations
and movements, the embedding of that scheme in the situation image
may well be unspecified as to the exact orientation and position,
perhaps only indicating the presence of the object in a particular
room. An indication in the situation image of such a general scheme,
a general structural potentiality with undefined specifics, is functional
to the system only insofar as the system's interactions are indifferent
to the actual interactive point of entry in the scheme, only insofar as,
in some sense, it doesn't matter where interactive processing within
that scheme is actually begun—that is, only insofar as the elements
of the frames and networks in that scheme are in some way(s)

functionally equivalent or insofar as some interactive functional significance of those elements is invariant under interactive transformations
through the scheme. Such functional indifference to point of entry in
a scheme will be particularly likely if three conditions hold: (1) the
scheme is cofunctional; (2) relevant network(s) are closed with respect
to the goal-directed transformations, that is, no such transformation
exists from the scheme; and (3) all elements of the scheme are
reachable as goals from any other element. If a particular element
in such a cofunctional, closed, and reachable scheme is functionally,
required it can simply be interactively constructed no matter what the
actual point of entry. These are some of the essential properties of
physical objects, with respect, say, to their visual orientation, and
will be taken as characteristic of object schemes in general (including
more abstract objects). [37]

Such schemes with an indifference to entry point, object schemes
in particular, are critical to the ability to give general characterizations of the situation, especially to aspects of the situation that are
out of sight and out of contact: to potential interactive aspects of the
situation that are themselves conditional on intermediate interactions,
for example, conditional on locomotion. Thus, a system could not
easily represent the interactive potentialities of a room down the
hall if that required the representation of the exact orientation of
every object in that room. Such general characterizations of the
situation potentials are functional to the system only insofar as there
is something general about the situation that is functionally worth
characterizing. Thus, the simple presence and, perhaps, rough location of an object in that room is functionally worth representing even
if its orientation is not known.

A second critical aspect of object schemes is that only with the
temporal stability of general interactive pattern (closure) that they
provide does it become possible to represent continuities in the overall temporal flow of time and space within the interactive field. [38]
One reason why object schemes are important is that they persist as
object schemes (are closed) under many variations of orientation,
location, and so forth. Without such levels of transformational
closure of potentialities there can be no level of continuity of the
pattern of potentialities through the ever changing details of interaction,
and thus no potential pattern outside of the immediate field of interaction which, nevertheless, continuously participates in the overall
temporal trajectory of the situation image. That is, there can be no
way to expand the representations of the situation image beyond that
immediate interactive field. A distant object, for example, can be
functionally represented as a pattern of interactive potentialities
based on explicit image indices from the past only because the general
scheme for that object is continuous and invariant (closed) under most

of the transformations that might have occurred in the meantime. The invariance, thus persistence, of object representations is the fundamental and skeletal characteristic that allows situation images to be extended in space and time.

Object schemes, thus, will for several important reasons be fundamental representational units in situation and world images. The primary representational category will be interaction types, as constituted by corresponding procedures, with the corresponding interaction events represented by the indices and index structures which they set. Interaction potentialities, in turn, will be structurally organized particularly with respect to patterns of structural invariance, that is, objects, in order for representations of anything beyond the most immediate and momentary situation to occur. Objects that change yet retain their object identity and thereby imply (the potentiality of) other events constitute the class out of which the representational category of agents is differentiated. [39] Similarly, particular forms of implication among events will constitute representations of causal connections. [40] Basic representational categories, therefore, will be founded upon interaction categories and will include actions, objects, agents, events, and causal relations. [41] Derivative representational categories will include, for example, the relations of object-property, whole-part, class-element, and object-location. [42] The development of such representational categories allows the situation and the potential world to be increasingly (though never fully) differentiated beyond the immediate and momentary.

The functionality of general interactive categorizations of the situation, of general schemes, is not limited to transformationally distant potentialities (though distance and degree of generality may correlate). No procedure can be defined with respect to or operate on every detail of even a part of the contextual situation. It must function with some generality in order to exist as a procedure at all: a procedure must function with respect to and (as an apperceptive procedure) upon types of schemes within the general situation image structure. Correspondingly, those types of schemes must be indexed (procedurally recognizable) as types and must exist within appropriate schemes of transformational possibilities. Some degree of generality of interactive characterization is, thus, necessary for the existence of general schemes.

This necessary generality is not really a constraint on situation image structures for even the most specific single index is, in effect, a partial and not a full description of an interactive potentiality: it is an index of a scheme type which is capable in principle of further specification. The situation image is differentiated out of the world image about the situation and differentiated only to a finite depth: the situation image in toto constitutes only a partial interactive description of the external situation, and similarly for each of its elements. There is no direct or total knowledge of the world, only fallible and partial knowledge of its interactive characteristics.

Thus, the world image is constructed from the specific to the general, out of the basic elements of knowledge in the procedures innate to the system, while the situation image is differentiated within the world image from the general to the specific by the outcomes of various interactions. The world image is a hierarchicalized network of general interaction possibilities and dependencies, while the situation image is a scheme structure of current possibilities. The world image is a representation of part of the structure of interactive potentialities between an agent and the world, while the situation image is a partial description of the potentialities instantiated by the current situation. [43]

DISCUSSION: INTERACTION, COGNITION, AND SITUATION

The Intuitive Appeal of Picture Models

Picture models of knowledge have a definite intuitive appeal, and for good reasons that go beyond and underlie the historical and cultural dominance of the picture model perspective. I would like to indicate the nature of these reasons.

Essentially, the appeal of the picture model approach derives from its being a simplified, asymptotically limiting case of the interactive approach. This appeal is mediated by the appeal of physical structures and their relationships as a primary metaphor.

The first logical step in the picture model approach is the assimilation of knowledge to structural representation. The underlying reason for the temporal priority of this step is that processes, and certainly control structures, cannot be conceptualized in a sophisticated way except in the context of already sophisticated conceptualizations of physical objects. Thus, object-based approaches must occur first, both historically and ontogenetically, and it is exactly the physical structure metaphor that leads to a structural representation conceptualization of knowledge. This step was undoubtedly aided in its historical version by a tendency toward an intellectual denigration of more clearly nonstructural physical skills knowledge in favor of the more static (even eternal) and structural seeming knowledge of the reflective mind.

The second logical step in the picture model approach is the assimilation of structural representation to structural isomorphism. There are two aspects to such an isomorphism, the elements and the structures, and each needs to be addressed. The discussion will focus first on physical objects and their relationships and then turn to other objects of knowledge.

Physical objects are patterns of interactive potentiality that remain invariant under certain classes of interactions, thereby anchoring other organizations of interactive potentiality. In particular, they anchor and differentiate interactive representations of space and time. The simplest version of the picture model approach is the taking of the objects as elements and their relationships in space as structure and considering some sort of model or picture of those objects in space as constituting knowledge of those objects in space. There are two errors in doing so, however, one involving the elements and the other their relationships, which both have the form of a simplifying misapprehension of interactive functional properties.

Regarding the objects and their representative elements, the error is in the assumption that there is an unproblematic one-to-one relationship from the element to the object it represents. The one-to-one correspondence will generally hold, but its nature is far from unproblematic. The interactive representation of an object is by implicit definition, and there is no absolute assurance that the differentiations of such an implicit definition are sufficient to identify uniquely a single object. As object representations develop in children, the principles of differentiation become increasingly sophisticated, but there is no natural point of completion to that process, and even in adults the presence of a uniquely identifying structure of differentiations remains a strictly contingent matter subject to potential falsification at any time. Furthermore, there always remain expressly problematic issues of identity and individuation about objects, such as the criteria of continuity of identity for objects that change their substances, structures, and properties over time, such as flames, butterflies, and people (for example, Wiggins 1967). The assured one-to-one correspondence between representational element and the object it represents, thus, is a simplified and simplifying asymptotically limiting case that is arrived at by misapprehending the contingent differentiations of functional implicit definition as being unproblematically assured natural connections. Since this conceptualization is falsified or expressly problematic only rarely or with respect to unusual circumstances for adults it tends to be retained uncritically.

Regarding the spatial relationships among objects, the error is in the assumption that the interactive functional relationships that implicitly define those spatial relationships need themselves be spatial in nature or, at least, have any particular structural correspondences to those spatial relationships. Our representations of space are constructed over time, in childhood and continuing into

adulthood, just like our representations of objects, and are constituted
as organizations of interactive functional relationships among our own
potential actions and the relatively invariant patterns of potentiality
that represent objects. The problematicness of these constructions
can be indicated by pointing to the slow and progressive differentiations
of space from self and other objects in infancy, the similarly slow
and progressive movement from topological to metric appreciations
of space in childhood (Piaget and Inhelder 1967), and the encounter
with non-Euclidean conceptualizations of space in adulthood. As with
objects, the error is in a simplifying assumption of a nonproblematical
natural correspondence between that which represents and that which
is represented: in the case of objects, a correspondence of identity;
in the case of space, a correspondence of structure. Again, as with
objects, the assumption works most of the time—our adult representations of space are surely sufficient for most of the spatial relationships that we normally encounter—and thus the errors of the assumptions of unproblematicness and structural correspondence seemingly
can be retained.

Regarding knowledge of things other than familiar physical
objects in space and time, the basic question is, Why does the physical object metaphor work as well as it does? In particular, why
does it work well enough to carry the basic picture model errors
along with it? The answer is fairly simple: all knowlege, at all levels
of knowledge, is organized a functional relationships among patterns
of relative invariance. The natures of the relationships, the patterns,
and the invariances can vary widely, but they remain interactively
functional and necessarily organized with respect to invariances.
This basic similarity with the representation of objects in space is
the reason that the physical object and spatial metaphor works as
well as it does, and the similarity is with respect to precisely those
representational properties (functional organizational with respect
to implicitly defining invariances) whose limiting cases yield the
picture model approach. It is interesting to consider, in this regard,
that interactive functional organization with respect to interactively
implicitly defining invariances is as much a requisite of the nature
of interactive representation as it is of anything represented, and
that that point holds for representation of the physical world as much
as for anything else.

Thus all knowledge, whether of the physical world or otherwise,
is organized as interactive functional relationships among relatively
invariant patterns of functional relationships. If the differentiations
of the implicit definitions in such representations are taken to the
asymptotic limit of direct correspondence then we have a picture
model conceptualization of knowledge. But the differentiations of
those implicit definitions are not and cannot be unproblematically
direct. Representational differentiations, whether of elements or of

structures, are always contingent and context-dependent, even for the seemingly paradigmatic case of physical objects in space. Conceptualizations of knowledge based on asymptotically unreachable picture model assumptions, however, have both the appeal of simplicity and approximate (asymptotic) validity and the necessity of historical precedence.

Gibson

The model of apperception developed in this section has a number of similarities to Gibson's (1966, 1979) theory of perception. In particular, it is a model of an interactive agent actively extracting information from and about the world. Furthermore, the apperception of an interactive scheme in which the elements of the scheme are themselves object representations constitutes an apperception of the interactive potentialities of those objects (or that object), that is, it constitutes an apperception of Gibson's "affordances" offered by those objects. In spite of such parallels and convergences, there are significant differences between the two models, though I will suggest that they are less substantive than they might at first appear.

The basic difference is that Gibson argues ubiquitously against mental processing theories in general as being potentially valid theories of perception and against memory and inference as being involved in perception in particular. Rather clearly, the model presented here is a mental processing model. Furthermore, memory is involved in the temporal persistence of both situation and world images, and inference is involved in the apperceptive computations and interactions. The gulf between the models, then, would appear to be wide.

Gibson's arguments for these claims, however, tend to be of two forms: (1) against discrete "snapshot," or warehouse, models of memory and similarly discrete models of inference; and (2) against any form of preparatory processing of sensations, inputs, or information prior to perception. His argument against discreteness is simply that it is inadequate to the facts. His primary argument against preparatory processing is that it leads to an infinite regress of homunculi who ultimately do the perceiving (of the processed inputs). On the one hand, Gibson's metatheoretical arguments seem to me quite valid. On the other hand, neither memory nor inference is discrete in its involvements in this model, nor is the interactive processing preparatory to perception: such progressing is, rather, constitutive of perception. Gibson's negative conclusions, thus, are too broad. In particular, he does not acknowledge the possibility or the potentialities of nondiscrete, nonpreparatory (constitutive) mental processing models. Gibson's own model, in fact, in such notions as "tuning" and "resonance," would seem to be itself a version of a constitutive interactive processing model. (For an expanded analysis of Gibson's position, see Richie et al. 1980.)

One genuine difference that seems to hold between Gibson's model and my own is that in mine apperceptions are based on inter-action outcomes and the basic nature of those apperceptions does not depend on whether or not the interaction has accomplished primarily a detection or a transformation of the environment (or both). Gibson's perception, however, is a rather pure process of information pick-up with little or no effects on the environment. This fits our general intuitions about perception but leaves somewhat unclear such phenomena as walking around to get a better look at something or picking something up in order to examine it more closely and leaves such technologically aided detections as with infrascope or X-ray, seismograph or sonar, in a state of classificatory suspension. More fundamentally, a strictly nontransformational model of perception could not accommodate such phenomena as eye scans or head movements, phenomena whose importance Gibson rightly emphasizes. In effect, Gibson is trying to have an active (interactive) model that is not transformational. (Gibson does not focus on this facet of his model, but he would seem to be committed to it by his claim that perception is strict and direct information pick-up, while cognition, presumably, involves something more than that.) I have suggested that the detection and transformational aspects of interactions and of the apperceptions based on them are just aspects, and are aspects of all interactions; they are not characteristics that fundamentally differentiate one kind of interaction from another. Gibson's tendency toward a transformation-free concept of perception would seem to be a vestige of the passivity of the classical sensation-based picture conceptions of perception which he has argued so forcefully against.

4

SITUATION AND CONVENTION

THE OBJECT OF LANGUAGE

In the preceeding sections, a general model of action systems has been outlined, with a particular focus on relationships among interaction, situation image, and world image. Briefly, the model conceptualizes an interaction as an execution of a world image in the context of a situation and in accordance with a situation image. It is intended as a model of sufficient generality to apply to all action systems, including linguistic and other communicational systems, and of sufficient specificity to permit the differentiation of linguistic from other action systems, such as for walking or vision.

The question arises, however, of exactly how to proceed with such specification and differentiation of an action system. An interaction per se is a particular flow of actions, not an action system. Similarly, a particular situation or situation image is a circumstance for which some interaction may be appropriate, but this will be an interaction within some action system and will not suffice—will not be broad enough—to define that system. An action system is a structure of potential interactions, [44] and such considerations of potential are the province of the world image. It would seem, then, that the action system constituting linguistic ability must be differentiated within the world image.

Potential interactions, on the other hand, are in the context of potential situations and in accordance with potential situation images. Thus, although the world image is the only actual structure within which an action system might exist, it corresponds to several conceptual realms of potentiality[45]—interactions, situations, and situation images—and an action system might be differentiated within these conceptual realms as well as within the world image control structure per se. I find it most convenient to differentiate linguistic systems initially (as well as other action systems) in terms of the class of potential situations with which they interact.

Many action systems can be differentiated at least initially in terms of the objects with which they interact. It is to be recognized, however, that, at least for the system itself, these "objects" are characteristics of the situations: an object is an instantiation of a certain class of interactive properties of a situation. Thus to differentiate an action system in terms of its appropriate objects is to differentiate it in terms of some specific interaction characteristics common to a class of potential situations. With this broadened understanding of object, [46] then, as a set of interaction characteristics characterizing a class of potential situations, the differentiating question becomes, What is the object of language? What is it that language interacts with?

MIND AS OBJECT

It would seem obvious that in some sense language interacts with mind. An utterance is standardly considered to have the function of inducing a belief or an action in another person, that is, to have the function of inducing some particular state or process in another's mind. [47] Mind is a quick and intuitive candidate for the object of language.

It is my contention that this view of language and mind, while not simply wrong, is nevertheless at least partly wrong and is at best highly uninformative. The basic problem is that the analogy with physical objects and physical action systems is easily and commonly taken too literally. Mind is taken as a substantive entity which is pushed around and manipulated by language. The analogy would be closer between mind and atoms than between mind and objects: it is not strictly wrong to say that physical action systems interact with atoms, but it leaves a lot to be desired in explaining how you pick up a teacup. Similarly, although an audience for a lecture might seemingly be accommodated as simply a set of simultaneous instances of a basic language-mind relationship, an audience consisting of a team coordinating its efforts toward a common goal cannot be atomized into component minds without losing its interactive significance as an audience. As with the teacup, the relationships among the component minds (atoms) are what constitute the actual interactive object of the action; the participation of mind is genuine, but it is indirect and at least one step removed from the proximal object of linguistic interaction. [47] Absent audiences and written languages provide still other difficulties.

More fundamentally, mind cannot be the proximate object of language interactions, even in dyadic situations; if it were, language acts would be successful or not depending solely upon their effects on others' minds. But a command can be a command even if disobeyed. What is the object of interaction in that case? Further, what is the object of language whose patterns of interactive possibility and impossibility, of acceptance and resistance, can make an interaction fail to be a command? Without an interactive characterization of the object of language, the interactive character of language itself cannot be accommodated.

An acceptable interactive characterization of the object of language would provide at least general answers to such questions as: What are the perceptual and transformational implications of linguistic interactions? What are the constraints on those actions? Perhaps most generally, What is the character of the apperceptive structures and trajectories involved?

I wish to argue that the interactive objects of language can be characterized as situation conventions. I will provide a preliminary analysis of such situation conventions, explore some of their interactive characteristics, and, primarily, explore some of the implications of this view of the object of language for language itself.

SITUATION CONVENTION

A situation convention is a consensual understanding about a social situation among the participants in that situation.[49] It is a commonality of understandings about what that situation is. A situation convention is a convention in the sense that it solves a coordination problem among such participants concerning how to characterize the situation they are in. The first point developed in the following discussion is that social situations intrinsically do pose coordination problems to their participants.

The situation image constitutes an interactive characterization of the situation. It is developed on the basis of prior interaction outcomes and functions as a determinant of following interactions. It constitutes what is known of the interactive potential of the situation.

Most of the content of a situation image consists of the implicational structures of apperception, structures which cleave into situation components and aspects such as objects, space and time, causality, and so on. These apperceptive structures are learned as situation potentials as part of the world image and become salient in a particular situation image upon the appropriate outcomes of particular interactions.

The interactive characterization of a situation involving other persons, however, poses special problems. The directly available cues for apperceptive grounding sustain apperceptive inferences only with regard to the physical body involved in the situation,[50] but such physical body apperceptions constitute only a small, and often not particularly important, part of the interactive potential constituted by that person.

This dearth of apperceptive grounding derives from the fact that much of the interactive potential of an individual is constituted by the individual's world image, which is not necessarily particularly redundant with respect to any immediately available cues, thus making apperceptive characterization of it quite difficult. Furthermore, even though the general structure of a particular individual's world image might become known over time, therefore redundant with respect to physical (bodily) cues, and therefore subject to apperceptive construction in someone else's situation image for appropriate situations, the actual interactive manifestation of that world image in a particular situation (that is, the interactive potential of that individual in that particular situation) depends critically upon that individual's situation image in that situation (world images are executed in accordance with situation images). Situation images are not only not readily apperceived from direct physical cues, they are also potentially highly transient, thus eliminating the possibility of the slow construction of person-specific apperceptive structures, as in the case of world images. [51] Situation images, then, are intrinsically difficult to interactively characterize in someone else's situation image; so the interactive potential of an individual in a situation is correspondingly difficult to characterize.

This difficulty of interactive characterization of persons in situations inheres in the situations in whose constitutions persons participate. That is, situations involving other persons are difficult to characterize in the situation image because critical aspects of the overall situations—the other persons' situation images—are not readily subject to apperceptive construction based on instantaneous redundancy. Furthermore, it is a difficulty of characterization that cannot merely be avoided because, at a minimum, the characterization must at least proceed to a classification as irrelevant to the goals of the ongoing interaction. [52] Examples of situations in which relatively rudimentary characterizations of other people suffice might be of fellow members of a symphony audience or fellow pedestrians on a sidewalk. [53] Paradigmatically, of course, the details of others' interactive potential will be highly relevant to an individual's goals in a particular situation.

It is clear that the problem of interpersonal situation characterization is mutual, that is, that an interpersonal situation is interpersonal for all persons involved, [54] and therefore that all share in having a problem of situational characterization. It is also symmetrical, in the sense that each participant's characterization problem is about the other participants: the mutuality of their problems is not merely parallel but reciprocal.

This symmetry of situational characterization problems among participants imposes itself as a necessary equivalence of characterizations within their joint potential solutions to those problems. Any set of situation image characterizations of an interpersonal situation by the participants in that situation that are mutually valid for that situation, that constitute, in other words, a mutual solution to the respective characterization problems, must be consonant with the fact that each situation image characterizes all other situation images (as aspects of the total situation), each of which in turn characterizes all others, including, in particular, each original situation image. Each situation image thus characterizes the entire situation, including its constituent situation images, including, in particular, itself. Each situation image, which in fact constitutes part of a mutual solution to a symmetric characterization problem, must, therefore, characterize the same situation as each of the others, a situation characterized from differing perspectives but, nevertheless, the same. Simply put, any situation image whose situation characterization is incomplete or inaccurate relative to any other situation image (with respect to any interactively salient aspect of the situation) cannot have a fully valid characterization of that situation, and thus the set of constituent images would not constitute a mutual solution. [55] If, for example, I construe an interpersonal situation between you and me as including mutual knowledge of an eavesdropper and you do not (for example, either you don't know or you do not assume that I know about it), then certain of our interactions are likely to be uninterpretable to the other, and we will not have arrived at a mutually complete joint characterization of the situation.

This argument carries over from the subject of the situation image characterizations to their content; not only must the constituent images of a mutual solution characterize the same situation, they must characterize it in the same way, that is, they must be interactively compatible. If any characterization in a supposed joint solution is different from, that is, interactively incompatible with, any other, then that difference must be accounted for in the other images in order for them to constitute a true joint solution, which, in turn, must be taken into account in the original supposedly incompatible image. The overall situation, then, must be characterized in the same way by all participants in a solution: any true interactive incompatibility constitutes a failure of joint solution. [56] Thus, any mutual solution to any interpersonal characterization problem must be constituted by interactively compatible situation images of the same situation: any solution to such a problem must be a joint solution. [57] To return to the example, if we do have mutual knowledge of the eavesdropper on our conversation but you think we have mutual knowledge that the eavesdropper is friendly and I think we have mutual knowledge to the contrary, then, again, we will have interactively incompatible characterizations of the situation, and certain of our interactions are likely not to be mutually interpretable.

Finally, it must be noted that any interpersonal characterization problem has many potential joint solutions, as many as there are potential equivalent characterizations of the situation. Thus, there is no a priori way to determine which characterization must constitute the solution. Together with the mutuality of the problem, that is, with the common interest in arriving at a joint solution, the multiple potential solutions imply that the mutual interpersonal characterization problem is a coordination problem (Schelling 1963). Correspondingly, a solution to the problem constitutes a convention (Lewis 1969). I will call such a solution a situation convention.

In effect, I am proposing the concept of situation convention as an explication of the classical concept of a consensual definition of the situation (Thomas 1967; Goffman 1959). A consensual definition of the situation solves the situational coordination problem, and, conversely, "a failure of definition will cause failure of interaction" (McHugh 1968, p. 3). [58] I will use the terms interchangeably.

INSTITUTIONALIZED CONVENTIONS

An interpersonal situation is never merely interpersonal. The characteristic of being interpersonal is always an aspect of a broader situation of objects and events, bodies and actions. An interpersonal situation will always involve other characteristics and corresponding apperceptive structures which, while not necessarily relevant to the interpersonal coordination problem, may nevertheless participate in its solution, participate in the sense of forming part of the apperceptive base for the solution-constituting situation images.

If some particular type of apperceptive structure does participate in a solution to interpersonal coordination problems for a particular individual, and does so more than once, then the participation of that apperceptive structure in that solution may become habitualized for the particular individual. Habitualization, in this case, means that the presence of the original apperceptive structure comes to serve as a cue (index) differentiating some interpersonal situations from others and that the situation convention associated with that cue becomes part of the apperception of the cue. That is, the interpersonal situation together with the cue comes to be directly apperceived in terms of a particular interactive characterization, and the apperception of that characterization in that situation constitutes that individual's participation in the overall situation convention. I may, for example, habitually assume a situation convention of hushed voices in a church.

If one person's habitualized apperceptions or attributions of interpersonal situation characterizations come to be apperceived as a characteristic of that first person by some other individual, then the first person's habitualized assumptions of situation conventions are said to have been typified by the second individual. A typification of a situation convention thus implies that one individual, the one who holds or has the typification, will apperceive as a characteristic of a second individual that that second individual will apperceive (assume) a particular definition of the situation in an interpersonal situation in the presence of a particular cue. In other words, a typification of a situation convention is a habitualized attribution (apperception) of a habitualized situation convention to another person. Thus, you may come to typify me-in-a-church as a situation in which I will assume a convention of hushed tones.

Note that such a typified attribution to an individual must be based on some differentiating characteristics of that individual. These differentiations may be based upon cues or cue structures that are specific to a particular individual or upon cues that serve to group many individuals or situations with regard to the relevance of the typification. Typifications, then, may be across general categories of people and situations.

If within some group of individuals there is a mutual habitualization of a particular situation convention and a mutually reciprocal typification of that situation convention, then that situation convention will be said to be an institutionalized convention. [59] Thus, if we all habitually assume situation conventions of hushed voices in churches, and we all (implicitly) typify each other as (implicitly) having such assumptions, then hushed-voices-in-churches is an institutionalized convention among us.

Institutionalized conventions are, basically, situation conventions whose appropriateness is stable across recurrences of a particular kind of situation within the reciprocally typifying group of people—stable across time and people. This stability of recurrence derives from the intrinsic temporal stability of habitualizations and typifications. Note that if the differentiating cues for an institutionalized convention are themselves temporally stable, for example, physical objects, such as insignia of rank, then the salience of the convention will be correspondingly temporally stable within appropriate situations as well as across instances of those situations. If the differentiating cue is itself transient, for example, an event, such as a gesture, then the appropriateness of the corresponding convention might also be transient.

CHARACTERISTICS OF CONVENTIONS

I have argued that joint solutions to interpersonal situation characterization problems are conventions (situation conventions) in the sense that they are solutions to coordination problems (Lewis 1969), where a coordination problem is taken to be defined by the equivalence of interest among the participants in selecting among alternative potential solutions to the problem (Schelling 1963).[60] In deriving institutionalized conventions from situation conventions, that is, as special (institutionalized) cases of situation conventions, I have, in effect, made the stronger argument that the interpersonal situation characterization problem is the fundamental coordination problem. Thus, I suggest that all other coordination problems are specializations of this fundamental problem and, correspondingly, that all conventions are special cases of solutions to the interpersonal characterization problem. I will adopt this perspective on conventions from this point on, using convention as a broad concept within which differentiations of (among other things) degree or form of institutionalization can be made.[61]

Apperceptive structures in the situation image are potentially highly context-dependent: the apperceptive significance of some cues may depend greatly upon the presence or absence of other cues. Such context dependence involves the possibility of hierarchies of significance and thus of potentiality. A particular cue, for example, might indicate a particular apperceptive significance for a particular second cue, should that second cue occur. Thus, part of the significance of the first cue is an indication of a particular significance for the second. In terms of the interactive potentialities indicated in the situation image, this implies that part of the interactive potential apperceived from the first cue is the potential of the structure of interactive potentialities that would be apperceived from the second cue, should the second cue occur. Thus, the situation image can contain hierarchies of indications and potential indications of interactive potentialities.

Such a hierarchy of potentiality is present at at least two levels for any institutionalized convention. Briefly, the typifications that constitute the institutionalization are themselves apperceptions of potentiality, the potentiality of the convention, while the convention itself is, in turn, constituted by apperceptive structures of the interactive potential of the situation. Logically, then, the situation must first be apperceived as one in which the convention is available (potential). That is, the persons and other situation characteristics must be appropriate to the typification apperceptions. Second, the situation must be apperceived as one in which the convention is operative (actual) before an interaction in accordance with that convention can take place.[62] First potentiality, then actuality. Note that a particular situation may remain one in which a particular convention is available (potential), but is never actualized: the two steps of apperception are, in principle, completely separable. Thus, any of the conventions of Robert's Rules of Order are potential given that the convention for formal parliamentary procedure has been invoked, but not all will be actualized.

The reciprocal typifications that constitute institutionalization, based on their appropriate cue structures, are themselves, when actually apperceived in a situation, equivalent characterizations of that situation by its participants, characterizations of the situation as one in which the relevant convention is a potentiality. These equivalent characterizations solve a particular aspect of the interpersonal coordination problem, that concerning the availability of the particular convention, and, thus, themselves constitute a convention. An institutionalized convention, therefore, consists of a convention concerning the availability of a convention.

Clearly this can be iterated: we can have hierarchies of conventions concerning the availability of other conventions, which concern the availability of other conventions, and so on. In effect, hierarchies of context dependence among the apperceptive significances of cue structures can constitute corresponding hierarchies of conventions. The overall hierarchy of such hierarchies of situation convention potentiality in the world image constitutes one of the primary resources that each individual brings to each new interpersonal situation characterization problem.

Conventions, whether potential or actual, [63] consist of relationships among the individuals involved. Certain relationships of symmetry of interests among alternative situation characterizations constitute coordination problems, and certain equivalencies among such characterizations constitute solutions to those problems, that is, they constitute conventions. Conventions, then, do not exist within a single individual but rather as relationships among individuals. Conventions are supra-individual. [64]

One implication of this supra-individual characteristic of conventions is that their existence is independent of their origin: they exist as the appropriate relationships independently of how those relationships came to be. In particular, conventions do not have to be based on agreement nor necessarily on language at all (Lewis 1969). As an example, consider two people who meet accidentally at a certain time, restaurant, and day of the week and have lunch together and who both, without discussion (but, presumably, with motivation), return in the following weeks to continue the luncheon relationship. This soon becomes an institutionalized (reciprocally typified) convention between the two people that is based entirely on precedent (habitualization followed or accompanied by typification) and without explicit agreement.

Another implication of supra-individualness is that conventions may exist implicitly, without the awareness of some or all of the participants of the particular characterizations comprising the convention or of the existence of the coordination problem qua coordination problem it solves. Thus, the characterizations that comprise a language are not fully available to awareness for any of us,[65] and the coordination problem(s) that language solves are not recognized as such by, for example, young children, for whom language is a reified component of the world on a par with rocks and trees.

Combining independence of origin with implicitness, it becomes apparent that conventions and structures and hierarchies of conventions could originate and evolve without there ever necessarily being any intentional design or explicit awareness of either those conventions or their evolution.

REFLEXIVITY

Consider a situation image participating in an actualized (not just potential) convention: the situation image represents the situation, one aspect of the situation is the convention, and one component of the convention is the situation image. This cycle of relationships constitutes a reflexivity inherent in conventions, and this reflexivity in its various manifestations and implications constitutes one of the most important properties of conventions.

One implication of this reflexivity is derived by noting that each situation image in a situation convention, if that situation image is to be complete, must represent itself: it is a component of the convention, which is an aspect of the situation, which is being represented. This representation of itself as a part of its representation of the overall situation is also itself part of the situation image (itself) and, therefore, must also be represented: a representation of the representation of itself. Clearly, this iterates, and we have that a complete situation image (as a component of a convention) must contain an unbounded hierarchy of representations of the representations of itself.

An equivalent perspective on this hierarchy, with the focus on the situation per se rather than the situation image, can be derived by noting that a situation containing a complete convention contains representations of itself, therefore representations of representations of itself, and so on. That is, the situation potentially contains an unbounded hierarchy of representations, or perspectives, on itself.

This argument carries over to the third version of this reflexivity implication, with focus now on the convention rather than the

situation, by noting that the convention itself consists of representations (of the situation, therefore, potentially) of itself, therefore, of
representations of representations of itself, and so on. That is,
the convention is itself constituted by a potentially unbounded hierarchy
of reflexive representations, or perspectives. Because of its form
in this third version, I will call this implication of the reflexivity of
conventions ontological or structural reflexivity.

An example of a conventional structuring with (at least) two
ontological levels would be a marriage ceremony performed as part
of a play. The convention of being-part-of-a-play constitutes a
second-level perspective on the convention of participating-in-a-
marriage-ceremony, a second-level perspective, in fact, that alters
the meanings involved in the first-level ceremony, for example,
eliminating the otherwise incurred mutual obligations between the
partners.

Both ontological levels in the preceding example are constituted
by institutionalized conventions. A less institutionalized example
might by: (1) it is a part of the definition of the situation between us
that I am inflicting my terrible singing on you in order to get you to
leave the room; and (2) it is equally understood between us that I
intend you to leave in response to the insult involved rather than in
response to the suffering from my voice. [66] Again, the second-level
perspective affects the representational contents (meanings) within
the first-level situation convention.

An immediate implication of ontological reflexivity is that no
situation image can ever be complete: the situation image is finite,
the hierarchy of potential representations is unbounded, and, therefore, there must be some level of perspectives beyond which the
situation image does not go, beyond which it is incomplete. Such
perspective-level incompleteness is called egocentrism[67] and is one
reason why the possibility of interaction failure is always present.

The converse of egocentrism is that, while of necessity incomplete, situation images nevertheless potentially contain a very interesting hierarchy of reflexive representations. Manipulations of the
levels and contents of various participants' egocentric situation
images provide unbounded potential complexity in interpersonal
interactions. [68]

Whereas ontological reflexivity is of a fixed structural character,
the second major implication of reflexivity is of a more dynamic or
dialectical character. It is derived from the primary reflexivity of
conventions by taking into account the role of interactions in apperceptively constructing conventions.

Interactions proceed in accordance with situation images, and
their outcomes constitute the grounds for situation images. With
respect to conventions, this implies precisely that interactions

proceed in accordance with conventions and that their outcomes constitute the grounds for conventions. Thus, situation image apperceptions (of conventions) ground interactions, whose outcomes ground further situation images (and conventions). The validity (justification) of the apperceptive constructions in the situation image, thus, is dependent upon the validity of the prior situation image, which grounded the interactions whose outcomes now ground the second situation image. Thus, the apperceptions of situation images presuppose the validity of prior situation images.

With regard to conventions, this relationship is even stronger. The validity of the apperception of a convention in a situation is dependent on the validity of the apperceptive significance of some grounding interaction(s). But the apperceptive significance of those grounding interactions, assuming that significance is, in fact, valid, is itself a solution to the interpersonal situation coordination (characterization) problem (the problem of characterizing the significance of those interactions): it is itself a convention. Thus, the validity of the apperception of conventions presupposes conventions. The validity of the apperception of these conventions, in turn, presupposes other conventions, and so on. I will call this second major implication of reflexivity the epistemological reflexivity of conventions.

Thus, if I walk into a room full of people and see you making peculiar finger movements, I am not likely to understand those movements as making a bid unless I have previously understood the situation convention to be that of an auction. Similarly, if you say "It didn't work," I will ground my understanding of what didn't work, my understanding of the meaning of the utterance, on a prior (understood) situation convention which provides the referent for the pronoun.

While ontological reflexivity yields a hierarchy of levels of perspective on top of the basic situation, striving for a nonexistent all-encompassing representational perspective, epistemological reflexivity yields a hierarchy of levels of presupposition underneath the basic situation, striving for a nonexistent ultimate ground of certainty. Similarly, inherent in both forms of reflexivity are limitations on and potentialities of the structure of conventions.

It is clear that the regress toward a ground of certainty for conventions is unbounded and thus not encompassable within a situation image. [69] Therefore, it must have some lower ground of initial level of apperception (attribution) of convention that is itself ungrounded. Interactions based on this initial ungrounded-level convention both assume and constitute that convention, insofar as it in fact exists. [70] Such interactions are "as if" the convention exists. If false, they have served to test the hypothesis of that convention; if true, they have served to initiate and ground that convention. [71] They are both tentative and presumptive, both perceptual and transformational, and, therefore, in a derivative sense so are all further conventions based upon them. In all cases, if an interaction based on a particular convention fails to yield expected outcomes, if that grounding convention is falsified, then some more fundamental convention must be sought upon which recovery of the definition of the situation can be based. [72]

As with ontological reflexivity, the structural limitation implied by epistemological reflexivity itself implies, and is implied by, a corresponding structural potentiality. The regress of presuppositions of conventions may never find certainty, but it does provide the possibility of highly complex structures of context dependence (context presuppositions) in the apperception (attribution and establishment) of conventions in the situation—that is, conventions which presuppose earlier conventions, which presuppose earlier conventions, and so on. These context dependencies among conventions may involve the establishment, cessation, maintenance, differentiation, or transformation of other conventions.

Furthermore, such apperception dependencies are grounded upon particular interactions occurring in particular contexts which are not, in general, repeatable, at least, not in those contexts and, therefore, not with the same apperceptive significances. Convention apperceptions, then, are in general based upon temporally transient and unique cues: there is little possibility of recovering the apperception of context dependencies if the relevant cues are missed and themselves not recoverable. Such potential transience of context dependency cues implies that instantaneous apperception of context-dependent conventions may be impossible. Thus, the possibility of such context dependencies based on transient cues implies that the apperception of conventions (especially situation conventions) may require the computation of complex temporal trajectories in the situation image. In fact, the apperceptive computation of a temporal sequence of context dependencies is the computation of a temporal trajectory. [73]

DISCUSSION: SITUATION AND CONVENTION

Lewis on Convention

The entire discussion of convention is dependent on Lewis' (1969) explication of convention as a solution to a coordination problem. It has required, however, some changes in Lewis' analysis, particularly the disentanglement of convention per se from institutionalized conventions. Lewis' definitions are stated directly in terms of "regularities" of behavior and "recurrent situations," and he claims that conventions must involve a property of "common knowledge," which implies reciprocal typification. Thus, in my terminology, Lewis defines institutionalized conventions rather than conventions in the broadest sense.

The separation of institution from convention involved another aspect of change. Lewis' concepts of behavioral regularities and recurrent situations are intrinsically extensional. Such extensionality commits his definition to an institutional perspective in that purely extensionally defined concepts can begin to make sense only with the potential for repetition and recurrence, which, in this context implies institutionalization. Thus the elimination of institutionality required the development of an intensional definitional base in place of Lewis' extensional base. This I have attempted to provide in terms of the situation and world images. It should be noted that Lewis (1975), following Bennett (1973), has revised his definition in the direction of intensionality but remains implicitly committed to an institutional perspective.

Another comment on Lewis' definition derives from the fact that Lewis contends that his final definition of convention is broader than, but inclusive of, the concept of the solution to a coordination problem (Lewis 1969, pp. 68-76). The basic argument is that some overall situations cannot be broken up into subsituations about which independent coordination decisions can be made; the decisions will be interdependent, and this interdependence will imply that there is no particular conventional solution to any one of the subsituations. Conversely, Lewis contends, the overall situation (without being "broken up") is not itself a coordination problem because there is no single action decision that is appropriate for the entire duration of the situation: it still requires interdependent sequences of action decisions. The problem here is the limitation to single actions as decision alternatives, and Lewis solves it by moving the focus of decision from actions per se to regularities of action (presumably taking into account the possibility of sequences of subdecisions). He furthermore seems to think that this shift from actions to regularities eliminates the general possibility of characterization in terms of coordination problems. Such a shift, however, is completely equivalent to a move from actions per se to action strategies as the decision focus, and this move is standard in game theory (Luce and Raiffa 1957, p. 311; Ferguson 1967, p. 9; or Von Neumann and Morgenstern 1964, p. 84). Thus convention remains definable in terms of coordination problems: it simply requires a more general conceptualization of them as problems for which the solutions can be strategies as well as simple actions.

Conventions, Society, and Information Cost

The factual structures of relationships among world images that constititute institutionalized conventions and the factual structures of relationships among those conventions together constitute the ontological ground of social structure. Social reality emerges as interactions within those relational structures.

Such structures of conventions, on the one hand, provide potentialities for successful interaction from the perspectives of the coordination problems they solve, but, on the other hand, their institutionalization constitutes constraints with respect to the perspective of alternative potential solutions. One apparent strategy to avoid such constraints on alternatives would seem to be simply to reach agreement with concerned agents for each instance of a coordination problem, that is, to avoid institutionalization. Even disregarding that such agreement reaching would in general require language, itself an institutionalized convention, in many, if not most, such cases, the information (transactions) cost of agreement reaching would be quite high, so high in some cases as to render the agreement impossible or meaningless (consider the case when a solution is discovered and agreement reached concerning it after the coordination problem is past). Thus, the institutionalization of conventions may well allow the solution of coordination problems at much lower cost (often paid in time) than otherwise possible, and, correspondingly, the solution of some that would otherwise not be solved at all.

It would seem, in fact, that much of the structure of society can be considered as structures of institutionalized conventions—consider law, money, and marriage—and that much (if not most) of the benefit to society of these structures is in terms of savings in information costs that would otherwise be incurred in attempting to solve (or in failing to solve) the corresponding coordination problems. Other social organizations, for example, cities, would also appear to be primarily responses to information costs (though also to transportation costs in the case of cities), though construable as conventions only with some straining. Savings in information costs, then, might well be the primary source of utility that makes social structure and evolution a non-zero-sum game. This pervasive importance of information costs seems to be a generally neglected perspective in anthropology and sociology.

5
MEANING AND LANGUAGE

COMMUNICATION

I intend to outline a sequence of differentiating criteria which begin with general actions and interaction systems and progressively differentiate increasingly language-like actions and systems out of that general background. I will be accepting certain stages and aspects of these differentiations as explications of familiar, though not necessarily understood, concepts. The first such explication will be of the concept of communication. [74]

Interaction outcomes are index structures upon which perceptual and transformational apperceptions are based. In an interpersonal situation, the initial actor will ground apperceptions directly on the outcomes of the primary interaction, while other participants will ground apperceptions on the outcomes of interactions that have detected the primary interaction. Such cross-apperceptions need not have any logical character different from those involving physical objects or animals, except, perhaps, somewhat greater complexity. They can be incidental and unintentional for all participants[75] and, of particular importance for my purposes, need not involve characterizations (situation image representations) of any of the participants.

However, an index structure that does involve a characterization of one or more of the participants in a situation will be called a significance. As a goal definition, it will be called a goal significance, [76] and as an apperception, it will be called an understood significance. Any interaction with significance will be called a communication, differentiated into the overlapping categories of goal communication and understood communication, depending on its significances. Any goal communication that is also understood by the initial actor will be called a complete communication, and, if the understood significance is the same as the goal significance, it will be called a fulfilled communication.

79

Consider an index structure representing someone as holding a particular belief. That structure will be a significance. An interaction taking that representation as a goal definition will be a goal communication, while an interaction grounding the apperception of that representation will be an understood communication. Note that I can understand you to hold certain beliefs on the basis of observations about you that you may not have intended and may be entirely unaware of: understood communications need not be goal communications. If I engage in goal communication and understand it to have had particular effects on you, then that is a complete communication. Those effects, however, may or may not be the ones intended in the original goal communication (my attempt may have misfired); if they are the same then that interaction is a fulfilled communication. Note that a fulfilled communication is defined by the agreement in my situation image between the initial goal and the resultant apperceptive understanding: it does not preclude the possibility that my understanding is in error.

Thus, if I leave Piaget's calling card in your office in order to make you think you had missed his visit, then that act of mine is a goal communication with the goal significance of your having that belief. If you, on the other hand, conclude that this is just another example of my neurotic maliciousness, then that act will be an understood communication with your conclusion as its understood significance. If I then realize what your conclusion is, then the calling card act is a complete communication, even though my goal has not been realized. I may, of course, falsely (or truly) think that you do believe that you just missed a visit from Piaget, in which case I think my act succeeded, and it will constitute a fulfilled communication. Finally, if you conclude from various gestures and expressions of mine that I am angry, then those gestures and expressions constitute an understood communication that is not (necessarily) a goal communication.

MEANING[77]

If any of those significances is constituted (in part) by an attribution of a situation convention, then I will term that convention a meaning. [78] Thus, there can be understood meanings on the parts of the participants in an interpersonal interaction and a goal meaning on the part of a primary actor. The primary actor can thus have both goal and understood meanings, while the remaining participants can only have understood meanings. I will call a communication with a meaning an utterance, the communicator, correspondingly, the utterer, and the remaining participants, the audience.

A goal or understood convention constituting a meaning need not constitute part of a significance qua convention. The situation image component must be appropriate to <u>constituting</u> part of a convention but need not be <u>understood as</u> a convention. Rather, the significance must be appropriate to a supra-individual convention in the sense that the significance represent the situation (in part, at least) with the symmetry of equivalence of indexing[79] among the participants that would, if that symmetry were true, constitute a convention. That is, a part of a significance, which, if true, would entail the existence of a situation convention, thereby attributes a situation convention to the situation and thereby constitutes a meaning. Thus, a young child knows nothing of conventions qua conventions but participates in many of them.

An apperceptive significance will, in general, be structured according to various components and aspects of the situation and, in particular, will be structured within the ontological reflexivity hierarchy of potential perspectives on that situation. With regard to this hierarchy, a meaning must be understood to be an aspect of the represented situation, must be represented as a situation convention within the ultimate (most encompassing) perspective on the situation constituted by the situation image and not simply within a (sub)perspective represented in the situation image. The reason is that it is possible for higher-order perspectives to contradict lower-order perspectives. For example, it might obtain that a particular convention is understood by the audience and intended to be so understood by the utterer but is not in fact true from the perspective of the utterer (the utterer is deceiving the audience about that convention). Such conventions-at-one-level contradicted at another would not constitute conventions if true and are therefore not meanings. [80] Thus, if there is any perspective level (level of ontological reflexivity) at which a lower-level attribution of a convention is contradicted, then that lower-level convention attribution cannot constitute part of a true convention, and, therefore, cannot constitute a meaning. Meanings, therefore, cannot be contradicted at any level of reflexivity (and remain meanings).

In effect, I am suggesting that the apparent regress of noncontradicting (nondeceptive) intentions in Grice's model (Schiffer 1972) exists not because the communication of meaning is necessarily conventional (for example, Lewis 1969; Kempson 1975) but rather because the ontology of meaning is convention. As such, the potential regress of explicit intentions is eliminated by constraints on what constitutes a convention (symmetry and equivalence): since self-contradicting reflexivities are incompatible with the nature of the situation conventions and since meanings have the ontology of situation conventions such self-contradicting reflexivities are therefore derivatively eliminated in the goal or apperceptive structures that constitute meanings, without having to invoke a regress of positive (noncontradicting) reflexivities to avoid them.

If an interaction does, in fact, yield a situation convention, then that convention will be called the occasion meaning of the interaction. This is the pivotal explication of meaning. An interaction with an occasion meaning will be called a complete utterance. If the occasion meaning of a complete utterance is the same as the goal meaning of that utterance, then it will be called a fulfilled utterance.

If I say a sentence or perform some other interaction and either intend or understand that interaction to determine a situation convention, then that interaction is an utterance, and the situation convention associated with it in my situation image is its meaning (to me). If that interaction (or any other) does, in fact, yield a situation convention, then that convention is the occasion meaning of the interaction, whether or not it was the goal meaning or even if there was no goal meaning for the interaction. A complete utterance, then, may not necessarily have been intended as an utterance at all, and, if so, it may have yielded a different meaning than that intended. If a complete utterance had a goal meaning and if that goal meaning is the same as the occasion meaning then the interaction is a fulfilled utterance. Note that an understood meaning is an individual's attribution of a situation convention, and such an attribution can be in error, while an occasion meaning is a situation convention, and it either exists or it doesn't.

Thus, if I shout and wave my arms in order to warn you of some danger, and if you understand my actions in that way, then those actions will constitute both a complete and a fulfilled utterance with that warning as the occasion meaning. If, on the other hand, it becomes immediately and mutually clear to both of us that I have made an error in thinking there was danger, then my-having-made-an-error becomes the occasion meaning, and the actions will constitute a complete utterance but not a fulfilled utterance: not a fulfilled utterance because, even though the action had an occasion meaning, that occasion meaning was not in accord with the goal meaning under which the action was performed.

CONSTRAINTS ON MEANING

An occasion meaning consists of a convention constituted by the apperceptions of an interaction. These apperceptions, therefore, must meet those constraints implied by their constituting a convention. In particular, apperceptions constituting a convention must attribute a convention to the situation. Such attribution need not be qua convention, but, on the one hand, any apperception lacking the necessary symmetry and equivalence properties cannot participate in the constitution of a convention, and, on the other hand, the possession of such properties is the attribution of a convention. Furthermore, the attributed convention must be the one actually obtaining: if the attribution is incorrect, then the apperception does not solve the coordination problem, and there is no convention. [81] Therefore, an occasion meaning is understood by all participants.

From this conclusion—that an occasion meaning must be an understood meaning—it follows readily that, since an understood meaning must be part of an understood significance, any complete utterance will also be an understood utterance, and an understood communication.

CONVENTIONAL MEANING AND LANGUAGE

Meanings are constituted by (context-dependent) apperceptions of utterances (interactions). If a kind of utterance becomes reciprocally typified as having a particular apperceptive effect on the situation image attributions of situation conventions, then that institutionalized convention significance will be called the conventional meaning of that utterance type. For example, the utterance type of banging a gavel can have the conventional meaning of calling a meeting to order.

Utterance types (together with their conventional meanings) are themselves conventions and are thus, in principle, subject to the same context dependencies of generation as any other convention. If a system of (context dependencies of) generation of utterance types should itself be institutionalized (evolve as a convention), then that system will be called a quasi-language. Quasi-languages, in turn, can be classified according to the (principles of generation of the) classes of utterances, for example, in increasing complexity, as finite, regular, context-free, context-sensitive, or recursively enumerable. [82] I suggest that a quasi-language that is not context free (for example, at least context-sensitive) be called, simply, a language.

A language, then, is a conventional system whereby conventional utterances can be generated that have conventional effects on situation conventions. [83]

DISCUSSION: MEANING AND LANGUAGE

Grice: Meaning and Intention

Grice's (1967) analysis of meaning and its developments since
its first proposal (for example, Tice 1969; Schiffer 1972) have formed
both a stimulus and a counterpoint to the explication of meaning
developed here: a stimulus in the sense that Grice's analyses seemed
clearly to be capturing something correct, and I wished to understand what that was from the perspective of the model I was
developing; a counterpoint in that the differences between Grice's
analyses of meaning and my own are not matters of detail but, rather,
of basic approach. The approaches have not yielded identical outcomes
though the relationships remain strong, and the ultimate explications
seem extensionally similar. Intensionally, however, the explications
are quite different; in particular: (1) my explication purports to give
some sort of an ontology to what the entity meaning is while Grice
in effect disregards that question, focusing instead on the verb form
of "X means Y"; and (2) Grice's analysis is based fundamentally on
the concept of intention, while mine is founded on apperceptive representations.

I argued earlier that, as a strict consequence of the definitions
involved, a complete utterance must be an understood utterance. A
more subtle question, however, and a critical question with respect
to the extensional relationship between this model and Grice's is
whether a complete utterance must be a fulfilled utterance. If so,
then any meaning actually constructed must have been a goal meaning
(a meaning intended), and these definitions of meaning in terms of
situation images could be recast in equivalent form in terms of goal
definitions. Such an approach would be largely equivalent to Grice's
definitions in terms of intentions but developed from a different
perspective. A complete utterance necessarily being also a fulfilled
utterance would obtain only if the utterer's understood meaning was
necessarily the same as the (utterer's) goal meaning. Therefore,
the necessity of the first identity entails the necessity of the second.
In this second form, the question, then, becomes one of whether or
not an utterer's understood meaning must be the same as the goal
meaning.

It seems clear that an utterer's understood significance need not
be the same as the goal significance—things do not always turn out
as intended. The critical issue, then, is whether such a "miss" can
construct a genuine definition of the situation. I contend that this is
easily possible and that, in fact, the experience of belatedly realizing
the full meaning of what we have just said, and everyone else realizing
it, too, has happened to everyone. [84] I would not want to argue that

such an event is common, rather the opposite; but its very possibility renders any identity between utterer's understood meaning and goal meaning, and thus between complete utterances and fulfilled utterances, at best statistical. In particular, it implies that occasion meaning cannot be defined in terms of intentions.

This, however, applies only to occasion meaning as explicated here (in terms of situation images) and certainly not, for example, to Grice's explication. Therefore, some more direct comparison must be made. The focus of this comparison is between the general theoretical strategies of grounding an explication of meaning on intentions and grounding it on apperceptive representations.

The focus of explication is the sense of "mean," as in "the utterance x meant that p," and as it might be differentiated from "the spots meant measles"; the focus is on Grice's non-natural meaning. I contend that "mean," in the sense of "his utterance x meant p, though he didn't intend it," would seem to be a case of the non-natural meaning that Grice initially set out to explicate but which is excluded by his, or any, explication in terms of intentions (or goals). The exclusion is clear: the meaning involved cannot be explicated in terms of intentions because it explicitly violates the relevant intention. [85] That such cases exist also seems clear. The basic question, then, is whether or not such cases are in fact instances of non-natural meaning. The instantiation of non-natural meaning would seem to be established by comparison with Grice's own criteria for non-natural meaning (Grice 1967, p. 40): (1) "x meant that p" in the above sense does not entail p; (2) the case can be rendered in the form "x meant ' . . . ' "; and (3) "the fact that he uttered x" does not necessarily have the same meaning as x, all three points in distinction from "natural" meanings. [86] Thus, this class of exceptions to Grice's explication strategy (unintended meanings) would nevertheless seem to meet the criteria for the concept to be explicated (non-natural meanings).

I would suggest, in fact, that the distinction between natural and non-natural meaning is fundamentally that non-natural meaning involves the attribution of convention and thus has potential alternatives equally valid as potential meanings, while natural meanings are (naturally) fixed. Such a potential for alternatives can be derived from the variability of goals but is derived more fundamentally from the reflexive arbitrariness of conventions.

The issue, then, is ultimately one of whether or not there is something fundamentally different about inadvertent meanings from other "non-natural" meanings. I contend, on the basis of the explication of meaning in terms of situation convention, that the differentiation of intended (goal) meanings from understood meanings should be considered as a differentiation within the concept of meaning rather than definitive of it. [87] I suggest, in other words, that the similarities as situation conventions between intended meanings and inadvertent meanings are more fundamental and important than the dissimilarities in terms of intentions.

The Expression of Thought

The expression of thought, in some sense, is one of the most important functions of language. It has often, in fact, been taken as the essential and definitive function of language. When this view is taken, the transmission model approach appears to be especially appropriate, since the most simple and natural way to express thought would seem to be to encode and transmit it. This leads to two questions: (1) why has the expression of thought had such an appeal as being the quiddity of language; and (2) how can the expression of thought be accommodated within a view of language as being essentially a conventional tool for the transformation of social reality?

There are at least four reasons why the expression of thought has such an appeal as the paradigmatic function for language: (1) it is, and has been for a very long time, the culturally dominant view of language; (2) it derives from a picture conception of knowledge with its own intrinsic appeal and history of dominance; (3) it is readily consonant with encoding-transmission models, and they have the appeal of apparent simplicity; and (4) the examples of language that are most readily available to someone contemplating the nature of language are the thought expressions of a contemplative mind.

One powerful example of the dominance of the thought expression approach to language is the division of the field of study into syntax, semantics, and pragmatics. Syntax is the study of the vehicles of thought expression; semantics is the study of the expressive coding relationships; and pragmatics is concerned with the uses of and purposes for such encoding expressions. Thus, the thought expression approach is intrinsic in this way of conceptualizing the field, yet it is considered to be an outline of topics within the study of language, not as itself embodying a theoretical approach to the study of language.

It is also interesting to note that those areas which have moved the furthest from strict transmission perspectives, for example, the study of the acquisition of language, sociolinguistics, and ethnomethodology, tend to be areas of study that look at actual language behavior rather than at contemplative thought expressions.

The appeal of thought expression models seems clear: dominance, simplicity, and a natural choice of examples. The question, then, becomes focused on how thought expression can be accommodated within a transformational, basically communicational, model.

Thought expression is so strongly thought of as an encoding of static beliefs or propositions that it tends to be forgotten that thought is an activity and not a static structure. Thought is an activity of internal transformations of situation and (with higher knowing levels) world images, sometimes tightly goal-directed, sometimes very loosely so. Insofar as those internal objects and goals of transformation participate in situation conventions, then language is the tool for engaging in those transformations with respect to the social realm as well as the strictly mental realm. That is, in this sense, language behavior is a direct expression of thought as a social activity. The social expression of thought, then, is at least as natural from a transformational perspective as from a transmission perspective and even more so when it is recognized that thought is an activity. (This still does not make language an encoding, however, for the relationships of an utterance to its goal meaning, its context, and the transformation itself do not in any case have the context-free structural correspondence of an encoding. Utterances are context- and goal sensitive indicators of situation convention transformations, not encodings.)

Among the strongest challenges to social communication-based models of language, however, especially relative to classical thought expression models, are cases of utterances without an audience, such as by a hiker alone on a trail (for example, Yu 1979). Part of the power of such examples derives from the fact that it is difficult to attribute communicative intent to people in audienceless situations, and, thus, intention-based models such as Grice's seem particularly vulnerable. The transformational model proposed here is not based on intent, but it might still seem that audienceless thought expression would constitute a counterexample.

The basic form of the answer is quite simple: once a means is available for the social expression of thought as an activity so also is it available for the audienceless expression of thought as an activity, including strictly internal private expression. The apparent problem is, if language is a means for the manipulation of social reality, then how can it function if there is no social reality immediately available? The question assumes that if social manipulation is the ground for the evolution and ontogenesis of language then that is all it can be used for. The assumption is simply false.

It is clearly possible for human beings, from childhood through adulthood, to engage in an activity, or some direct derivation of an activity, as if some condition obtains that in fact does not. This ranges from play fighting and other forms of play (Bruner, Jolly, and Sylva 1976), to symbolic play (Piaget 1962), to the multitudinous instances of keyed behavior in everyday life (Goffman 1974). Clearly, then, there is no problem in principle for a fundamentally social activity to be engaged in privately. Furthermore, the presumptions involved do not have to be explicit "pretend," or "subjunctive," cognitions. The participations of most people in situation conventions most of the time are strictly implicit, with no explicit cognitions of situation conventions per se involved. This is true for all children and most adults all of the time and for everyone most of the time. It is only in problematic or complex situations that there is any need to focus explicitly on conventions and their potential reflexive layerings. The potentiality for and likelihood of such implicit participation is an aspect of the supraindividual character of conventions. If such participation is generally implicit, however, then the "as if" or subjunctively social character of audienceless and private language can be equally implicit. Such cases, therefore, are quite compatible with the transformational perspective and, furthermore, interestingly so.

6
PERSPECTIVES ON
COMMUNICATIVE ACTION SYSTEMS

LANGUAGE AS AN ACTION SYSTEM

To this point, the focus has been primarily on communicative and meaningful acts per se, independent of how those acts were produced. Attention will now turn to the systems underlying those acts. An action system is a procedure (control structure) or structure of procedures organized around a space of potential goal definitions. When a goal definition in that space is constructed in the system, the procedure computes interactions in accordance with the situation image and the goal so as, if successful, to transform the situation image in accordance with the goal. As long as the situation image is not itself faulty, the actual environmental situation will be transformed correspondingly.[88] An action system thus has three primary analytic aspects: the space of possible goals; the generation of the interaction in terms of the goal and the situation image; and the transformational relationship between the actions and the situation image.

The analysis of language that has been presented makes an initial sequence of differentiations concerning general actions in terms of the goals and consequences of the actions (communications and utterances), followed by a sequence of differentiations in terms of the transformational and generative properties of those actions (utterance types and languages). If we now restrict consideration strictly to aspects of action systems (thereby disregarding consequences) and, thus, shift attention from action types per se to underlying interaction system capabilities, we can define a communication with a goal significance as a prelocutionary act, an utterance with a goal meaning as an illocutionary act, an utterance with a goal meaning that is dependent on a conventional meaning as a locutionary act, and a locutionary act generated by a productive system as a linguistic act.[89] If, for example, I deliberately move a rock, I have performed a general goal-directed activity. If I shove something that glitters under the rock in

order to entice you to move the rock I have performed a prelocutionary act. If I pantomime pushing and lifting motions with respect to
the rock for you as an audience, I have performed an illocutionary
act. If you and I are members of a work crew for which moving rocks
is a common activity, and I give you the simple work crew hand signal that indicates that I need help in moving a rock (perhaps work
conditions are noisy and, thus, hand signals are necessary), I have
performed a locutionary act. If I say "Help me move this rock," I
have performed a linguistic act. The analysis thus yields a sequence
of increasingly language-like action systems, each differentiated
within the preceding, culminating in an explication of language in
terms of both its goal structure and its transformational structure.
Thus, if valid, it succeeds in explicating the framework of communication and language as action systems.

Furthermore, the unique manner in which convention is the
object of language as well as constitutive of it provides a dual framework for the embedding of the action system perspective on language
within an institutional perspective on language.[90] Situation conventions and institutionalized conventions constitute the ontological reality
of society, and language is the institutionalized action system for
creating, maintaining, and transforming that reality. The intimate
relationship between language and society is thus not simply functional but logically necessary.

THE SEQUENCE OF DIFFERENTIATIONS

The differentiations within general action systems of increasingly communication-specialized action systems, beginning with prelocutionary systems and yielding linguistic action systems as the most
specialized, are based on varying principles of differentiation that
might appear to wander across the three aspects of systems of action.
This variation in principles of differentiation might give the appearance that the principles themselves, or at least their sequence, is
arbitrary and ad hoc, and thus perhaps raise doubts about the naturalness of the definitions produced.[91] One possibility, for example,
might be that the differentiations all cross one another and thus form
a factorial structure of differentiations rather than a sequence. I
wish to argue to the contrary, that the principles are natural and
that their sequencing is, with one interesting exception, intrinsic.

There are two differentiations based on the nature of the action
goal definition: prelocutions in terms of the goal as characterizing
an agent and illocutions in terms of the goal as characterizing that
structure of relationships among persons which constitutes a situation convention. Locutions and linguistic acts are differentiated in

terms of the conventionality of the act and of the productivity of the system by which the act is generated, respectively. All four of these differentiating principles would seem to be natural in the sense of designating boundaries between qualitatively different classes of properties: the context sensitivities of the interactive characterizations of persons, the symmetries and reflexivities of situation conventions, the institutionalization of utterance types, and the productivity of linguistic systems.

Thus the focus of examination shifts from the principles of differentiation to their sequencing. The direction of differentiation from general action systems to prelocutionary systems clearly cannot be reversed. Furthermore, it is evident that prelocutions must be differentiated within general actions: they are related as species to genus.

Similarly, to transform the interactive character of persons is clearly broader than to transform those particular characteristics participating in the structure of relationships that constitutes a convention. Thus, the direction of differentiation from prelocutions to illocutions is irreversible. Also, it is again a genus-species differentiation and not a simple crossing or intersection of characteristics: an illocutionary act must be a prelocutionary act.

The first sequencing question with interesting consequences occurs in the differentiation of locutions within illocutions. Superficially, it might appear that actions with conventional apperceptive significances can be used toward many kinds of goals, therefore it might seem that the principle of the conventionality of the act crosses other principles of action differentiation and therefore that the differentiation sequence from illocutions to locutions is arbitrary.

It is clear, however, that conventions can only exist among persons, and, similarly, that conventions can have proximate effect only on persons. Thus, any system of conventional acts must be prelocutionary. Furthermore, any conventional act must be institutionalized. That is, it must be reciprocally typified among the relevant individuals as having that particular conventional significance or else it will not, in fact, have that significance and thus will not be a conventional act. But this is to say that the conventional significance must be symmetrically available to all participants, thus that the transformations induced must be symmetrically available, and thus that a conventional act, used conventionally, will change situation conventions only into other situation conventions.

There are two directions of exception to this, however, involving, respectively, the introduction or the maintenance of deception: conventional acts used nonconventionally in situation conventions and conventional acts used nonconventionally in situations that are not themselves constituted by situation conventions. Conventional acts used conventionally must have symmetric transformation effects and thus must leave conventions as conventions. Conventional acts used nonconventionally (for example, verbal deception) will transform the attributed definition of the situation in accordance with the conventional significance for those who take the act as being used conventionally. For those who do not take it conventionally but expect others to (the utterer in particular but not necessarily exclusively), it will transform their attribution of others' attribution of the definition of the situation differently than it transforms their own situation image. Thus it destroys symmetry and thus destroys the factual existence of a situation convention, though not necessarily the attribution of one on the part of those participants taking the action as conventional.

Similarly, in a situation that already has an asymmetry (thus a lack of conventionality) among the situation images of the participants, a conventional act may be used for its conventional transformation effects on the attributions of those who do attribute a convention, thus maintaining the asymmetry, but simultaneously maintaining the attribution of conventionality for those who began with one.[92] Thus, conventional acts used nonconventionally can both introduce and maintain nonconventional asymmetries among the various situation images.

The critical point to note, however, is that conventional acts that are not taken conventionally by somebody in the situation have no conventional effect at all (though they might have many indirect and derivative effects). Furthermore, an act will be taken conventionally only by someone who begins with the attribution of conventionality to the situation in which the act is performed. Thus, although conventional acts can be used prelocutionarily and nonconventionally, such usage is completely derivative from the attribution of situation conventions and the taking of the acts as conventional on the part of the relevant participants.

This necessary derivativeness implies first that locutions are only meaningful relative to situation conventions, whatever else may be derived from such basic significances, and thus that they must be defined after and differentiated within illocutions. Second, although locutions may be used strictly prelocutionarily through the introduction of false situation convention attributions on the part of some participants, this is only possible derivatively from the hypothetical consideration of the locution as if there were some particular situation convention operative, with that hypothetical consideration inserted in the context of the actual asymmetric attributions involved. Thus, in no case will the conventionality of acts simply cross with prelocutions: all such "conventional prelocutions" begin as and remain parasitic upon illocutionary systems. Therefore, the differentiation of locutions within illocutions is again of necessary direction and of genus-species form.

The principle of productivity, which differentiates linguistic acts within locutionary acts, is the exception to the pattern. It is evident that action systems that are not even prelocutionary can, in principle, be productive in the sense of generating an unbounded number of acts (for example, locomotion) and undoubtably in the sense of the higher-order generative capacities as well (for example, tool use and design), though this productivity has not been formally investigated except in the case of language. Thus, in particular, we can posit productive systems of strictly prelocutionary and strictly illocutionary acts and inquire into their nature and structure.[93]

It would seem likely, in fact, that the productivity of an action system is dependent more on the complexity of its object than on anything else. Thus, the class of potential locomotions may be an unbounded set, but its complexity is exhausted by relatively few transformations. Beginning with prelocutions, however, the potential complexity of the object (mind) is as great as the potential complexity of the action system itself, and within this general class of action systems and its subclasses we probably see expressions of maximal individual processing capacity.[94]

We have been inquiring into the potential productivity of potential action systems of various kinds. We might also inquire into the potential systemness of such potential action systems. This also would appear to be dependent on the complexity of the object but in a somewhat reverse manner. In particular, the greater the object complexity, the more complex the action system transformational capacity that must be acquired in order to realize a servomechanism capability on the relevant space of interactive potentialities. Therefore, the more complex the interactive object, the more time required for the generation (both cultural and personal) of appropriate action systems, and the less likelihood that such systems would in fact be acquired.

It is interesting to ask, in this regard, whether the hierarchy from strict prelocutions to linguistic acts involves an increase or a decrease in object complexity. That is, are situation conventions more or less complex in principle than minds, and does the conventionality of a locutionary act increase or decrease its potential complexity relative to that of strict illocutions? It would seem plausible that a decrease of complexity is involved, to the point that most people acquire a productive language system while those same people might have relatively rudimentary strict prelocutionary or strict illocutionary skills. This is precisely what would be expected if illocutions picked out relatively simple structures relative to the potential complexity of prelocutionary systems, while institutionalization imposes still greater relative simplicity on illocutions.

SITUATION CONVENTIONS AS OBJECTS

It is evident that situation conventions can exist as structures of factual relationships among situation images and equally evident that such structures can be affected by various interactions. It might seem, however, that the presence or absence—and the content if present—of situation conventions is a strictly analytic distinction within situations that are fundamentally prelocutionary in structure. It might seem, in other words, that situation conventions are strictly epiphenomenal relative to minds, that minds are thus the fundamental object of language, that situation conventions are essentially "transparent" to the primary goal definitions concerning minds, and thus that illocutions are at best an analytic subset of prelocutions but do not in any sense differentiate an actual and separate potential kind of action system within the overall control structure model. Put simply, how can a system know about a situation convention, and why should it care? I wish to examine the status of situation conventions as objects and to argue that they are objects, and are very important ones, to all persons.

The sense in which situation conventions are knowable to interactive systems is the same as the sense in which any object is knowable: it is manipulable, and it offers resistance. The patterns of possible interactive transformations arising within the structures of impossible transformations serve to define the interactive reality of situation conventions just as the functionally equivalent patterns of potential transformations serve to define physical objects. It is true that such transformational patterns are generally inferable about physical objects through instantaneous apperceptions from visual scans and that such instantaneous apperceptions are not generally possible with situation conventions, but, to make the comparison stronger, consider a blind man learning about and keeping track of particular physical objects. In both cases, the only available information for apperception is the results of actual attempts to perform the transformations whose structures define the objects to be transformed. In both cases, the object is known, and is only known, by (directly and presumptively) testing transformational hypotheses concerning its presence. Furthermore, the feedback concerning the structural reality of situation conventions is separable from feedback concerning the constituent minds, as, for example, in the case of a situation in which everyone knows a certain fact but no one knows that everyone knows:[95] a presumptive test of the simple individual knowledge of that fact may receive quite a different response from a presumptive test of the presence of that fact in the definition of the situation.

The status of situation conventions as knowable is thus established. Their status as object is dependent on what we choose to mean by object as differentiated from state or characteristic or process. I have not offered a full theory of objects to this point but will be satisfied with pointing out that situation conventions, though potentially quite variable in content, also have the potential for being of long duration, even institutionalized, in time. Furthermore, such persistence is not simple continuity, as with, for example, the process of fire or the state of being green, but is rather a continuity of invariance under a class of transformations, as with physical objects. That is, situation conventions are closed under various classes of transformations, in particular, of locutions,[96] and this implies the invariance under those transformations of the property of being subject to those transformations (unlike, say, the transformation of fire applied to a piece of wood, but like the property of being manipulable under the class of manipulations), that is, the invariance of the property of being situation conventions. Fundamentally, I suggest that the interactive reality of an object is precisely such a structure of potential transformations which is invariant under some other class of transformations (perhaps the same transformations), that the transformations involved define the kind of object, and that the invariance—and resultant savings in cognitive bookkeeping—is what makes objects useful cognitive units.

The status of situation conventions as knowable and as invariants leaves yet to be answered the question of their usefulness. Their potential bookkeeping usefulness as cognitive units is dependent upon those units' being functionally embedded in broader goals for, if not functional, no degree of simplicity will make them useful.[97] Thus, the issue is one of the functionality of situation conventions as situation conventions with respect to more fundamental goals.

A partial answer is derived from the fact that illocutions are functional as prelocutions. That is, operations on situation conventions can transform the beliefs and actions of other people, as with my pushing and lifting motions to get you to help me move a rock. Illocutions, then, are a means of extending one's own agency through that of another, and situation conventions are important as both means and constraints on any such prelocutionary extension. Thus, situation conventions, and therefore illocutions, must ultimately be taken into account by a satisfactory prelocutionary system.

This point is only a partial answer, however; although it explains why situation conventions and illocutions must be taken into account, it doesn't explain why situation conventions should be taken as the objects of a separate goal structure, that is, why illocutions should ever form a distinct action system. Such "taking into account" would seem to be manageable within the action computations of a strictly prelocutionary system.

Again, part of the answer derives from the functionality of situa-

tion conventions for prelocutionary goals. Combine this basic functionality with the cognitive savings from the invariance properties,
and it becomes clear that any efficient prelocutionary system will
have to have a subsidiary illocutionary system.

Again, however, the answer is only partial, because, although
it explains why most prelocutionary goals might be approached through
subsidiary illocutionary goals, it doesn't explain why situation conventions would ever be taken as objects of interaction and units of cognition in their own right. The points made thus far establish that situation conventions are important prelocutionary tools or instruments
but not that illocutions would ever have any sort of functional autonomy.

This final point of functional autonomy is made by first broaden-
ing the perspective somewhat from the strict action or transformational
characteristics of action systems to their perceptual and cognitive
characteristics. Interactions do not simply do things; they also ground
apperceptions concerning the potentialities for other interactions, that
is, they provide information about the situation, about what else might
be done. Thus, prelocutions can be used not only to proximately affect
another's actions but also to affect the grounds upon which the other's
future actions will be determined. It is here that situation conventions
and thus illocutions have their true flowering.

In particular, strictly prelocutionary acts with such indirect
goals of affecting the grounds for others' actions, that is, such indirect prelocutions without the involvement of the mutuality and symmetry of situation conventions, are extremely limited by the uncertainty concerning the possibility of intervening interference in accom-
plishing the goal. Prelocutionary goals which involve the establishment
in the recipients of particular policies or perspectives for action over
time, rather than simply a particular action at a particular time, are
susceptible to all conceivable intervening influences on those desired
strategies or perspectives, including, in general, mere whim. Especially if such a policy orientation has been established in the first
place by a strictly prelocutionary act, such interferences will have
free play, and the prelocution is likely to fail.

If, however, the policy perspective is a component of a mutual
and symmetric definition of the situation, established (therefore) by
illocutions, it will remain constant through most such potential interferences: situation conventions are immune to most experiences, ex-
cepting further illocutions. The existence of the mutuality of such a
definition of the situation assumes, of course, the existence of a
mutuality of interest in maintaining a situation convention. That is,
the circumstances must involve a coordination problem in order for
there to be a situation convention. It is precisely, in fact, when such
mutuality of interest is not present, or at least not sought, that strict
prelocutions must most often be attempted: there is no need to main-

tain the asymmetry of a strictly prelocutionary communication, with all of the problems of such maintenance, when the natural symmetry of coordination is possible. [98] Conversely, when coordination is sought, it is essentially impossible to obtain except through situation conventions. Thus, we have an important form of prelocutionary extension of agency, coordination, or cooperation that is not only more efficiently performed through illocutions but, in effect, can only be performed through illocutions.

Furthermore, such indirect policy-level prelocutionary goals make essential use of the potential duration and institutionalization of conventions and, thus, for the first time, bring into relevance the complex structurings and transformations that are possible with conventions. Goals may be defined strictly with respect to these structures and transformations of conventions without necessarily being directly derived from or subordinate to particular prelocutionary goals of physical actions. Therefore, a level of analysis has now been reached at which the potential functional autonomy of illocutionary systems is explicable. Conventions provide not only for the coordination of actions but also for the coordination of the realm of conventions. Conventions provide the opportunity not only to know about and act upon the world but also to define it. [99] It is at the level of such definitions that we find the full pervasiveness and importance of conventions: it is in terms of our (situationally conventional) participation in such conventions that we define our selves and our identities and in terms of structures and relationships among such conventions that we define our roles and institutions.

Thus, conventions provide not simply an epiphenomenal or instrumental level of goal definitions but, rather, a distinct ontological level about which goals can be defined. Illocutionary systems, therefore, can be developed autonomously around goal spaces concerning that ontological level.

Finally, it should be noted that, in general, locutions do not take objects distinct from situation conventions but rather remain instrumental as highly efficient types of actions toward illocutionary goals. Thus, locutions (and linguistic systems) will tend to remain subsidiary systems to illocutionary systems and will not develop similar functional autonomy. The exception to this is of major importance but of relatively narrow scope relative to language communities in general: when a locutionary (linguistic) system develops that takes the (conventions of) locutionary systems as objects, as in mathematics. [100]

THE SEQUENCE OF LANGUAGE GENESIS

The sequence of differentiations of action systems culminating with linguistic systems that has been developed has implications for language genesis in all three of its senses: phylogenesis, ontogenesis, and microgenesis. In this section, I would like to point out some of these implications.

It is evident that, insofar as the sequence of differentiations of communication and language acts is intrinsic and necessary, that sequence will impose itself upon any progressive construction of language systems out of general action capabilities, including, in particular, the constructions of phylogenesis and ontogenesis. Thus, prelocutionary actions depend upon the evolution, or development, of a minimal cognitive capability to represent the context dependency of others' interactive characteristics, while illocutions depend on the ability to base that context sensitivity on the implicit relational structure of situation conventions. Correspondingly, prelocutionary capability will occur only insofar as the representation of context dependence is possible, and illocutionary capability will follow prelocutions in both evolution and development.

It is of interest to note that both of these characteristics are present in an implicit and degenerate sense in young infants. The efficacy of an infant's hunger or discomfort distress calls, for example, is a context-sensitive result, sensitive, in fact, to contexts constituted by such distress calls. That is, the infant is dependent upon the context sensitivity of the behavior of others (adults) without being able actually to represent cognitively that sensitivity. Such distress calls, then, form a prelocutionary system at the level of the evolutionary gene pool (the distress call system constitutes a genetic representation of adults' context sensitivity) but not at the level of cognition. That is, it is at the genetic level rather than the cognitive level that the selection has been made among the logically possible alternative solutions to the relevant coordination problem. Such innate prelocutions obviously also exist in species whose organisms never do develop the cognitive capability of prelocutionary acts.[101] It seems highly likely that such innate prelocutions form a substrate out of which cognitive prelocutions develop and differentiate, given sufficient cognitive capacity, again both evolutionarily and developmentally.[102] Furthermore, there appear to be innate prelocutionary systems that have evolved in human beings for the primary purpose of providing such a foundation for the development of cognitive prelocutions, and, thus, language: for example, cooing and babbling (Freedman 1974).

Not only are such innate "interpersonal" actions implicitly prelocutionary, they are also implicitly illocutionary in the sense that they define a situation mutually for all participants: the significance of such innate actions is "available" to all members of the same species.[103] In this case, however, the existence of a situation convention is not only implicit and simple, as with innate prelocutions, but is so simple as to be degenerate or vacuous: situation conventions are present in fact but with nothing in the system being dependent upon or making use of any of the special properties of situation conventions. That is, none of the properties of conventions as distinct from context-sensitive agents is made use of or responded to in these cases. The illocutionary character of innate prelocutions is truly epiphenomenal, both genetically and cognitively.

Again, however, the presence of situation conventions, even if epiphenomenal and of degenerate simplicity, may provide the foundation for the differentiation and elaboration of illocutionary systems once the requisite cognitive capabilities are present. The cognitive requisite in this case is the ability to compute complex temporal trajectories of situation interaction characteristics. Only when such trajectories are computable can situation conventions be taken as true objects of interaction rather than simple instruments, or even epiphenomena, of prelocutions. In this regard, it is of interest to note that the hidden translations of object permanency (Piaget 1954) also require the ability to compute temporal trajectories, and, although object translations constitute relatively simple trajectories, the onsets of object permanence and of early language in development seem closely connected. Presumably, simple object permanency trajectory capabilities would not be sufficient for the species-level evolution of language,[104] the possibilities are still too limited, but such a capability does suffice to ground the development of simple language in the individual once language has evolved in the species.

Analytically, the progression from prelocutions to linguistic acts is a sequence of logical differentiations, each within the preceding. Systemically, however, these differentiations are based on differing kinds of principles that have correspondingly differing consequences for the sequencing of language genesis. Thus, prelocutionary systems and illocutionary systems are both full action systems in the sense of being servomechanisms with their own goal spaces and principles of interaction computation. Moreover, each of them is subordinate to its preceding structure in the sense of a means-end subordination of the goal spaces, and this subordination visits itself as a sequencing constraint on the constructions of the action systems, be they phylogenetic or ontogenetic constructions.

Locutions, on the other hand, do not form a distinct action system. They have the same goals as illocutions. They are, in fact, a variety of illocutions rather than a distinct and subordinate means to illocutionary goals. Locutions are differentiated by the conventional nature of their illocutionary efficacy rather than by their goals. Thus the analytic sequencing does not in this case have quite the same effect on the genetic sequencing: this differentiation has no necessary impact on the sequence of construction of language. The genesis of locutions is, therefore, very possibly coextensive with that of illocutions, and, in view of the relative power and simplicity of locutions, the construction of illocutions is likely to be to a large extent in terms of the construction of locutions. From an evolutionary perspective, this would imply that the earliest locutions were likely to have been habitualized and institutionalized (within a band, perhaps) interactive forms derived from, probably simplified from, earlier illocutionary precedents (for example, pantomime)[105] and that such locutions would from an early time constitute a large portion of the cognitively available illocutions. Ontogenetically the same point holds, except that the early locutions are likely to be only dyadically institutionalized between mother and infant, with the child only later beginning to make use of the locutions institutionally available in a wider language community. This subsequencing of dyadically institutionalized locutions before more widely institutionalized locutions derives from the relative greater availability to the infant of the opportunity for precedent setting and habitualization of dyadic locutions and possibly also from the timing of sufficient neural maturation to be able to master the more widely institutionalized vocal locutions.[106]

The sequencing considerations for the construction of linguistic systems are, corresponding to the difference in the relevant principle of differentiation, somewhat different from those for the other action types. Like locutions, linguistic acts can be a variety of the prior category of acts: locutions a variety of illocutions distinguished by their conventionality; linguistic acts a variety of locutions distinguished by their productivity. Unlike locutions, however, linguistic acts are an intrinsically more complex variety of the prior form of action, not simply a distinct variety. Thus, although this increased complexity is not necessarily of the form of a distinct action system, as with illocutions relative to prelocutions, it is, nevertheless, a complexity differentiation and therefore will have consequences in the sequence of constructions. In particular, while locutions would be expected to occur very quickly in the construction of illocutions, the construction through the various levels of productive complexity of quasi-languages would be expected to be somewhat more delayed and protracted relative to the onset of strict locutions.[107]

Both prelocutionary and illocutionary systems are capable of productive complexity, but linguistic systems for the first time involve institutionalized productive complexity and thus for the first time have the possibility of partaking of the greater power of cultural evolution relative to individual development (or genetic evolution). Correspondingly, with the creation of an institutionalized linguistic system, either culturally or in the individual, we encounter the probability that the institution has developed greater power and resources than the individual would be likely to develop de novo and almost certainly greater than the individual would have developed to that point in his prior prelocutionary and illocutionary systems. These greater institutional resources, as they are assimilated in the individual's linguistic system, become available to the superordinate illocutionary, prelocutionary, and general-action systems, thus greatly expanding the individual's entire range of powers of agency. Thus, whether considered culturally or individually, the institutionalized resources of linguistic systems provide much of the complexity, power, and flexibility of available illocutionary and prelocutionary systems and thereby of action systems in general.

Linguistic acts generally, and certainly initially, would not be produced by distinct linguistic action systems but would instead correspond to an increased power in the production of (locutionary) illocutions. It is possible, however, (though not necessarily common) for a linguistic system to be constructed as a distinct servomechanism with a distinct goal space—with goals consisting of the construction of a particular locution suitable to a particular illocutionary goal and contextual situation. Thus, while locutions have transformations of situation conventions as their goals and productive locutionary systems (linguistic systems) will have great power with respect to such goals, a distinct and autonomous linguistic system servomechanism will take as its goal definitions not directly the transformations of situation conventions but, rather, the construction of locutions appropriate to such transformations. Consider, for example, the construction of such a locution which is then not uttered. That is, it is possible for the very constructional productivity of linguistic acts to be differentiated as a distinct action system. Such a system is no longer just a system of locutions with productivity but a productive system about locutions. It takes locutionary systems and, potentially, productive locutionary systems, as objects in the same sense that illocutions take situation conventions as objects: it encounters and functions within the structure of flexibilities and constraints, of possibilities and impossibilities, of conventional illocutions. As such, it forms a metasystem and, if institutionalized, a metalanguage, for language[108] and provides corresponding possibilities for the deliberate refinement and expansion of the power of language. The development of such a metasystem in the individual probably requires formal operations, since it involves a cognitive differentiation between language form and content and should be a prerequisite for maximal power of language use, whether logical or expressive. One historical development of such a metalanguage was probably during the period of the pre-Socratic Greeks, with particular emphasis by the Sophists, and resulting in the first language formalizations by Aristotle.

Unlike phylogenesis and ontogenesis, microgenesis is not constructional. Microgenesis has to do with the computational origins of a particular act within a given control structure rather than with the construction of that control structure. The construction of a subordinate action system clearly requires the prior construction of a superordinate action system, [109] but the execution of an interaction within a given control structure does not necessarily require an immediately prior computation in a superordinate system. In fact, precisely to the extent that an action system is fully developed with a distinct goal space involving distinct interactive objects, that action system will have a potential functional autonomy, that is, will be capable of microgenetically initiating actions toward goals concerning those objects independently of any particular current goals of superordinate systems. Thus, the sequence of differentiations, insofar as it involves differentiations of action systems, has somewhat opposite consequences for microgenesis (execution) than it does for (constructive) phylogenesis and ontogenesis. In particular, insofar as an action of a particular system level has originated epiphenomenally or instrumentally from the execution of a "higher" level, then that action will be, respectively, either computationally identical or subordinate to the computation of that higher action. But insofar as an action of a particular level has originated in terms of goals concerning interactive objects specific to that level and goals derived from prior goals concerning those objects rather than from concomitant higher-order goals, then that action system is functionally autonomous and that action is microgenetically autonomous.

THE ANALYSIS OF LANGUAGE

The sequence of differentiations from general goal-directed action systems to linguistic systems generates, with one exception, a corresponding hierarchy of potentially autonomous action systems, each of which introduces qualitatively new characteristics of communication and language. The one exception is the level of locutions, which, when organized as a productive (even if not autonomous) system, becomes linguistic. Such a hierarchy of system levels provides a framework within which various characteristics of language may be differentiated and analyzed, and from which certain language characteristics can be deduced. Some implications of this hierarchy for the sequencing of language genesis have been mentioned.

This basic hierarchy of levels of action is further differentiated by the various levels of functional autonomy discussed earlier which a given system can reach relative to the action level immediately above. In particular, an action level can exist as strictly epiphenomal to the one above, as strictly instrumental, as productively instrumental, and as functionally autonomous from the level above. Each level of autonomy supercedes and incorporates the preceding level.[110] In particular, a functionally autonomous system can still be used instrumentally by the higher level; the distinction is that it can also function without necessarily being in such a direct instrumental capacity. Differentiation of such levels of autonomy adds further structure to the analysis of language and its genesis.

An additional dimension of differentiation is obtained from the consideration of the general form of an action system. An action system is organized around a goal space in such a way that, given a current goal definition and a current situation image, it will compute an interaction (likely a feedback-controlled interaction) so as to transform the situation (image) in accordance with the goal. There are thus three analytic aspects to an action system: the nature and structure of the goal image; the computations of interactions given a goal and a situation image; and the actual transformations performed by the interaction on the situation and situation image. Various characteristics of language arise within differing ones of these aspects and thus add still further structure to the framework for the analysis of language.

This framework, however, is from a strictly systemic explanatory approach to language, and it is clear that that is not the only available approach. If we consider the general problem of analyzing a system in interaction with its environment, there are two fundamental perspectives that can be adopted: (1) we can attempt to describe that system's class of interactions from an external perspective; and (2) we can attempt to explain those interactions in terms of the interior processes of the system.[111] It is evident that no interior process explanation can be attempted without at least some external description to begin with, and it should be equally evident that any exterior description is of ultimate use only insofar as it participates in an interior explanation: a description that describes with explanatorily useless principles or categories is always to be rejected in favor of one that does not.[112] Thus, both description and explanation must be pursued simultaneously and dialectically, each providing primary criteria of evaluation for the other.

It should also be evident that description is not merely observation. Observation is the ground for description, but description must organize and go beyond observation. Description cannot be simply the class of interactions observed (as on a videotape); nor can it be a set of regularities and categories by which that class of observations can be generated: that is simply a more efficient coding of the observations. There can be strong and valid utilitarian grounds for being concerned with specific events (interactions) or sets of events, but a science must be concerned with the principles and regularities under-

lying those events and thus must consider not only what has been and
what is but also what might have been and might be. Science is concerned with the counterfactual as well as the factual, [113] and, therefore, description similarly must be concerned with what might have
been observed as well as what was observed. This directly implies
that description as well as explanation involves hypothesis generation
and testing. That is, they both involve inference beyond the data given
and thus the possibility of error.

In the case of system interactions, the descriptive (and explanatory) focus is, thus, on the potential interactions and not just the
actual. The concern is with interaction capacity, and a valid description is a representation of the class of potential interactions that constitutes that capacity. [114] Such a description has theoretical status:
it can be falsified by showing that it includes either too much in its
representation of capacity or too little.

Observations, the grounds for descriptions, are always partial:
they are of some particular category of events and of some particular
aspect(s) of those events and, correspondingly, of categories and
aspects of system interactions. Thus, events (and interactions) are
not analytically unitary: they are bundles of categories and aspects
only some of which are relevant to any particular task of observation,
description, or explanation. Categories of description in a particular
case are delimited by criteria that serve to select or reject interactions as relevant to the descriptive task at hand, and aspects of description are determined by criteria (perhaps the same ones) that
specify the nature of that relevance. In particular, an interaction is
descriptively relevant only insofar as it could serve to falsify a potential capacity description, and the criteria of falsification, therefore, determine the fact and the nature of that relevance, that is,
whether and in what way an interaction might falsify a description.
Thus, the criteria of descriptive falsification, the criteria of descriptive error, determine the aspect of the interactions to be observed, and, correspondingly, the nature of the interaction capacity
to be described. Interactive capacities are for particular types and
characteristics of interactions and not simply for raw sets of particular interactions, [115] and those types and characteristics—and thus the
capacities to be described—are determined observationally by the
descriptive error criteria.

If the interactions to be considered are language acts and the
error criterion is in terms of judgments of acceptability or nonac-
ceptability of those acts by fluent speakers of a particular language,
then the corresponding capacity to be described is generally called
the linguistic competence for that language. [116] If the descriptive error
criterion is in terms of a probabilistic match with the stream of sounds
produced by such a speaker, the capacity to be described will generally

be called one of <u>linguistic performance.</u>[117] It is important to note
first of all that, as defined, neither competence nor performance is
explanatory; both are capacities to be described <u>and</u> explained, and
each would likely require differing, though presumably related, descriptions and explanations.[118] It is also important to note that these
two are not necessarily the only capacities to be defined with respect
to language acts; any differing error criterion would define a new
capacity. It remains to be seen, however, which capacities are most
meaningful from an explanatory perspective.

A description of a linguistic competence is called a grammar
for that language and is classically understood to have three components: (1) a syntactic component, which "specifies an infinite set
of formal objects, each of which incorporates all information relevant
to a single interpretation of a particular sentence"; (2) a phonological
component, which "determines the phonetic form of a sentence generated by the syntactic rules"; and (3) a semantic component, which
"determines the semantic interpretation of a sentence" (Chomsky
1965, p. 16).

Pragmatics, sometimes considered a part of the competence
to be described (and thus requiring its own component in a grammar)
and sometimes not, is concerned with the uses and effects of language
acts.[119]

I wish to suggest that these definitions of the various aspects
or divisions of the study of language represent a confounding of the
sociological and psychological perspectives on language, and that,
as a consequence, their standard conceptualizations are at best
confused and at worst incoherent.

First of all, the acceptability of an utterance depends upon the
efficacy of that utterance in performing a (conventional) transformation on a situation convention in accordance with a goal. Therefore,
a judgment of the acceptability of an utterance type will depend, in
part, on the creativity involved in imagining situation and goal contexts within which that utterance might be conventionally efficacious.
Insofar as such contexts are rare or unusual for a particular utterance
type, that type risks being rejected invalidly (McCawley 1974, 1976).
Judgments of unacceptability are themselves fallible.

Furthermore, insofar as the syntactic acceptability of some
"formal object" is itself determined by such general judgments of
acceptability, then the syntax of a language will be subject to the
same constraints as the whole grammar for the language. If the error
criteria are identical, the competencies are identical. It might be
contended that syntactics and, say, semantics do describe the same
interactive competencies and thus that such an equivalence of error
criteria is legitimate but that they describe different "components"
of that competency. However, this accepts that distinct judgments of

syntactic acceptability and semantic acceptability are either not possible in principle or are rigidly equivalent; otherwise, they form capacities that are in principle distinguishable. If they are not distinguishable as capacities then it is not clear in what sense they differ as components (that is, in what ways are they not equivalent?); and if they are distinguishable as capacities, then syntax is improperly inclusive of semantics by virtue of its error criterion equivalence as capacity to all of grammar. [120] Such improper cross-dependence of error criteria is compounded by the aforementioned fallibility of unacceptableness judgments. Since equivalent arguments hold for pragmatic constraints on acceptability, it is not surprising that the study of "syntax" has expanded to encompass virtually all of grammar. A clearer separation of the capacities in terms of their corresponding error criteria might, if possible, greatly simplify their description (and explanation). [121] Such a possibility, however, is not guaranteed.

The problem is that, while general judgments of acceptability and unacceptability can be made, though fallibly, it becomes increasingly difficult to differentiate judgments concerning syntactic, semantic, and pragmatic constraints on acceptability and perilously close to circularity to make the attempt. On the other hand, some such judgments are desired and necessary because it is clear that the capacity defined by general acceptability judgments is not unitary: it is comprised of subcapacities in the sense of a correspondence of subcapacities to subsystems or aspects of systems within the overall system. Therefore, description of those interactive capacities ultimately must reflect the structure of the corresponding explanatory process structures. The deep source of this problem of the differentiation of subcapacities is that to attempt to ground conceptualizations of these capacities directly in terms of underlying interactive systems is to require some model of such action systems, which has been basically nonexistent, and also to cross from the institutional (external and ideal) perspective to the psychological (internal and real) perspective, which has been basically illegitimate; whereas to attempt conceptualizations of such subcapacities directly and solely in terms of observation error criteria, as has been standard practice, is to encounter definitional circularity and arbitrariness. In compromise, the capacities are generally defined with respect to intuitive and nonspecific models of the underlying system structure.

What are wanted are descriptive error criteria definitions of capacities that are as extensionally close as possible to interactive capacities as manifested by underlying explanatory (systemic) action structures. That is, definitions of capacities are themselves subject to judgment, improvement, and rejection relative to explanatory systems, just like the descriptions within (or of) a capacity relative to observations. It is evident, in fact, that such linguistic capacities are themselves part of the description of the overall interactive capacity of a system, that is, that they constitute subcapacities relative to the total system and are testable as such relative not only to observations but to corresponding explanatory structures. Thus, definitions of capacities as interactive capacities of subsystems of the total system (or aspects of such) optimally should coincide with definitions of capacities in terms of descriptive error criteria. Definitions of capacities in terms of systemic structure are, in fact, the fundamental definitions toward which descriptive error definitions are fallibly aimed. [122], [123]

The framework for the analysis of language outlined earlier in terms of the hierarchy of action systems from general goal-directed to linguistic and in terms of the three aspects of action systems is clearly an internal systemic framework rather than an external observation error framework. But each aspect at each level of that framework should correspond to a capacity in the sense of corresponding to a space of interactive potentialities, and these capacities should be descriptively approachable. Furthermore, insofar as the systemic framework is valid, it serves as an explanatory context within which the standard descriptive language framework must fit if that standard framework is to be valid. I contend that the definitions of syntax, semantics, and pragmatics are partially identifiable within the system framework, [124] but, as later sections will show, the issues normally subsumed under these categories do not fully conform to such an identification: the identifications are at best partial.

As a first approximation, it would seem that syntax is associated with the computational capacity for the generation of interactions. Pragmatics, then, as concerned with the uses and effects of utterances, would seem to correspond most closely to the capacity (space) of potential goals of an action system. Semantics, that by which pragmatic goals may be obtained, would then correspond to the transformational properties of interactions. This identification of syntax, semantics, and pragmatics with the three aspects of action systems has an attraction of simplicity and generality. One consequential result is that it leads to questions about the syntax, semantics, and pragmatics of all action systems, general, prelocutionary, and illocutionary, analogous to such questions about linguistic capacities.

Closer examination, however, shows that this identification is not fully coherent. In particular, pragmatics is generally considered to be concerned with both the interactive uses and the situational effects or consequences of utterances, thus appearing to include both the transformational properties of interactions and the goal space of an action system within its purview. Semantics, on the other hand, as being concerned with the means by which pragmatic goals can be reached, would seem to focus on interaction transformation properties, while, as being concerned with the meanings that utterances convey, would seem to focus on the goal space for those utterances. Semantics and pragmatics, then, appear to include identical aspects of action systems within their supposedly distinct realms of analysis. I contend, and will argue later, that this incoherence cannot be eliminated because it rests on a fundamental equivocation in the standard conceptualization of meaning.

There is, however, another sense in which this simple identification of the three components of grammar with the three aspects of action systems is unsatisfactory, and, in this regard, appropriate modification of the identification is possible. The unsatisfactoriness is simply that the identification as given makes syntax, semantics, and pragmatics exhaustive of the capacities of any and all action systems, not just language systems. But grammar, which they presumably comprise, is not normally taken to be the total interactive capacity it would constitute under such an identification. In particular, syntax and semantics are concerned with institutional language, not with any action system. They are concerned with <u>conventional</u> interactive computational forms and <u>conventional</u> interactive transformational effects, that is, with the capacities of forms and effects, respectively, of linguistic action systems (note that the goal capacities of linguistic systems are subsumed in those for illocutionary systems). Pragmatics, then, becomes concerned with all noninstitutional aspects of language, that is, with language as it relates to all aspects of illocutionary, prelocutionary, and general action systems. These identifications are much more consistent with the institutional-psychological distinction implicit in the standard categories, though they do not avoid the incoherence mentioned above, and will be adopted at this point.

The intent in the following sections is to present an illustrative analysis of some of the primary characteristics of language as they arise at each successive level of the analytic framework constituted by the sequence of differentiations of action systems. Considerations of perspectives for analysis in addition to this primary framework, such as the three aspects of action systems, or the syntactic, semantic, and pragmatic identifications, will arise as relevant to the discussions at the particular levels of differentiation.

GOAL-DIRECTED SYSTEMS

The section begins with a review of the nature of goal-directed systems, of some of the types of such systems that are possible, and of some of the internal relationships within such systems. The next part of the discussion is devoted to the relationship between the organization of goal-directed servomechanisms in the world image and the structure of the field of potential agent-world interactions. In particular, it is suggested that the world image is likely to capture only relatively decomposable structures in that field of potentialities. Last, it is pointed out that the typically linguistic issues of the truth and falsity of representations and of model theoretic possible worlds approaches in fact arise at the level of general goal-directed action systems, before even the first differentiation toward linguistic systems has been made.

A goal-directed system is basically a procedure for computing interactions, given a situation image and a goal definition, which transform the situation in accordance with the goal. The three aspects of goal-directed systems are, thus, the procedure for the interaction computation, the space of possible goals with respect to which the procedure is appropriate, and the relationships between the interactions and their objects by which the interactions effect their transformations. The situation image is a foundational component of all goal-directed systems that both defines the prior conditions for the interaction computation and represents the posterior situation as transformed by that action. Such updating of the situation image, in accordance with the interaction effects, will consist of apperceptive processes based on both the outcomes of the primary goal-directed interactions as well as on the outcomes of auxiliary testing or "perceptual" interactions (which may themselves also be goal-directed).

The computation of an interaction from a situation image and a goal definition is basically a problem-solving format: a state (situation) and a goal are given, and the problem is to find a transformation (interaction) that will transform the state into the goal. Thus, a goal-directed system functions as an interactive problem solver. As a problem-solving system, it may proceed either heuristically, that is, based on procedures with a high likelihood, but no certainty, of relevance and success, or algorithmically, based on procedures with an assurance of success.[125] Within either of these categories, goal-directed interactions may depend upon the outcomes of interpolated or simultaneous testing interactions, and thus be subject to feedback, or they may be computed solely on the basis of the initial situation image and goal definition without intermediate information, and thus be uncorrected or ballistic. Interactions with feedback may be further subdivided according to whether or not the feedback contains information used in the computation of the subsequent portion of the interaction. If not, then the feedback is "simply" an indication of success or failure in a trial-and-error process, and the system will be called error-sensitive. If so, then the feedback can be used in an iterative approximation or approach to the goal, and the system will be called error-corrected.

Thus, a goal-directed system may proceed with respect to its primary goal space in any of six modes, generated by the intersection of the heuristic-algorithmic dichotomy with the trichotomy of ballistic, error-sensitive, and error-corrected computations. It is to be noted that these categories of interactive problem-solving modes apply at every distinct servomechanism level and to every distinct goal space within a level in an overall action system, and that the modes found may will differ from level to level and from servomechanism to servomechanism.[126] The optimality of various modes will be subject to such considerations as computation cost and error cost, while the availability of modes will depend upon the knowledge that the system has of the relevant object of interaction.

Availability, however, is ultimately constrained by the interactive tractability of the object of interaction: an algorithm cannot be used if none exists or if it would be too complex to be computed; similarly, feedback of error information is possible only insofar as it is detectable and, again, if its computational complexity is not too great. Thus, while system and situation conditions will determine the problem-solving modes used for a particular interaction in a particular system, the ultimate availability of these modes is a feature of the object of interaction and is, therefore, analyzable without reference to particular systems. The availability of goal-directed problem-solving modes will, accordingly, be analyzable in principle at each distinct object level in the sequence of language differentiations.

The goal definitions of a goal-directed system cannot be identical in all respects to the situation image "definitions"—goals to be accomplished must be distinguished from outcomes already obtained—but otherwise they must be in equivalent representational form: they are both "about" the same thing, the situation; and goals, once accomplished, become part of the situation image. Therefore, although it is conceivable that a particular system would use quite different internal representational conventions for its goal definitions and for its situation images, they must, nevertheless, be intertranslatable[127] and thus representationally equivalent. In particular, goal definitions must share whatever representational structuring is to be found in situation images.

Situation images, consisting of structures of indices in various registers, will be organized partly in accordance with the structure of the hierarchy of servomechanisms that generate them but primarily in terms of the structures of apperceptions among them. The apperception outcomes, in turn, will be organized with respect to the procedures that use them. Situation images, therefore, are constrained in structure by the organization of the procedures in the world image in terms of both their constructive origin and their referencing function. That is, just as goal definitions, when accomplished, must be translatable into situation images, so must situation images, when referenced, be functional as inputs to procedure executions. The relationships between individual situation image indices and individual computation decisions, however, are in general complexly many to many, rather than one to one, and, thus, although situation images ultimately must be organized for utilization by procedures and procedures must be executed in accordance with situation images, the structural similarities thereby induced between them will be of major importance but will be far from simple equivalences.

The ultimate constraint on the structure of the world image and thus on the structures of situation images and goal definitions[128] is, in part, whatever organization of procedures happens to be innate to the system. Fundamentally, however, that constraint is the functional structure of the agent-situation interaction relationships, the structure of the field of potential interactions. Thus, the boundaries and hierarchical organization of servomechanism procedures must conform to the boundaries and hierarchies of particular goal-directed problem-solving possibilities in the general agent-world interactive relationship. The apperceptive structures of situation images similarly must conform to the implicational structures that actually hold within that agent-world relationship.[129]

It is conceivable that the agent-world interactive relationship would allow only a sparse servomechanism hierarchicalization with correspondingly highly complex problem-solving procedures within each servomechanism. Since a servomechanism is generally of minimal utility until it is well organized around its goal space, and since the construction of procedures (servomechanisms) must proceed progressively with increments of interactive success at each step,[130] a servomechanism structuring with too high a complexity within each servomechanism component would be unlikely to have been constructively realized either phylogenetically or ontogenetically. Since each servomechanism's goal space corresponds to the space of potential transformations on some object of interaction, the hierarchicalization of servomechanisms actually found among human beings is evidence for the corresponding hierarchical decomposability of the structure of interactive potentialities between agents and the world.[131] Furthermore, since any structure of interactive potentialities with insufficient decomposability is unlikely to be captured in a corresponding procedure (servomechanism), we can expect such a hierarchical structuring of objects and corresponding spaces of transformation (servomechanisms) to be relatively ubiquitous, including with respect to language.

Thus, just as phylogenetically and ontogenetically early procedures are hierarchically organized around material objects within spaces of physical transformations and with causal apperceptive implications in time,[132] so will language procedures be hierarchically organized around situation conventions within spaces of occasion meaning transformations, and with apperceptions of conventional meaning in time.

Situation images are about the current contextual situation in which a system is located, and world images are about sets of potential situations and the potential transformations among them. As such, both situation images and world images may be in error. They may yield interactive computations that have unanticipated effects. Thus, issues of truth and falsity arise at the level of general action systems[133] before even the first differentiation toward language has occurred. Since truth and falsity are relationships between representations and that which is represented, this is not particularly surprising unless language is taken as representationally (cognitively) fundamental.[134] I contend that all involvements of truth and falsity with language are particularizations of, or derivations from, this basic involvement with situation and world images.

The world image is representational in that it corresponds to the interactive potentialities of the world and to the interactive relationships among those potentialities. That is, the world image constitutes the system's knowledge of how the world might be—the possibilities of the world, or the possible worlds. Correspondingly, the situation image constitutes the system's knowledge of the current location of the actual world (the situation) among those possibilities. This structure is similar to that of the common model theoretic location of the actual world in a space of possible worlds (Hughes and Cresswell 1968), but there are two fundamental differences. First, the characterizations of worlds and possible worlds in this model are strictly interactive and are thus characterizations of possible world-agent interactive relationships, not of worlds per se. Second, the characterizations are never complete in the sense of entirely specifying any particular possible world; they are always finite and therefore have the nature of partial descriptions of classes of (interactive) worlds. Similarly, the situation image does not define the current situation so much as it indicates a class of (interactive) possible worlds within which the current situation (actual world) is located.[135] I contend that the utility of model theoretic semantics in the study of language (for example, Creswell 1973; Montague 1972) is derivative from this connection with world and situation images as they relate to general action systems. That is, I contend that, insofar as a model theoretic "possible world" formalism is appropriate to language, it is so because of its appropriateness to cognition and action systems in general.

PRELOCUTIONARY SYSTEMS

Prelocutionary systems are differentiated by their property of accepting goal definitions concerning agents, and the special properties of such systems, therefore, are derived from the special properties of agents as objects of interaction. The special property most focused on in the following discussion is that special context sensitivity of agents constituted by their being apperceivers. Correspondingly, the discussion is primarily devoted to an exploration of the consequences of the fact that communications must be apperceived by their recipients in order to be successful. In particular, the section analyzes the constraints that those necessary apperceptions impose on the possibility of decomposing a communication into subcommunications, or, conversely, of constructing a communication out of "smaller" pieces. It is concluded that communications can be decomposed but not in such a way as to violate certain natural context-characterization structures of apperceptions. The possibility of decompositions within those natural structures requires situation conventions and thus illocutions.

The effects of an interaction on any situation are always dependent not only on the interaction itself but on the situational context within which the interaction takes place. That is, interaction effects are always context-sensitive. However, when an agent is the object of action, as is the definitional case for prelocutionary interactions, then that context to which the interactions are sensitive is itself context-sensitive: the agent as object of interaction is a context-sensitive context. Therefore, the sensitivities that a prelocutionary system must take into account in computing an interaction will themselves be sensitive to other aspects of the situation: the computation of sensitivities must become recursive.

Agents as objects of interaction are not only context-sensitive contexts, they are also contexts with memory.[136] The internal state of an agent and thus the nature of its sensitivity to the current context is itself dependent upon past contexts and states. Furthermore, such internal states and their relevances to current context sensitivities are not necessarily directly apperceivable, and thus cannot be simply subsumed under the direct apperception of the current situation. In effect, the context sensitivity of an agent as object extends into the past as part of the relevant context, bounded ultimately only by the birth of the individual (and, indirectly, the cultural memory which he or she represents), thus providing both vast potential scope for the recursions of context sensitivities and a correspondingly vast potential for the complexities of computing the context sensitivities of agents as objects of interaction.[137]

The context within which a communication significance is computed is the situation image within which the interaction detecting (or constituting) the communication occurs. The context sensitivity of the computation of the situation image is the source of the potential recursiveness of the context sensitivity of the significance of the communication. Thus, a communication may have differing significances depending on the contextual situation image within which it is apperceived, while that contextual situation image will itself be sensitive to current and past interactive contexts. The aspects or components of a situation image to which a particular communication significance computation is sensitive, that is, those aspects or components which, if different, would yield a different significance, will be called the pragmatic (or communicational) presuppositions of the significance (whether a goal significance or an understood significance). The pragmatic presuppositions of a goal significance will be called the prelocutionary presuppositions of the interaction. Thus, if I know that you have been concerned about losing your job and I interpret your current sad expression as indicating that you have, in fact, lost it, then that prior knowledge constitutes a pragmatic presupposition of the significance I have given to your expression. Similarly, if I then tell you about some new opportunities I have heard about with the intent of helping you feel better, then the assumption that you lost your job is a prelocutionary presupposition of my goal significance of improving your mood.

A prelocutionary communication becomes part of the apperceived situation for the agent(s) to which it is directed. Those apperceptions of the recipient(s) of the communication will depend upon the prior situation image within which they occur and upon the apperceptive procedures available to the recipient. Finally, those apperceptions, and thus the communication, will affect the interactions of the recipient (either current or future) through their participation in the recipient's computations of interactions toward the recipient's goals.[138] Thus, a communication affects its recipient's actions by means of, and only by means of, its effects on its recipient's situation image, and, therefore, a communication, in order to be effective, must be consonant with both the logic of the apperceptions involved (the rules of apperceptive inference) and with the salience of those apperceptions to the recipient's goals.[139]

A received communication, as part of a recipient's situation, will give rise to apperceptions in that person's situation image only insofar as that communication is taken as redundant with respect to general interactive characteristics of the person's situation. The situation image is a representation of the interactive potential of the situation, and a communication will affect that image only insofar as it is taken as indicative of some of that potential. That is, the apperceptive logics by which a communication affects a situation image are reflective of an imputation of redundancies between such communications and other interactive characteristics of the situation.

A received communication is indicative most proximally of the internal situation image and goal structure of the communicator, and thus the apperceived significance of a communication must be logically mediated (though not necessarily explicitly cognitively mediated) through such indicative force about the communicator. That is, a communication is fundamentally indicative of the communicator's interactive potential. Insofar as that potential is primarily reflective of the communicator's current motivational (goal) state, the significance of the communication, both goal and understood, will tend to be directly about the communicator's interactive potential. Insofar as that potential is primarily reflective of the communicator's situation image, that is, of the interactive potential of the communicator should those parts of the image become interactively salient, the apperceptive significance of the communication to the receiver will tend to be directly about the corresponding interactive potential of the situation, that is, about the situation, not about the communicator.

Thus, whatever the goal significance of a communication, to be successful it must be taken by the recipient as being apperceptively redundant with respect to that significance. There are two primary implications of this necessity. The first is that a communication, whatever its form, be of a form with which the recipient has learned such redundancies in the past; the apperceptive logics must be constructed before they can be used. The most primitively available such already formed apperceptive logics will be those formed within general noncommunicational action (and apperception) systems. That is, the most primitive goal communications will be goal-directed manipulations of the physical environment, or of bodily expressions, for the sake of (the consequences of) their already established natural apperceptions, for example, leaving a branch of a tree half submerged in a pool of quicksand in order to warn passersby. [140] Other grounds for communicational apperception will be those of apperceptive similarities (for example, resemblance or pantomime) or of conventions.

The second implication of this necessity for apperceptive redundancy is that if the computation of a communication interaction is decomposable (or separable) into subcomputations corresponding to subsignificances (for example, submessages in a message, or words in a sentence), then the structure of the subsignificances in constituting the overall significance and, correspondingly, the structure of the subcomputations in generating the overall communication must be consonant with the structure of the natural apperceptive logics that represent the redundancies and generate the significances. That is, decompositions of communications must be consonant with (not necessarily to say isomorphic with) the structure of the natural apperceptive logic of their significances if those significances are to be correctly apperceived.

The underlying natural logic of apperceptive significances will thus impose necessary constraints on the structure and form of communications. Some of these constraints may be reflective of strictly contingent characteristics of the biological realizations of apperceptive representations, [141] but there will also be other constraints derived from the strictly formal nature of apperceptions.

The most fundamental of these formal constraints will be those derived from the nature of apperceptions as contextual interactive characterizations, as interactive characterizations of some potential or actual interactive context. That is, an apperception will modify or update some region of the situation image. The region affected constitutes the context representation, while the index structure produced constitutes the interactive characterization of that context. From one perspective, this simply means that all communicational significances will have this same context-characterization form. From the decompositional perspective, however, it entails that any decomposition of a goal communication must be a decomposition consistent with this full natural apperceptive logic structure and must be a decomposition of all of that formal structure, otherwise the decomposition fails qua decomposition, and the communication, even though perhaps understood in some way or another, fails to be fulfilled.

In particular, a decomposed communication must provide a complete construction of a significance, including the specification of the relevant situation image (index structure) contexts and the interactive characterizations (further index structuring) of those contexts, or else the decomposition simply fails to be a decomposition of a significance and will have only indirect relevance to whatever significance the overall interaction might actually be taken to have. A significance, in other words, defines a minimal unit of communication and thus a necessary constraint on the outer form of a communication decomposition. A communication whose decomposition is complete and consistent with the natural logic of a significance will be called closed (or complete). [142] The units of decomposition of a closed communication will be called the constituents of a communication, while the participations of those communication constituents in the construction of a full apperceptive significance will be called the constituents of the significance.

A closed communication is necessarily complete and consistent with respect to both the context-specifying and the context-characterizing aspects of a significance. In particular, both aspects must be (fully) recoverable from the decomposition of the overall communication. [143] It is conceivable that the decomposition of a significance into constituents by a closed communication would not be computationally consistent with the context specification-characterization distinction. Specification and characterization might proceed simultaneously or in alternating pieces, for example. The natural computation of an apperception, however, is the construction of an index structure (characterization) within (relative to) some other index structure (context). That is, the context specification-characterization distinction, and corresponding computational sequencing, is part of the natural logic of apperceptive significances with which communication decompositions must be consistent. [144] The functional distinction between context specifications and context characterizations can thus be expected to be a universal constraint on constituents of significances and thus on communications. Situation image context specifications will be called subjects (of communication or of significance), and context characterizations will be called predicates (for a related distinction, see Strawson 1974). [145]

Apperceptions are structures of interactive implications. As such, issues of structure and consequence among those implications as they relate to their abstract form and representational content will be similar to those considered within formal logic. Correspondingly, the natural logic constraints on communication decomposition will have affinities to the issues of well-formedness and validity within formal logic (Lakoff 1972a; McCawley 1971, 1972). However, aside from issues of processing constraints, heuristic procedures, and so on,which will affect the actual computations of apperceptions, and thus of significances, relative to formal logic, apperceptions are embedded in a representational framework fundamentally different from most contemporary logic and mathematics. In particular, objects, space, time, subjects, predicates, and others are part of the definitional ground of logic and mathematics, but they are goals of construction and analysis from an interactive perspective. Thus, the affinities and connections from formal logic to communication decomposition will tend to be indirect, complex, and, especially, incomplete. Nevertheless, constraints discovered within formal logic generally will have some sort of counterpart in the natural logic of significances.

The primary constraints on natural logic will be the decomposability structure of the agent-world interactive relationship. This decomposability of interactive computations imposes itself proximally on the servomechanism structure in the system, indirectly on the apperceptive structure, and, through the apperceptive constraints, ultimately on the constituent structure of significances and thus of communications. Thus, communication decompositions will reflect the decomposability of the agent-world relationship into hierarchies of objects with corresponding spaces of potential transformations.

Natural logic is primarily a structuring of interactive implications and, thus, will fundamentally reflect the basic structure of interaction and apperception: a situational context, a procedure, and an outcome situation. The outcome is to be expected, given the context and the procedure, based on the underlying apperceptive logic, but the basis for the apperception may be either perceptual or transformational, descriptive or procedural. Differing foci within this organization lead to differing styles of formalization for natural logic. If the situational object of interaction is taken as fundamental from some metaperspective and used as a foundation for formalizing natural logic, the result will be an intrinsically perceptual (descriptive) logic, in the sense that the most natural lines of decomposition and inference will be descriptive, with procedural issues of both representation and transformation highly subordinated, along the lines of standard formal logic. If the procedure with which an interaction is computed is taken as fundamental, the resulting formalization should be primarily transformational in decomposition and inference, with description subordinate, as, perhaps, with recent developments of the logic of case (Fillmore 1968). From either perspective, the decomposability of the agent-world relationship into objects and their transformation spaces will be manifest.

This decomposability of the field of potential interactions provides the natural ground for the corresponding decomposition of communications and significances into complete constituents. The possibility of decomposition into incomplete constituents, however, of decomposition along non-natural lines, exists only in a special case.

For a strictly prelocutionary system the only apperceptive logics available for communication are the natural apperceptions of the physical or bodily environment. Such "natural" significances are intrinsically closed. Thus, the only decomposability actually available at the level of strict prelocutions is the decomposition of communications into subcommunications with full (sub)significances, each potentially able to stand alone (though perhaps different presuppositions would be operative in isolation).

Decomposition within minimal significances, for example, with respect to subject-predicate structures, is "non-natural" with respect to standard apperceptions: an apperception per se is intrinsically a complete interactive characterization of a specified context, a characterization of the context consisting of the situation within which the original interaction takes place. Thus, constituents of a minimal significance, constituents which do not specify a complete subject-predicate structure, are non-natural in the fundamental sense that they must contribute to an overall significance without themselves being significances. They must be in some sense incomplete components or aspects of significances (Dummett 1973).

Constituents within minimal significances, therefore, exist qua such constituents only as part or a potential part of a full significance. The corresponding constituents within minimal communications similarly exist as such constituents only insofar as they are potential elements of a decomposed communication; their function as constituents is above and beyond whatever natural significance they might have in isolation, for those isolated natural apperceptive significances will be full (complete) significances and not subliminal constituents. But such existence as a potential constituent in the construction of a communication is a highly context-dependent existence, dependent in particular on participating in the context of the construction of a communication.

A constituent within a minimal communication can be understood as such only if the communication is understood qua communication; otherwise, the would-be constituent will not be contextualized in a communication and, therefore, will be taken to have some full natural significance rather than as being a subliminal communication constituent. Since the constituent participation in the construction of a communication is non-natural, the decomposition structure that yields those constituents must similarly be understood as such in order to be understood at all. Thus, subliminally decomposed communications must be understood as such in order to exist as such. Furthermore, they must be understood by each participant to be so understood by all other participants, and so on. Basically, subminimal decomposition by definition cannot be based on natural apperceptions external to the communication situation. Therefore, such decomposition can only be based on apperceptive structurings (logics) affiliated with the communication as such. But there is no ground for it to be so affiliated except insofar as it is taken as such by all participants. Thus, a fulfilled decomposed minimal communication must have a significance symmetrically and mutually available to all participants. That is, its significance must include a situation convention. Decompositions of fulfilled minimal communications, therefore, are possible only if those communications are utterances with meaning.[146]

Thus, although the basic possibilities and constraints on decompositions of general communications arise in the natural logic of the context sensitivities of significances at the level of prelocutions, the interactive possibility of decomposition within minimal communications does not arise until the level of illocutions.[147]

ILLOCUTIONARY SYSTEMS

Illocutionary systems are distinguished by their taking situation conventions as their proximal objects of interaction; just as the differentiating properties of prelocutionary systems derive from the context sensitivities of their interactive objects, the differentiating properties of illocutionary systems derive from the characteristics of situation conventions. One of the dominant characteristics of situation conventions is reflexivity, and this will be the source of many of the illocutionary properties to be discussed. In particular, ontological reflexivity yields the possibility of decompositions within minimal significances, while epistemological reflexivity yields its own type of presupposition together with the special possibility of implicatures. Following these discussions, attention is given to a framework for classifying actions, including, in particular, differing kinds of pre-locutions and illocutions. The final topic is an analysis of the possibility of strict illocutions, of illocutions that are not locutions.

It should be noted first that the pervasiveness of illocutions in human interaction derives neither simply from their communicational usefulness nor solely from the immense power and usefulness that can be constructed, both autonomously and instrumentally, from the secondary properties of illocutions that situation conventions allow and make possible, but, fundamentally, from their simple unavoidable-ness. That is, the almost automatic mutuality and symmetry of images of the situation and the shared coordination problem of at least settling on a framework within which interaction can take place make at least epiphenomenal situation conventions very difficult to avoid in any pre-locutionary dyadic interchange. Strict prelocutionary acts would, thus, tend to be single unidirectional acts from communicator to recipient, since any dyadic interchange would tend to create automatically the symmetries of a situation convention. [148] Strict prelocutions, therefore, are products of either unusual circumstances or unusual efforts to maintain a fundamental asymmetry of definitions of the situation. [149]

However, the tendency toward the implicit construction of at least epiphenomenal situation conventions in dyadic interchanges does not necessarily constitute a corresponding tendency for the construction of the most striking characteristics of illocutions, including those which yield their tremendous power. Such epiphenomenal situation conventions, rather, constitute a framework of potentialities which can be realized, either phylogenetically or ontogenetically, only through the construction of explicitly illocutionary action systems, which reflect and exploit the various interactive properties of situation conventions. [150] Thus, although epiphenomenal illocutions are to be expected at a rather primitive level, the discussion that follows, like the corresponding case for prelocutions, is a discussion of action system potentialities that arise at the level of fully developed illocutions and not a discussion of the properties of any illocutionary system whatsoever. [151]

One of the most important possibilities to emerge at the level of illocutions is that of the decomposition of minimal significances into constituents. The basic problem involved in such decomposition

is that an apperception is always fully an apperception and a significance is simply a special kind of an apperception; so how could any
significance be decomposed into constituents that were not themselves
significances? That is, any interaction that affects anybody's situation image in any way does so by virtue of being apperceived in that
situation image. Therefore, any communication or utterance, or any
piece of a communication or utterance, can only give rise to an apperception and not to a "not-fully-apperceptive" constituent of an
apperception. Decompositions of communications and significances,
and of utterances and meanings, with respect to any constituents that
are not themselves significances or meanings would thus seem to be
impossible.

Nevertheless, such decomposition is possible within illocutionary systems, and this possibility emerges as a fundamental consequence of the ontological reflexivity of situation conventions. Situation conventions are structures of relationships among situation
images, and situation images are representations of the situation.
Furthermore, situation conventions are relations among situation
images in terms of their being representations of the situation and
in terms of their content as such representations. [152] Thus, although
the simple existence of a situation convention is definable in content-
free terms (at least, free of specific content), the definition and the
attribution within a situation image of any particular situation convention are possible only with respect to particular representational contents. That is, any particular situation convention exists only with
respect to particular interactive characterizations of the situation,
and, therefore, a situation convention itself constitutes a representation of the situation, a definition of the situation.

But a situation convention is itself a part of the situation, subject to being interacted with and subject to being the object of apperceptions in the respective situation images. Therefore, although apperceptions can be decomposed into subapperceptions only in accordance with the decomposability structure of the agent-world interactive
relationship, the fact that a representation of the situation (a situation
convention) is part of that situation entails that that decomposability
will include decomposability with respect to the representation of the
situation as well as with respect to the situation represented. A situation convention thus puts a representation of the situation into the
situation to be interacted with as a representation of the situation,
and, thus, corresponding illocutions and apperceptions can be decomposed with respect to the properties of such representations. That is,
a particular interaction must be, and can only be, fully apperceived,
but, if that apperception is about a situation convention (a representation of the situation), then that full apperception about that representation may constitute only a part of a full apperceptive structure within

that representation and thus give rise to a constituent of a minimal representation. Just as apperceptions may be about properties and characteristics of objects in the environmental situation, so may they be about constituent properties and characteristics of representations (of that situation) as long as that situation contains such a representation.

By constituting a representation of the situation within the situation (ontological reflexivity), a situation convention thus creates the potential for decomposition with respect to the characteristics of representations (for example, subject and predicate) as well as with respect to other structures in the interactive relationship. At the level of prelocutions, such decompositions with respect to representational characteristics are not possible because the situation does not contain such representations. Thus, decompositions within minimal significances of communications can occur only as the decomposition of minimal occasion meanings of utterances.

Another consequence of the ontological reflexivity of situation conventions is that occasion meanings can be about not only the wider situation, but, in principle, about any of the levels of situation convention perspective to which ontological reflexivity gives rise. Furthermore, given the possibility of decomposition, they can be about any aspects or characteristics of those levels or of the communication interactions taking place at those levels. Such metacommunication about the timing, structuring, or meaning of other interactions is ubiquitous in human interchange (Bateson 1972; Knapp 1972; Scheflen 1974), and at least in the form of play (that is, this act is playful, not serious), extends into the nonhuman species (Bruner, Jolly, and Sylva 1976; Freedman 1974; Hinde 1970). Like many other structures of action systems, many of these metacommunicational systems are specific and limited explorations of the potentialities of ontological reflexivity at the species level on the part of evolution (for example, the potentiality of playfulness metacommunications, but of no—or few—others), with genuine cognitive productivity with regard to that reflexivity probably not possible until adulthood in human beings, [153] where it is manifested as a general ability to transform, or "key," new meanings out of old behaviors (Goffman 1974). Again, however, such initial species-level limited manifestations provide the ground for the later evolution of the corresponding general capacity and, once evolved, for the development of that capacity in the individual.

Epistemological reflexivity also gives rise to new characteristics at the level of illocutions. The meaning corresponding to an utterance will depend upon the situation convention context within which the utterance is considered, and, since the epistemological reflexivity of situation conventions entails that that context must at some level simply be presumed, the meaning will depend on (be sensitive to) a presumed contextual situation convention. In other words, the pragmatic presuppositions of the meaning of an utterance may include presuppositions about the situation convention context as well as about the wider situation. Situation convention presuppositions of meanings will be called <u>indexical</u> (or <u>utterance</u>) presuppositions. Indexical presuppositions of goal meanings will be called <u>illocutionary presuppositions</u>.

Thus, if I understand your standing up at the head of the table as an act of calling the meeting to order, that meaning will be dependent on, will have as an indexical presupposition, a prior definition of the situation as a meeting about to begin. Similarly, if you in fact are standing in order to call the meeting to order, then that prior situation convention understanding of a meeting about to begin will be an illocutionary presupposition of the goal meaning of your act.

The presumption of situation conventions differs from the tentative presumptiveness of all other situational knowledge, and, correspondingly, indexical presuppositions differ from pragmatic and other action presuppositions in that, in addition to being intrinsically tentative, uncertain, and falsifiable—properties shared with all other presumptions—situation convention presumptions have the potentiality for creating themselves, for making themselves true (though not certain), even if false when initially presumed. In particular, an illocution based on an illocutionary presupposition may well provide the ground for the generation of the situation convention that was presupposed at the start. Conversely, an understood meaning may comprehend indexical presuppositions initially not part of the situation convention.

The construction of an indexical presupposition in the process of understanding a meaning can take place primarily because utterances must in some sense be apperceived <u>as</u> (potential) utterances in order to give rise to meanings at all, and this gives grounds for apperception of the indexical presuppositions underlying those illocutions. That is, if a communication is not taken as (if) an utterance, then whatever significance is drawn from it will not be attributed as mutually and symmetrically available to the participants; thus the significance will include no meaning, and the (understood) pragmatic presuppositions will include no indexical presuppositions. On the other hand, a communication that <u>is</u> taken as an utterance will, by virtue of that fact, be apperceived in terms of its potential appropriateness to the contextual situation convention (it must be appropriate as a potential transformation of that contextual situation convention), and maintenance of that attribution of appropriateness may well result in changes in, or additions to, the attributed situation convention. [154] That is, the indexical presuppositions of a meaning attributed to an utterance may constitute transformations of the initially attributed situation convention. In sum, in order to preserve the presumption that some particular interaction is an utterance, in order to preserve the presumption of appropriateness between that interaction and the contextual situation convention, the presumed situation convention may have to be changed.

Indexical presuppositions that constitute changes in the attributed situation convention will be called utterance implicatures,[155, 156] and the corresponding utterances will be called indirect utterances. As components of goal meanings, utterance implicatures will be called indirect goal meanings, or illocutionary implicatures, and the corresponding illocutions will be called indirect illocutions. [157] That is, an illocution whose goal meaning is dependent on the audience's computing an (utterance) implicature is an indirect illocution: an indirect illocution is an attempt to attain an indirect goal meaning. Thus, if I didn't understand that the situation was one of a meeting about to begin, I might, nevertheless, come to understand that from your standing at the head of the table to call the meeting to order, in which case that understanding would be an utterance implicature and your standing would be an indirect utterance. Correspondingly, if you were aware that I didn't know that a meeting was to be held but intended to convey that to me by standing to call it to order, then your standing would be an indirect illocution with the illocutionary implicature that a meeting was about to begin.

The concept of an indirect illocution raises the general issue of the categorization of illocutions. That is, the definition of an illocution needs elaboration in order to understand what different kinds of illocutions are possible and by what principles they might be considered to be different kinds. As actions, they should be subject to whatever categorization procedure(s) are appropriate for other actions and with whatever specializations of categories might be derived from their own particular nature. The primary principle of categorization of actions is the proximal object of the interaction. Within a particular object category, actions may be classified according to the nature of the interaction transformation, the goal definition, and the relationship of the proximal goal definition to other goals, a relationship which might be called the point of the interaction. Actions can also be categorized according to their effects, and some such categorizations relative to the proximal objects and goals, such as success or failure or inadvertence, can be particularly useful, but a general categorization by effects leads quickly into a consideration of anything and everything that could happen in the world and thus ceases to have any particular relevance to actions per se.

Categorization by goal is usefully subdivided into considerations of those goals or parts of goals which, on the one hand, concern the relationship of the object to the remainder of the situation, the external structuring of the object, and those goals or parts thereof which, on the other hand, concern the relationships internal to the object, that is, the internal structuring of the object. Thus, my desire to move an object concerns its external structuring, while my desire to rearrange its parts concerns its internal structuring. With this differentiation of aspects of goals there emerge five basic principles for the categorization of interactions: (1) the proximal object; (2) the nature of the interaction transformations; (3) the external structuring of the goal; (4) the internal structuring of the goal; and (5) the point. From some perspectives, and for certain purposes, consideration of effect can provide a sixth principle of categorization.

Thus, for example, an interaction with a physical object as the proximal object of interaction might be categorized with respect to the nature of the transformations involved in accordance with which muscle groups were used, tools (if any) involved, and whether or not the goal was attempted (in part) through prelocutionary extensions of agency through another person. Goal issues of external structuring include such possibilities as location, orientation, and velocity, while those of internal structure would similarly involve potentials of both static structure and dynamic process. The basic principle in the categorization of point is the microgenetic salience of the proximal goal to other goals. Thus, the proximal goal can be autonomous or an instrumental means to some other goal. As instrumental, the point can be further subdivided according to whether or not the second goal is a general action strategy, or course of events, or a specific action or event.

Interaction with an agent is through interaction with a situation image. Prelocutions may be strict and thus categorized with respect to the nature of the interaction transformation involved in accordance with the particular natural apperceptions that are being manipulated, or they may be accomplished through subsidiary illocutions. They might also be parasitic on illocutions. Issues of external structuring with regard to a situation image as interactive object are essentially issues of the contextualization of the representational characterizations in that image. Such issues of contextualization will involve either the mode whereby the characterization is embedded in the situation image context, for example, a direct embedding of an interaction potential (a directly available potential) contrasted with the indirect potential for some interaction potential, or they will involve the content of the situation image context, or representational subject, of the characterization per se. Issues of internal structuring with regard to situation images are simply issues of the contents of the characterizations that are in those contexts. Such characterization contents can be categorized according to the properties of what is being represented. As with general actions, the points of prelocutions may be autonomous, instrumental means to other general goals or means to other specific goals. The instrumental categories, however, can be split further according to whether the second goal is with regard to the physical situation or is still about the situation image, that is, whether or not the prelocution is itself instrumental for some general action system goal or whether its instrumentality is with respect to some other prelocutionary goal. Thus, the prelocutionary goal may be autonomous, a means to a general characteristic of situation image content, a means to a specific situation image content, a means to a general action strategy, or a means to a specific action on the part of the recipient.

The subjects of the characterizations in prelocutionary goals (part of the external structuring) provide a fruitful ground for further categorization. The subject of the characterization in the goal of the prelocution may be either specific to the communicator or about the wider situation. Concerning the wider situation, the goal subject could be the recipient or some other person or physical or temporal characteristic (or structure) of the situation. Concerning the communicator, the subject could be about the communicator's situation (or world) image qua image or the communicator's goal status or emotion and feeling status. Such issues of goal subject are fundamental to ecological differences in the interactions necessary to produce the goal significances and thus provide useful further differentiations of prelocutions.

As operations on situation conventions, illocutions cannot be based on strictly natural apperception manipulations. Illocutions must be taken <u>as</u> (potential) illocutions in order to have a meaning (and, thus, in order to be illocutions). Therefore, the transformations induced by illocutions will be based either on iconic resemblance, either of artifacts or of motions, for example, mime (in an extended sense), [158] or on convention (which makes it a locution). Illocutionary transformations may be further classified in accordance with whether or not they are decomposed[159] and, if so, whether or not any of those decompositions are within minimal units.

The external structuring of goal situation conventions, that is, the external structuring of goal meanings, is essentially constituted by the boundaries of the convention involved and by the inclusions of that convention in the broader situation convention. Situation convention boundaries will be primarily with respect to persons involved, which may be specified either by inclusion or by exclusion, and with respect to time. Temporal goal boundaries may be definite, thus requiring typified markers, or indefinite in the sense of having no limitation on temporal scope. It is also possible for situation convention boundaries to be defined with respect to particular actions or action characteristics, so that differing principles of conventional definition can be alternated depending on the particular actions, or modes or manners of action, engaged in. Such a coordination of conventions, of course, requires its own encompassing convention within which the principles of coordination are defined.

Issues of situation convention inclusions are constituted by the identities of the broader conventions within which a particular convention is embedded and by the relevancies of that particular convention to those embedding conventions. Such relevancies may be subdivided into those which are reflexive, that is, the broader convention is in some sense about the embedded convention, for example, a convention of theater within which a convention of marriage ceremony is performed, and those that are not reflexive and therefore are differentiations within the larger convention, for example, a convention for bidding within a definition of the situation as an auction.

The internal structuring of a situation convention goal is, as with prelocutions and significances, simply the contents of the apperceptive characterization involved and, similarly, may be classified in terms of those contents. Such characterizations can be of any aspect of characteristic of a situation convention; therefore, the potential principles of classification are essentially those of the structuring of conventions. Thus, the internal structuring of an illocutionary goal may concern the definition of the situation at any level of reflexivity, including, in particular, the lowest level, where the situation convention constitutes a representation of the extraconventional situation. At any level of reflexivity, such an illocutionary goal might involve the hierarchicalization of topics within the definition of the situation, especially the current most salient topic, the task definition of the situation, or the understanding of the manner and timing of the interactions within the convention. As special cases of the manner of interactions, the institutional type of the convention or the institutional status of the individual participants within such an institutional convention may be specified. Also, the current interactive status of the participants must be continuously both specified and, generally, changing, as with the dynamics of floor apportionment or audience specification. [160]

As with prelocutions, the point of an illocutionary goal may be divided into autonomous points, those as means to other general goals and those as means to other specific goals. Illocutionary goals as means, similarly, may be divided into those which are means to other goals concerning situation convention content and those which are instrumental to some prelocutionary goal. For example, an illocution may be instrumental toward a prelocutionary goal which is in turn instrumental toward some general action system goal, or, at the other extreme, it might be a microgenetically autonomous presentation of, say, the self. [161]

The basic structure for the categorization of illocutions, then, is derived within the principles of categorization of general action systems as they apply to situation conventions as interactive objects. These principles are the nature of the interactive transformation toward the goal, and three characteristics of the goal itself: internal structuring, external structuring, and point. The possibility of instrumental points toward prelocutionary goals, with perhaps still other layers of instrumentality involved, indirectly subjects illocutions to the possibility of classification with respect to the characteristics of superordinate goals as well as to the proximal situation convention goals.

Certain categories of illocutions within this general scheme of classification have such a dominance within the natural ecology of interpersonal interactions that they become marked lexically and syntactically in derivative linguistic systems. Thus, declarative statements are unmarked for any instrumental point for which they might be used, while questions and commands are specifically marked for such points. The advantages of efficiency in so marking such ecologically dominant forms of illocutions should create a gradient of explicitness of such conventional marking, becoming less institutional and fixed as the frequency of particular illocutionary forms decreases. It would seem likely that the dominance of the most dominant such forms would inhere in the interpersonal situation per se, and thus the fact, though not necessarily the form, of their conventional marking would be culturally universal, while illocutionary forms of lesser dominance might show interesting cultural variability in their dominance and corresponding markings. Clearly, the interactive ecology of interpersonal situations and the categorizations it selects within the general range of possible types of illocutions[162] are subjects of analysis in their own right.

The final topic concerning illocutions I wish to consider is the possibility of strict or pure illocutions, that is, of illocutions that are not conventional, not locutions. It might seem at first that any illocution must have the arbitrary conventional meaning of a locution in order to affect the situation convention and, thus, be an illocution at all. In fact, however, all that is required is that the utterance have a significance that is common to the participants involved, and is understandable as being common, and thus a meaning. The point here is that significances can be meanings in this sense without being necessarily either natural (prelocutions) or conventional (locutions). This in between status is attained by interactions that by themselves would not necessarily have any particular significance but that remind through some (perhaps iconic) similarity or other connection of something that does (or would) have such significance. Such an action, then, performed as part of (constitutive of) a situation convention, can affect that situation convention commonly for all participants and thus have meaning, and thus be an illocution, through a version of utterance implicature, except that the action is an utterance only through its implicature(s). Examples are the stylized actions of mime, with stylized intention movements as a special important case, ranging down to interaction rhythms stylized (keyed) from some natural rhythm or motion. [163] It should be noted that locutions (as a class, not necessarily individually) must originate, both phylogenetically and ontogenetically, out of the conventionalization of such pure illocutions.

LOCUTIONARY SYSTEMS

Locutions are illocutions whose effects on situation conventions are themselves conventionalized. That is, a locution is an action that falls under a reciprocally typified class of actions which, as a class, have a reciprocally typified transformational effect on situation conventions; a locution is an institutionalized action type with an (institutionalized) conventional meaning. [164]

A locution thus contains as a part of its indexical presuppositions the supposition of the availability or potentiality of the convention by which the utterance type has conventional meaning, that is, the availability of the convention by which the action is a locution. Such indexical presuppositions of locutions will be called conventional presuppositions.

Conventional presuppositions are constituted by the entire epistemologically reflexive ground upon which the invocation of a convention is based. In the case of locutions, the convention invoked is that of a conventionalized transformation of the prior situation convention. But, in order to invoke such a conventionalized transformation upon the prior contextual situation convention, that transformational convention must be a potential within that prior situation convention. The presuppositions of such potentiality constitute conventional presuppositions, and thus conventional presuppositions may range over any characteristic of situation conventions of relevance to such potentiality: the cultural or ethnic familiarity of the participants, [165] topic definition, task definition, timing, relative participant status, conventionalized ritual, and so on.

Conventional presuppositions, as special cases of indexical presuppositions, can also give rise to implicatures and can thus be used to make indirect utterances. Thus, I might applaud simply in order to express appreciation and approval, but I might also applaud in order to implicate that a current focus of the situation definition is deserving of appreciation and approval or that the current situation contains an element which ought to be the current focus because it is so deserving. [166] Similarly, I might use a formal utterance style in order to implicate that the situation is itself formal or serious, or I might choose particular forms or styles in order to implicate relative status among the participants in the situation. [167]

Implicatures based upon conventional presuppositions will be called conventional implicatures, [168] and the corresponding utterances will thus constitute conventional indirect utterances. Conventional implicatures within indirect goal meanings will be conventional indirect goal meanings or locutionary implicatures, while the corresponding locutions will be indirect locutions. [169]

Thus, in the case of the work crew with a hand gesture requesting help in moving rocks, the assumption that the audience to that gesture is included in the work crew convention by which that gesture has that meaning will be a presupposition (conventional or locutionary) of any instance of that gesture. Correspondingly, I might use that gesture to implicate (a locutionary implicature) that you are a member of the work crew (perhaps you were a visitor, or an apprentice rock mover, before), in which case the gesture is an indirect locution and your understanding of it will constitute the understanding of the conventional implicature of a conventional indirect utterance.

The potentiality of a locutionary transformation within a prior situation convention constitutes a potentiality of whatever posterior situation convention that locution will transform the prior situation into, but what is institutionalized about a locution is its transformational power and not its transformational consequence. [170] Thus, just as an apperception will serve to update a situation image through the induction of an appropriate transformational trajectory, so also will the apperception of a locution serve to update (an attribution of) a situation convention through the induction of the conventionally appropriate transformation. The conventional meaning of a locution, then, is an institutionalized transformation which, when invoked, operates on the prior contextual situation convention to yield (usually) a posterior situation convention whose modifications constitute the locutionary occasion meaning. [171]

Occasion meanings, then, are of the same sort as situation conventions, while conventional meanings are operations on situation conventions. One primary implication of this relationship between conventional meanings and occasion meanings is that locutions are intrinsically context-sensitive with respect to their occasion meanings. A conventional meaning is of the form of a (partial) function operating on situation conventions to yield other situation conventions, [172] and, thus, its value (occasion meaning) is dependent upon its argument (contextual situation convention). Context sensitivity is, therefore, analytically present for all locutions. [173]

A second implication is that conventional meanings, when invoked, yield occasion meanings, which have truth values, but that conventional meanings themselves do not have truth values. [174] Thus, no locutionary type can be directly analyzed with respect to truth value. That is, conventional meanings (of locutionary types) transform representations (situation conventions) but are not themselves representations. Representations have truth values; their transformations do not.

LINGUISTIC SYSTEMS

Situation conventions can be created and transformed with strict illocutions, but the available repertoire is limited to those underlying natural significances which a strict illocution iconically invokes. Correspondingly, the applicability of strict illocutions is limited to those situations in which such invoked natural significances will, with some assurance, implicate the intended meanings. Strict locutions offer large-scale improvements over strict illocutions with respect to the assurance of effect and, in part, the scope of applicability, but the repertoire is at best still limited to a fixed categorization of conventional meanings. Linguistic systems constitute a fundamentally different order of efficacy with respect to interactions with situation conventions: they productively compute utterances for each and every locutionary use. Limitations on situation convention transformations thus cease to be primarily limitations of illocutionary means and become primarily those of the conceptualization of ends. The essential concerns regarding linguistic systems are with those structures and processes whereby such productivity is made possible.

The following discussion will focus primarily upon the means by which, and the sense in which, such productivity is possible, especially with regard to the construction of complete meanings (closed utterances) out of elements that are not complete (closed). The possibility of such decomposition within minimal units has been established in earlier discussions, but the productive realization of that possibility in an action system remains to be examined. The basic results of that examination are, first, that incomplete meanings function as transformations on machine configurations (index structures) which are intermediate to the processes of natural apperceptions. Second, such external transformations of intermediate machine configurations are meaningful and possible only insofar as those configurations participate in special linguistic situation conventions. Third, the representations constituting linguistic situation conventions must have a special conventional representational structuring called semantic structuring. Fourth and last, there must be special procedural schemes, called conventional meaning schemes, to function with respect to such semantic structures. A number of structural and computational properties of conventional meaning schemes are analyzed, and the discussion closes with a brief consideration of the computation of complete utterances within the framework thus developed for incomplete utterances.

This exploration of linguistic productivity will involve a number of shifts of discussion among a number of dichotomizations of analytic perspective, with differing perspectives illuminating and explaining differing aspects of the nature of linguistic productivity. The dominant perspective contrast is that between the supra-individual level of conventions and the intra-individual level of machine structures and processes. Conventional meanings have an existence at both levels, and both are necessary to an understanding of their nature. The second contrast is that between complete conventional meanings and incomplete conventional meanings. In many respects, linguistic productivity is the ability to construct the one out of the other, yet incomplete meanings would seem to be a special case of complete meanings. This contrast, too, requires exploration. The third contrast is that duality already mentioned between the representational and computational aspects of interactive knowing systems, between potential situation images and world images. This contrast shows up in its own special way in linguistic systems. The fourth perspective contrast is that between issues of microgenesis and ontogenesis, which are particularly interdependent with respect to conventional systems. It is hoped that the multiple aspects provided by these multiple perspectives begin to fill in a full outline of, a full apperceptive frame for, linguistic systems.

Definition of Productivity

In considering the productivity of linguistic systems, a preliminary question concerns the definition of productivity given in the initial definition of language. The concept of productivity at that point was defined somewhat arbitrarily in terms of the abstract computational power of the system. The meaningful focus is on the functional productivity of the system: the ability of the linguistic system to transform whatever situation convention happens to exist in accordance with whatever goal meaning happens to be generated. A functionally productive (creative) system, then, would be one that could serve as an all-purpose functional instrument (McCawley 1974), and the definition in terms of computational power is intended as a surrogate for one in terms of functional power.

It would seem desirable, then, to define a productive linguistic system directly in terms of its ability to transform any situation convention in accordance with any goal meaning. Such unlimited transformational power, however, is clearly not possible. It might be possible to define a locutionary system as being linguistic (productive) insofar as it had no limitations of transformational power intrinsic to the system itself, that is, no limitations attributable to the system rather than to the situation, but neither the coherence of such a definition nor its applicability to any candidate system could be demonstrated at the present time.[175] Thus, it remains necessary to approach functional power through some computational surrogate.

The relevance or validity, however, of such a surrogate has yet to be established. Some indication of correspondence between computational and functional power is required.

Compositional Dependence

It is conceivable that a linguistic system would produce an appropriate linguistic act for each required occasion meaning but that the structures of such acts would have no connection to the structures of their meanings. In such a case, the constituents of an utterance would have no systematic relationships to the meaning of that utterance. This is clearly not the case, and its possibility seems highly counterintuitive. Demonstrating such impossibility, however, requires an argument of some subtlety and provides a connection between computational and functional power.

Linguistic systems are productive action systems that compute and construct locutionary utterances. The construction of such linguistic locutionary acts must be recursively compositional; otherwise they would form a finite set (a list) corresponding to minimal and, in particular, nonproductive, computational power. They are constructed so as to transform the contextual situation convention in accordance with a goal meaning, and, therefore, their construction must be in some sort of correspondence with those contextual situation conventions and goal meanings, or else the conventional meanings produced would not be functionally appropriate, and the utterance would fail relative to its goal. [176] Furthermore, that correspondence or dependence must include the representational structures and organizations of context and goal, for such structure is part of what situation conventions and goal meanings are. It follows that that compositional construction will not only be dependent upon the structures of contextual situation conventions and goal meanings, but will be in some structural way correspondent to those structures. That is, linguistic acts will not only be in some sort of a one-to-one (or many-to-one) correspondence to the simple identities of the relevant contexts and goals but also in some sort of an internal recursive compositional (structural) correspondence to them. The reasoning here is that, in order to maintain a simple computational correspondence with such structures while simultaneously avoiding a compositional (structural) correspondence, some basis for computing the compositional structure of a linguistic act would have to be found that would simultaneously preserve the simple correspondence with context and goal and obliterate any structural correspondence, that is, that would simultaneously preserve the structural identities of context and goal while obliterating their structural character. Such a structure-obliterating (structurally orthogonal) recoding of structure would require excessive and unnecessary computational resources and, perhaps, infinite and impossible resources, at all levels of genesis:[177] microgenesis, ontogenesis, and phylogenesis. More fundamentally, it would require some sort of a priori knowledge of such an orthogonal coding: it could not be learned from experience since that orthogonality must be with respect to an infinite and, thus, mostly unexperienced, set of potential structures. Thus, linguistic utterances will be action structures that are compositionally dependent upon and in some way compositionally correspondent to the structures of the prior situation convention and the operative goal meaning.[178]

Increased linguistic computational ability will, therefore, correspond to increased functional range across situation conventions and goal meanings.[179] That is, though the exact nature of the correspondence is far from clear, computational power cannot be irrelevant to functional power, and the validity of a computational surrogate to functional power is demonstrated.

Constituent and Lexical Meanings

The necessity of a computational surrogate for functional power in the definition of language has no bearing on the fundamental questions concerning the nature of the systems by which that basic functional productivity is attained. The necessary compositional dependence of linguistic utterances on situation conventions and goal meanings provides at best a necessary functional characteristic of linguistic systems. The essential question, then, is still how linguistic productivity is computationally possible. Explication of the structures and processes that constitute such systems and manifest such functional characteristics ultimately requires, in fact, a refinement of the representational and interactive foundations of situation conventions.

Being dependent upon prior situation conventions and not just situation images, linguistic acts are capable of being decomposed within minimal units of significance.[180] Their compositional dependence on context and goal structures, therefore, will include a dependence on the sub-apperceptively minimal components of those structures. Thus, a linguistic utterance will, in general, be composed of a structure of sub-acts (sub-action structures), each of which corresponds in some way to a constituent of the decomposed conventional meaning of the utterance and thereby compositionally contributes to the conventional meaning of the utterance but which would not necessarily in itself have a well-defined transformational effect. The contribution to the conventional meaning of an utterance that is made by a sub-action of that utterance will be called the constituent meaning of the action constituent. [181]

Such constituent sub-action structures may themselves have a decompositional structure with respect to meaning, but clearly at some point the meaning decomposition must reach a minimal level of typified action types together with their corresponding typified contributions to the conventional meanings of utterances. [182] Such minimal action typifications will be called lexical items, and their typified structural contributions to conventional meaning will be called lexical meanings. [183] A linguistic utterance will, thus, consist of a structure of lexical items, with a conventional meaning derived from the constituent lexical meanings as they participate in that particular structure. A linguistic system is, correspondingly, an action system that constructs out of available lexical items utterances whose conventional meanings, generated by those particular structurings of lexical meanings, are appropriate to the given situation images (with their situation convention attributions) and goal meanings.

Sentential Presuppositions and Implicatures

In accordance with such a functional structuring of linguistic systems, the presuppositions of a linguistic utterance will exist at two levels: those involved in the potentiality of the linguistic system as a conventional system and those involved in the potentiality of the utterance. Furthermore, the utterance-level presuppositions will be separable into two aspects: the presuppositions of the potentiality of the particular decomposition structure of a linguistic utterance and the presuppositions of the potentialities of the particular lexical items of the utterances. Presuppositions of linguistic acts thus can be differentiated into three categories: systemic, decompositional, and lexical. These presuppositions and their corresponding implicatures will be called systemic, logical, and lexical, respectively, with sentential as the generic term. As aspects of goal meanings, they will be called linguistic, and the corresponding actions will be called indirect. The use of the word "accuse" in order to convey by implica-

TABLE 1

Presuppositions, Implicatures, and Indirect Actions

	Illocutions	Locutions	Linguistic Acts
Presuppositions Of meaning	Indexical presupposition	Conventional presupposition	Systemic, logical, lexical presupposition; Sentential presupposition
Of goal meaning	Illocutionary presupposition	Locutionary presupposition	Linguistic (systemic, logical, lexical) presupposition
Implicatures As effect	Utterance implicature	Conventional implicature	Systemic, logical, lexical implicature; Sentential implicature
As part of goal meaning	Illocutionary implicature; Indirect goal meaning	Locutionary implicature; Conventional indirect goal meaning	Linguistic (systemic, logical, lexical) implicature; Linguistic indirect goal meaning
Actions In terms of effect	Indirect utterance	Conventional indirect utterance	Systemic, logical, lexical indirect utterance; Sentential indirect utterance
In terms of goal meaning	Indirect illocution	Indirect locution	(Systemic, logical, lexical) indirect linguistic act

ture a negative evaluation, for example, would be an indirect linguistic act with a linguistic lexical implicature as part of its goal meaning, while the utterance of "the king of France is bald" to implicate that France does, in fact, have a king would involve a linguistic logical implicature. [184] The rote utterance of a line of a German poem by a captured American soldier in order to convince his Italian captors that he is German (Searle 1969) would constitute an indirect linguistic act with a linguistic systemic implicature.

Complete and Incomplete Conventional Meanings

At a preliminary level of analysis, the productivity of a linguistic system is a consequence of its ability to construct appropriate conventional meanings out of available lexical meanings. The explication of linguistic productivity, therefore, turns to the processes of linguistic construction and the nature of the subminimal meanings upon which such construction is based. The question of the nature of such subminimal (incomplete) component items and meanings will be addressed before that concerning the processes of construction.

The examination of subminimal meanings begins with a review of apperceptions at the level of prelocutions and illocutions and proceeds to an analysis at the level of conventional meanings. Fundamentally, conventional meanings, both complete and incomplete, are constituted by apperceptive procedures, which operate on prior situation convention contexts. It is pointed out that incomplete conventional meaning procedures differ from those for complete conventional meanings in requiring for their execution not only an appropriate prior situation convention context but also an appropriate context of other constituent meanings: incomplete meanings are doubly context-dependent. This explication of the double context dependence of incomplete meanings in this section is the first step in a more thorough analysis of incomplete meaning procedures and their situation image counterparts in following sections.

Significances and meanings are products of apperceptions in the situation image, contextualized within schemes for agents and situation conventions, respectively. Communications and utterances function to construct such structures in the situation image through the outcomes of the apperceptions involved: the apperceptive procedures that have been learned with respect to such inputs serve to transform the situation image along some network possibility within the appropriate schemes. Such apperceptions may be context-dependent in the sense that the apperceptive process will function within differing transformational networks depending on which such networks are indicated in the current situation image: an animal sound in a jungle may have a different significance from the same sound in a zoo. In these respects, significances and meanings differ from other potential structures in a situation image "only" with respect to certain facts about their contextualizing schemes (representing agents and situation conventions respectively). [185]

Conventional meanings, however, are of a different kind. A conventional utterance will, in accordance with its conventional meaning, transform or update (an attribution of) a particular contextual situation convention. That is, the potentiality of a conventional meaning can exist in a situation convention, but the invocation of that meaning operates on the situation convention, rather than "simply" being contextualized (embedded) in it. At the level of the individual, that transformation or updating process is an apperceptive process: the (context-dependent) apperceptions of the utterance yield changes in the situation images constituting the situation convention and thus in the situation convention itself. The conventional meaning of a locution, then, resides not in the situation images of the participants (except as potentiality) but in the structures of (conventionally cross-typified) apperceptive procedures whose computations have been learned as constituting the apperception of the locutionary type. Conventional meanings, in other words, are procedural, are constituted in the world images of the relevant participants.

Correspondingly, the conventional meaning of a linguistic act is constituted by the context-dependent composition of the conventionally typified apperceptive procedures forming the lexical meanings of the lexical constituents. The difference between the complete meanings and the lexical meanings is that, whereas the execution of the apperceptive procedure constituting a complete conventional meaning will complete a situation image (thus convention) transformation if given an appropriate contextual situation convention to operate on, the execution of an apperceptive procedure constituting a lexical meaning requires, in addition to a contextual situation convention, the execution of other contextual lexical apperceptive procedures in order to complete a situation image (convention) transformation. The contextual dependency of a conventional meaning is on situation conventions; the contextual dependency of a lexical meaning includes both situation conventions and other lexical meanings. Just as any apperception yields an index structure representing current agent-situation interactive possibilities (situation image) so also does an apperception of a lexical item, but the interactive possibilities indexed by a solitary lexical apperception are primarily with respect to potential apperceptive interactions with other constituents (all in the context of a current situation convention). Lexical meanings, then, as incomplete meanings, are doubly context-dependent: on the situation convention context and on the constituent context.

Such double context dependence is characteristic of any incomplete meaning, lexical or constituent. Since any level of constituent meaning, including full conventional meanings, can, in principle, be lexicalized (conventionally typified), the primary distinction with regard to the cognitive nature of transformational meanings is between complete and incomplete meanings, whether lexicalized or not. Complete and incomplete meanings must both be psychologically instantiated as apperceptive procedures, [186] and they are differentiated from each other by their respective context dependencies, but their respective differentiations within the general class of apperceptive procedures requires further explication.

Intermediate Products

Apperceptive procedures, including those for conventional meanings, operate on the situation image products of prior apperceptions to yield resultant apperceptive products. For complete conventional meanings, those prior and resultant products must be situation image attributions of situation conventions. For incomplete (constituent) conventional meanings, it is pointed out that those apperceptive products may be in some sense intermediate between an initial (before the utterance begins) situation convention attribution and a final (after the full utterance) situation convention attribution. The focus of analysis thus turns to the nature of such intermediate apperceptive products.

To begin with complete meanings, a conventional meaning procedure is first differentiated as operating on and yielding meanings in the situation image. This differentiates conventional meanings from procedures for general apperceptions or significances but is shared with apperceptions of any utterance; it also shares the possibility of the resultant meanings, being only epiphenomenally represented (qua meanings) in the situation image.

Further, the applicability of conventional meanings is dependent on appropriate contextual situation conventions. That is, their potentiality is itself a matter of convention. This fact uniquely differentiates conventional meanings among procedures.

Such dependence and thus the differentiation, however, are subject to varying degrees of epiphenomenal representation. First of all, the context dependence may not be represented at all: if no bounds of potentiality have been learned, conventional meanings will in effect be reified as natural components of the potentialities of the world, just like causal potentialities. [187] Secondly, even if context dependency of applicability is represented, it may not be represented as a dependency on situation conventions (and clearly cannot be if situation conventions themselves are epiphenomenal) but rather on more mundane cues such as dress or age or physical setting (for example, a church). [188] Whatever the epiphenomenality of representation, however, a procedure constitutes a conventional meaning procedure if and only if it itself constitutes (part of) a convention, if its efficacy as a procedure is dependent upon the mutuality and symmetry of a convention.

A secondary, but quite important, characteristic generally associated with conventional meaning procedures (though not necessarily) is that they are not only procedures for recognition (and apperception) but also procedures for production. In particular, they produce what they recognize. That is, they are cofunctional. Cofunctionality is not specific to conventional meanings[189] (nor even necessary: procedures for comprehension and production of locutions can exist in isolation), but such a dual organization of the task potentialities of a scheme is highly functional when possible. [190]

Incomplete meanings are a species of conventional meanings and thus function like them in the sense of requiring appropriate prior contextual characterizations and executing particular transformations upon them. The difference is that, while a conventional meaning computation begins with a situation image attribution of a situation convention and apperceptively ends with some other such situation convention representation, an incomplete meaning begins with some intermediate product of a situation convention apperception and ends with some other such intermediate product. An apperception of a linguistic structure of incomplete meanings begins with the overall subject frame of the apperceptive transformation (the prior situation convention frame), ends with the overall consequent frame of the apperceptive transformation (the posterior situation convention frame), and, in between, progressively constructs the apperceptive path from the one to the other through its various intermediate steps. The prior situation convention frame is the "intermediate" apperceptive "product" before the apperception has begun, and the final frame is the "intermediate" apperceptive "product" after the apperception is completed. These initial and final "products" are common to all apperceptions. The in-between strict intermediate apperceptive products, however, are different from the prior case of complete meanings (which function with respect to complete apperceptive products) and thus become the focus with regard to the nature of incomplete meanings. Exploring the nature of those intermediate products will involve an explicit shift from the supra-individual realm of conventions (conventional meanings) to the machine theoretic structures that constitute those conventions.

Intermediate Configurations

Intermediate apperceptive products are part of the situation image; thus in some sense they must be structures of indices. This section explores the sense in which such index structures could be said to exist.

If the state of the system is the set of all its contemporary indices, as defined earlier, then any change of state is constituted by some change(s) in indices. If a procedure is of any complexity at all, then its execution will involve sequences of state changes and, thus, of register changes. A procedure execution, therefore, is constituted by register changes; it does not simply result in them. Procedures have been implicitly individuated in accordance with their correspondence to various redundancy characteristics or task aspects of the environment, and the indices considered have been selectively only those which represent the outcomes of those characteristic tests or task attempts to other procedures. [191] It is clear, however, that procedure executions involve intermediate index register operations with no particular representational significance for the external situation: they are simply intermediate steps, perhaps even internal communications, of the execution, and they are generally more dependent on and thus more representative of the structure of the procedure than of the situation being interacted with. Similarly, an intermediate machine configuration in a computer performing an addition is on its way from a pair of numbers to their sum, but that intermediate configuration is not itself a number.

Such intermediate configurations are as present in apperceptive computations as in any other; in particular, they are present in conventional meaning apperceptions. An incomplete meaning apperception, then, yields a transformation of one intermediate machine configuration, one intermediate apperceptive product, into another, beginning with a full situation convention frame and eventually ending with one. Correspondingly, an incomplete meaning is a scheme for transformations of such intermediate configuration. How this is so, or even possible, however, is not yet clear.

Linguistic Situation Conventions

The machine theoretic possibility of intermediate index configurations does not in itself entail the possibility of special apperceptive procedures (incomplete meaning procedures) to operate on them. It is argued that this latter possibility of apperceptive access to intermediate configurations is brought about insofar as the intermediate configurations themselves constitute situation convention attributions.

Apperceptive procedures will be learned and organized in accordance with structures of redundancies in the world and for the sake of generating interactively functional indications about the situation. An intermediate machine configuration as final output from a natural apperceptive procedure would, therefore, constitute a failure of computation, a failure to complete the interaction, a failure of apperception, and, thus, no output at all. An intermediate configuration as communication between procedures, as procedural outputs, cannot generally be functional to the system because there is nothing in the external situation to correspond to the apperceptive process organization that the intermediate configuration reflects. Thus, the transformational relationship of incomplete meanings to intermediate configurations presents a puzzle: how can intermediate configurations be the final configurations of incomplete meaning processes?

A situation convention is about an interactive situation with other agents, in particular, with other apperceivers. If intermediate configurations of apperceptions of the situation convention are themselves validly representative of the mutual and symmetric, that is, situationally conventional, intermediate apperceptive statuses of all the participants in that situation, then those configurations will be functionally valid representations of real interactive potentialities in the external situation: mutual and symmetric potentialities of the completion of the incomplete apperception.

Intermediate configurations of a linguistic apperception will thus themselves be elements of the situation image and situation convention, though their interactive relevance will be largely restricted to the linguistic apperception underway. As such, they do not constitute the products of incomplete apperceptions of the situation convention as much as products of full apperceptions of mutual and symmetric stages of transformation of the situation convention. The situation conventions concerning such stages of linguistic transformation, constituted by mutualities of "intermediate" configurations, will be called linguistic situation conventions. Incomplete meanings, therefore, constitute complete (transformational) conventional meanings with respect to the stages involved in constructing other conventional meanings; that is, they constitute complete conventional meanings with respect to linguistic situation conventions.

Access to Intermediate Configurations
Requires Conventionality

Incomplete meaning procedures are schemes for the transformation of intermediate products of situation convention apperceptions, for the transformation of linguistic situation conventions. The conventionality of the transformational objects of incomplete meanings, of intermediate configurations, is not simply definitional, however, but necessary as well.

Incomplete meaning procedures can be defined only with respect to intermediate configurations. Intermediate configurations can be taken as representative of potential objects of interactions and, thus, as index structures with respect to which interactive procedures may be defined (that is, incomplete meanings) only insofar as they correspond to interactive potentialities of the external situation. If they represented any natural potentialities of the situation they wouldn't be intermediate. Insofar as they represent situation conventions about the status of incomplete apperceptions, however, they can be both externally representative and externally incomplete. Incomplete meanings, therefore, are possible—and only possible—with respect to linguistic situation conventions.

Furthermore, linguistic situation conventions constitute conventionalized intermediate transformational (apperceptive) statuses. Such a conventionalization of transformational status, clearly, can only be defined with respect to a situation convention as object: it would be absurd to consider the conventionalization of the intermediate products of a natural apperception. Therefore, incomplete meanings are possible only with respect to linguistic situation conventions, which are possible only with respect to situation conventions. Ultimately, then, the external access to intermediate configurations through incomplete meanings is possible only because of the conventionality of occasion meanings. That is, the functionality of individual-level procedures operating on intermediate configurations derives (solely) from their participation in the supra-individual level of conventions.

Linguistic situation conventions, as stages of an interactive process, will be sensitive to the situation conventions that constitute the objects of those interactions. They will, therefore, constitute representations, or (partial) descriptions, of the prior and posterior conventions within the temporal trajectory of the conventional situation. That is, they will constitute (partial) representations (linguistic situation conventions) of representations (contextual situation conventions). Thus, as in an earlier discussion, decomposition into incomplete

meanings becomes possible only through the presence in the situation
of a description of the situation (the definition of the situation), thus
yielding the potentiality of the decomposition of a transformation of
that representation with respect to its structure as a representation
(description) rather than with respect to what it represents.

Semantic Structuring

The basic point of this section is that the representational principles of linguistic situation conventions will always involve some
degree of (arbitrary) conventionalization. The basic argument is that
only with respect to such conventionalized structures will conventionalized apperceptive procedures be possible.

Incomplete meanings interact with, and operate on, linguistic
situation conventions, which are constituted by intermediate apperceptive configurations. The fact of the supra-individual conventionality
of those configurations in a situation, however, and thus the potentiality of appropriate incomplete meanings, is not given a priori, nor
is it accidental. Accordingly, the issue of the potentiality of the existence of incomplete meanings, the potentiality of the linguistic situation conventions upon which they depend, must be addressed before
the issue of their execution.

The transformation of a situation image by a particular apperception is logically a transformation of the entire situation image,
but it is clear that no apperceptive procedure functions that massively
and generally: situation images and situation conventions alike are
transformed a piece at a time. This is because any procedure is
learned only with respect to the generalities of repetitious executions.
That is, it gets constructed (learned) only as it demonstrates functionality in repetitions of executions, and only components (types) of
situations and not whole situations in all their variation and detail
have sufficient general recurrence for such learning to take place.
Any procedure, then, including in particular apperceptive procedures,
will be defined with respect to some general type of representational
element or structure and will function within (constitute in part) some
scheme appropriate to that type.

Conventional meaning procedures, like any other apperceptive
procedures, must function with respect to particular types of structures in the situation image, changing them into other types, or alter-
ing the relationships or values of structures within that type. For conventional meanings of strict locutions, these situation image structural types will tend to be fairly simple, and the transformations
correspondingly straightforward.

However simple or complex, the relationships between those

representational structural types and the corresponding conventional meanings must be equivalent among participants in the occurrence of a conventional meaning, otherwise the conventional meaning transformation itself cannot be (conventionally, supra-individually) defined. These functionally equivalent and common representational structurings within the participant situation images of the prior situation must themselves constitute (a part of) the prior situation convention, for, even if their representational content is relatively nonarbitrary (for example, a shape or color of a physical object) and thus not strictly a convention, the common and symmetric attribution of such (functionally equivalent) structurings among the participants in the situation is a conventional solution to an interpersonal coordination problem. Such structurings can also be highly conventional in content as well as form, as with the situation convention representation of "being in an audience after a juncture in performance" (general condition for applause). In any case, the presence of such appropriate conventional structurings of the representations of the situation constitutes at least part of the required conditions on the prior situation convention for the potentiality of the conventional meaning.

Like complete conventional meanings, incomplete meanings will require conventionalized structurings as prior conditions. Also similarly, those conventionalized structurings will have varying degrees of arbitrariness of representational form with respect to underlying nonconventionalized representations:[192] they might match closely in representational form, perhaps even being simply direct conventionalized attributions of underlying nonconventional representations; they might be constituted by explicit learned indices for fully conventionally arbitrary, though conventionally quite functional, structural types of underlying representations;[193] or, in between in representational arbitrariness, to the extent that representations of the nonconventional world are not fully constrained by that world and thus themselves have a degree of arbitrariness of form, that arbitrariness might be further constrained during the original learning of the relevant natural representational schemes by the concurrent learning of the structurings appropriate to the relevant conventional meanings, and thus the "underlying" natural representations might themselves come to have a degree of conventional form.[194] Thus, such conventionalized structuring will range in form from the naturalness of physical objects to the arbitrariness of conventionalized ceremony. Whatever the degree of conventional form, the appropriate conventionalized prior conditions must be present, either as explicit indications or as potential (apperceptive) recognitions. This conventionalized aspect of situation image structures, though not necessarily in all cases structurally distinct from the "underlying" nonconventionalized structures, is, nevertheless, analytically distinguishable at least as an aspect, if not as a structure, and thus forms a distinct level of organizational structuring in the situation image—a distinct class of potentialities (with respect to appropriate linguistic conventional meaning schemes) in the world image. Such representational structuring with respect to conventional meanings will be called semantic structuring. [195]

Specification Only by Functional Differentiation

Linguistic situation conventions, then, must be constituted by appropriate (conventionalized) semantic structures in the participants' situation images in order to be linguistic situation conventions; otherwise, there is no potentiality of conventional meanings. Given the potentiality constituted by such structure, however, the question shifts to how (complete and incomplete) conventional meaning procedures function within it. It is argued that such procedures can proceed only by progressive functional differentiations of contexts within the situation image (subjects) and characterizations within the world image (predicates). The necessity for such an approach by differentiation is indicated, and then the possibility of such an approach is analyzed.

An apperception, whether conventional or not, is basically an update of some specific substructure in the situation image. A conventional meaning apperception, therefore, must have specified an appropriate (semantically structured) subject frame (representational context) in the prior situation convention and must define a transformation (predicate) appropriate to that frame. The issue, then, becomes the manner in which such subjects and predicates can be specified.

The subject frame for a strict locution is often specified simply by being the only candidate in the prior situation convention that is appropriate for the invoked conventional meaning. The predicate transformation can be defined in terms of some procedural type, or, if the schematic potentialities are sufficiently clear and conventionally characterized, the transformation can be specified in terms of its consequence on the frame structure (a definition by specification within a network of potential new frames); that is, in some cases, the update procedure might be specified in terms of a procedural type, while, in other cases, it might be specified in terms of the outcome it is to produce.

A linguistic act must also specify a subject and a predicate and, in fact, becomes complete insofar as it has completed those specifications. The productivity of a linguistic system is constituted precisely in its flexible ability to specify a transformational component of a scheme to be applied to a representational component of the situation convention. The manner of such specifications, however, depends on fundamental characteristics of the situation image.

In particular, the indices that constitute a situation image have no properties by which they might be specified other than their functional relational properties. Thus, internal relational forms (structural types) and external relational positions exhaust the possible characterizations of a situation image component. In particular, neither indices nor index structures have any weight, size, color, shape, or any of the other characteristics whose representations they might constitute. Specification of a subject within a situation convention, therefore, can only occur by way of differentiations in terms of such relational forms and positions.

Similarly, a transformational procedure can be distinguished only with respect to its internal structure or its relational position in the world image scheme. Therefore, correspondingly, specification of a predicate must also be in terms of either structural or relational differentiations.

Structural differentiations of subject or predicate, however, are in fact special cases of relational differentiations. Specifications of schemes by general structural form, whether in the situation image or the world image, can in principle occur directly and independently of any other structures, and, if there is only one instance of that form available, such a form specification may suffice to specify a particular scheme or scheme component in the system. Even in such optimally powerful circumstances, however, specification by form is simply a special case of specification by relational position: even form specifications must be with respect to functional properties, that is, relational properties: a form can only be a functional form. A form specification, then, is simply an invocation of some typified type of functional relation, and a form specification with only one instance is, therefore, a relational differentiation with only one instance.

Fundamentally, differentiation is the only basis for specification because there are no independent one-to-one relationships between (any) lexical items and any particular schemes; there are only context-dependent differentiations of varying degrees of specificity. Even proper nouns as lexical types merely have a strong and explicit differentiating power for particular one-element functional types (and that power, of course, is only with respect to an appropriate contextual situation convention). Specifications of conventional meanings, therefore (both subject and predicate aspects, and whether complete or not), are not by naming a container or matching a label, but by differentiations of functional position. [196] The direct context-independent one-to-one naming relationship is an unattainable limit of generality of decontextualization and of specificity of differentiation. [197] Specifications of subjects and predicates, therefore, must be in terms of functional relational differentiations.

Differentiations of position within structures of functional relationships require differentiations with respect to something. If a scheme is specified in terms of its functional position with respect to other schemes, then those other schemes must somehow be specified as well. But they would seem to be specifiable only in terms of differentiations with respect to still other schemes, and a potential problem of infinite regress looms. Some point must somehow be given from which differentiations can begin.

Within the structure of alternatives comprising the world image, at any particular time there will be one particular structured alternative available as the ground or beginning for differentiations: the situation image. In a natural way, the situation image is the point in the world image with respect to which all schemes are organized; apperceptive, perceptual, or cofunctional. [198] Every scheme is either an element of the situation image or is connected to an element through structures of intermediate schemes. Furthermore, within the situation image, for schemes with conventional meanings, there exists (in relevant situations) the organizing focal point for differentiations constituted by the situation convention attribution. The situation image (convention), however, is itself a complex structure, and there must be some means of differentiation within as well as with respect to it.

Within the structure of current indices comprising the situation image, at any particular time there will be one particular component structure of primary functional salience and, as such, the natural (necessary) origin for any further transformations of functional focus, that is, the necessary origin for the specification-by-differentiation of any alternative functional foci. This is the situation image structure specified by the current goal definitions as the current subjects of goal-directed change. Deriving from this primary component will be structures of relevancies to the achievement of that goal: the relevant task environment. Within that structure of goal subject(s) and direct task relevancies, there is, if necessary, the natural specification of that particular set of indices which are of direct relevance to the transitions of the single current state of the system. Thus, in a strictly logical sense, the current system state always provides the locus of origin for differentiations of other parts of the system, [199] in particular, for the specifications of subjects and predicates.

Conventional Meaning Schemes and Linguistic Systems

The apperception of a locution, thus, will consist of the computations of the differention specifications of the subject and predicate and the transformation of the subject frame in accordance with that predicate, all in accordance with the semantic structurings involved. Such computations will not necessarily be simple nor, correspondingly, will the procedural schemes that engage in them. The concepts of semantic structuring and linguistic situation convention, therefore, provide only one perspective, a strictly representational perspective, on the nature of the construction and understanding of linguistic acts: the computational perspective remains, and its examination promises to illuminate still further aspects of linguistic systems. In particular, the discussion will touch briefly on issues of the computational organization of relevant schemes, their ontogenesis, and the principles of representational structure with respect to which semantic structures and linguistic computations alike are organized. This section, in particular, will focus on the procedural counterparts to complete and incomplete meanings, especially on their interrelationships. In consonance with the duality of structure between situation images and world images, this procedurally focused discussion proves to be similar to the corresponding earlier situation image-focused discussion of conventional meanings. It is suggested that certain organizations of such conventional meaning procedures with the capability of recursive interations are what constitute linguistic systems.

Schemes for operations within and upon semantic structures, that is, schemes for the interactive computation of conventional meanings, will be called conventional meaning schemes. [200] Particular conventional meaning schemes exist only with respect to particular forms of semantic structures: they must be functionally compatible. Conventional meaning schemes and semantic structures constitute, in effect, dual aspects of conventional meanings in the sense that each provides the functionally relevant contexts for the other, and together they constitute the instantiation of conventional meanings in a particular individual and situation. Conventional meaning schemes and semantic structures are, respectively, the world image and the potential-situation-image aspects of conventional meanings.

Conventional meaning schemes for strict locutions, as with semantic structures, will be relatively simple. The functional point of linguistic conventional meaning schemes, however, is to provide flexibility and power in the computation of such interactions with meaning. Correspondingly, transformational networks in linguistic conventional meaning schemes will tend to be well developed. In fact, the intended constructions, differentiations, and transformations of a linguistic act can be of unbounded complexity, far more complexity than any finite set of meaning schemes could accommodate as a simple list of alternatives. In general, therefore, the specifications of subject and predicate in linguistic conventional meanings cannot be in terms of some list of simple one-step differentiations from current functional foci. Instead, those specifications must be made progressively, in terms of iterations of successive basic forms of differentiations. Conventional meaning schemes, correspondingly, must function compositionally in order to compute such progressive (iterative) differentiations. Some meaning schemes, in fact, may specifically require others as prior (preliminary) computational contexts, as well as being able to accommodate compositionally others as contexts. Conversely, some meaning schemes will coordinate others as subroutines. Conventional meaning schemes, thus, will have potentially complex computational relationships.

Furthermore, some subject and predicate specifications will be in terms of structurally subordinate components that in themselves could constitute complete meanings. Insofar as such subordinate complete meanings require linguistic decomposition, meaning schemes must function recursively. That is, meaning schemes may be required to decompose complete meanings into (among other things) subordinate complete meanings (for example, embedded sentences) and then to recursively further decompose those subordinate complete meanings.

Within such a system there must be some procedure for determining the overall compositional sequencing of the various meaning schemes. Such sequencing decision making itself constitutes operations upon and with respect to semantic structures, and such a procedure would, therefore, constitute a meaning scheme. Conventional meaning schemes, then, will constitute a compositionally coordinated hierarchy with a highest coordinating element. Clearly, the whole hierarchy will be a meaning scheme as well. It is likely that, when such a hierarchical meaning scheme ontogenetically acquires the capability of recursive iterations of itself, it probably has thereby acquired sufficient functional power to constitute a (productive) linguistic system. [201]

Characteristics of Linguistic System Ontogenesis

Principles of operation for linguistic system meaning schemes must be in terms of the structures of the contextual situation conventions and, further, in terms of whatever structural particularities have been imposed by the semantic structuring. In the simplest possible locutionary case, the semantic structuring and the situation convention will be epiphenomenal, and the locution will likely be a cross-typified "gesture" that was originally a pure illocution. The apperceptive selections and transformations in such a case will take place primarily in terms of the "underlying" nonconventional (natural) structures of actions and objects, [202] perhaps with some small element of conventional arbitrariness (in either selection, transformation, or both) derived from particularities of the conditions of original habitualization. [203] All more complex locutions and linguistic systems must be constructively differentiated (historically and ontogenetically) out of such primitive locutionary percursors.

The ontogenetic development of such meaning-scheme structures and coordinations, therefore, constitutes the development of a linguistic system. At any particular stage in the ontogeny of a linguistic system, each meaning scheme will provide a compositional structuring of its appropriate semantic structural types, and some meaning schemes will be available to provide further substructuring to the decompositional types produced by other meaning schemes. The linguistic system will develop by further specializing meaning schemes and semantic organizations for the decomposition of semantic structural types yielded by already existing meaning schemes. [204]

The lexical meanings available within a linguistic system at a particular time will depend on the level of development of that system. In particular, lexical meanings cannot be more decompositionally specific than the subcategories produced by the current lowest-level meaning schemes. Correspondingly, as a linguistic system develops, the available lexical meanings should progressively differentiate from essentially complete meanings through the progressive substructurings and sophistications of additional meaning schemes, until the specifications provided by those differentiated incomplete meanings generally conform to the wider linguistic community. [205]

Characteristics of Linguistic System Functional Organization

Given that the entire system could in principle be simulated by a Turing machine with an extremely simple structure (Minsky 1967), it is undoubtedly the case that some small set of primitive principles of differentiation and transformation (and thus of conventional meaning schemes) would logically suffice to compositionally accomplish any given task of conventional meaning specification. The knowing system, however, is not (usually) a designed system; its schemes, including those for linguistic system operations, are constructed through a quasi-evolutionary, or hypothesis-testing, learning process in accordance with the structure of the agent-world interactive field as experienced by that system. Accordingly, meaning schemes are ontogenetically and interactively constructed within a primitive attentional orienting (focusing)[206] response in concurrence with the ontogenetic construction of the corresponding (semantic structuring) schemes with respect to which those linguistic operations take place. Meaning schemes, thus, will operate not in terms of principles of minimal logical sufficiency but in terms of principles of maximal functional efficiency (within the compatibly functionally organized semantic structures).

The development of semantic structural categories will be responsive to constraints of functional efficiency and will thus be organized in accordance with the primary types of situation convention structures with respect to which such semantic categories must be specified. Situation convention representational structures, in turn, will have developed out of and will share many of the structural principles of general situation images. This sharing of structural principles between semantic and natural representations will be for three fundamental reasons: (1) a partial overlap of that which is being represented (the physical situation); (2) a commonality of need for invariances of interactive pattern (objects, whether physical or abstract) with respect to which other relevances can be defined;[207] and (3) the ontogenetic (and phylogenetic) origin of the semantic within the natural. Semantic categories, thus, are going to have ontogenic and logical foundations in the representations of the perceptual and transformational relevancies among the fundamental representational forms of actions, objects, and agents, including such particularizations as relationships of object to property, class to element, part to whole, entity to location, entity to state, and situation to change. [208] These are all "merely" particularizations of the general relationship of interactive relevance, but they are the particularizations with respect to which world images will be organized and, thus, with respect to which semantic categories will be defined. [209]

The development of linguistic systems will be constrained by the underlying structures with respect to which semantic structures are defined, but that constraint is not total. Just as the world constrains—but does not completely fix—the structures of the schemes that represent it, so also do those schemes constrain, but only partially, the semantic and meaning-scheme structures by which their linguistic transformations are decomposed. This incomplete constraint is especially true in the latter case because meaning schemes mediate between complex scheme structures, on the one hand, and linearly sequential decompositions of transformations on them, on the other, and there is a distinct a priori arbitrariness in the correspondence between the two. Thus, the underlying constraints on linguistic meaning schemes, that is, the underlying representational structures upon which they are defined, should be largely of universal (natural) form, while the semantic structurings of those forms by meaning schemes should show variations across linguistic communities within the decompositional possibilities. [210]

Characteristics of Linguistic System Utterances

A linguistic utterance is a locution computed by a productive system. Such computations will involve the construction of complete conventional meanings out of incomplete conventional meanings. The discussion to this point has focused primarily on the individual and supra-individual nature of such incomplete meanings and on some representational and procedural characteristics of their microgenetic and ontogenetic potentiality. Thus, incomplete meanings are constituted by conventional meaning schemes, which are interactive with linguistic situation conventions; the potentiality for linguistic situation conventions requires an underlying semantic structuring; and semantic structuring of representations is developed concurrently and in accordance with conventional meaning schemes, which operate within and upon such structuring. Clearly, meaning schemes (cofunctionally) compute incomplete meanings, and the issue of the nature and potentiality of incomplete meanings has been explored at least skeletally. The focus of the discussion will therefore shift to some of the characteristics of the construction of complete utterances with respect to such incomplete meanings.

The specifications of incomplete meanings produced by meaning schemes in accordance with available semantic structures correspond to constituent meanings in the computation of an overall linguistic act. These constituent meanings will be further subdivided until the incomplete meanings produced correspond to directly institutionalized meanings, to the lexical meanings of lexical items. Such a progressive differentiation within conventional meanings implies that the constituent meaning structuring of a linguistic act will be a partial ordering, with a greatest element (the complete meaning) (Birkhoff 1967) and with no overlapping constituents: in other words, a tree structure.[211]

Each constituent meaning will be of a type or category appropriate to the meaning scheme producing it. Correspondingly, it will be of a type appropriate to the types of other constituents in the linguistic act so as to jointly constitute a valid decomposition of that next higher constituent. The linguistic decomposition of a particular conventional meaning, thus, will proceed in accordance with the potential structures of types (categories) of constituents as constrained by the semantic structures and provided by the meaning schemes, with the constituent categories defined by the decompositional positions they occupy and with the structures of constituent categories defined by the decomposition heuristics computed by the meaning schemes.[212]

Conventional meaning schemes, thus, implicitly define logical structures of categories of subconstituents in accordance with which particular types of constituents may be further decomposed.[213] Such subconstituents must themselves be specified, perhaps through further decomposition, perhaps through direct lexicalization, in order for the particular constituent at issue to be specified in an actual utterance, but there is no logical constraint upon the position(s) within the sequential linguistic act in which those subconstituent specifications occur. That is, logical trees of constituent decompositional specifications in principle might have highly complex relationships to the actual lexical sequences in linguistic acts.

The relationship of a linguistic sequence of acts to an underlying structure of constituent meanings will be a product of the coordinations, or context sensitivities, among the meaning schemes of a linguistic system hierarchy. [214] The principles of such coordination and the corresponding relationships between structures of constituent meanings and sequences of lexical items will be potentially of high complexity. [215]

The constraints on those relationships are simply that they be computable and that the underlying structure of constituent meanings be recoverable, recoverable both in logical principle and in computational practice. [216] There are four kinds of foundations available for such recovery: the lexical meanings and corresponding mutual constituent structuring constraints involved; the lexical sequence; the contextual situation convention; and parallel channel phenomena, such as gestures, stress, and emphasis. [217] Meaning-scheme coordinations must be sufficiently indicated, either lexically or in terms of sequencing organization, for the underlying constituent relationships to be contextually recovered. Such linguistic coordinative indicators will themselves constitute linguistic meaning scheme conventions, and may themselves become specifically lexicalized.

The actual coordinations, and corresponding lexical sequencings, produced in the computation of a linguistic utterance will be constrained by the possible forms of coordination conventionally available and will be selected within those constraints with respect to the structures of the prior situation conventions, relevant goal meanings, and whatever higher-order interactive goals and strategies generate those goal meanings. [218] Sources of general constraint or lexical sequences will, therefore, be differentiated among underlying representational constraints on semantic and meaning-scheme structures, functional computational and goal-directed constraints on meaning-scheme microgenetic processes, and constraints of particular linguistic conventions embodied within specific linguistic systems.

Linguistic Systems as Goal-Directed Systems

A goal meaning for the construction of a linguistic utterance must specify in some internal way a structure in the utterer's current situation convention frame and define some alteration in it. [219] Similarly the linguistic act produced must specify a subject frame and an update for its audience, but it must do so without direct internal access to either. It must do so by apperceptive differentiations and specifications within the overall structure of the relevant situation and world images.

Any apperception involves the two phases of contextualization of interactive focus within current representations and updating within or of that context. A linguistic apperception differs from a natural apperception in the conventional nature of the updating significance and in the iterative compositional structure of the context and update specifications. Essentially, a linguistic act is structured by an iterative subdivision of the overall apperceptive process, in accordance with the available constituent structurings and constituent indications in the linguistic system and as constrained by the situation and world images with respect to which those apperceptive processes must be defined, until each lowest level subconstituent has been directly lexicalized. [220, 221] Conversely, a linguistic act is understood by the apperceptions of its elements and, consequently, the apperception of the entire act with respect to the situation convention.

An issue that has been left open to this point concerns the internal organization of the computational process whereby a complete conventional meaning is subdivided into ultimately lexicalized constituent meanings. There are two basic possibilities. The first is that the linguistic system may in some sense explicitly compute a transformation from prior situation convention to goal situation convention, and this explicit transformation is what constitutes the complete meaning that is subdivided. The subdivision may computationally occur either after the construction of the transformation, that is, as a distinct phase, or simultaneously with that construction: the critical point is that it occur with respect to that explicit transformational construction. This possibility is essentially a direct microgenetic interpretation of the previous discussions of the logical progressive constituent structuring of linguistic complete meanings. The other possibility, however, is that (most of) the constituent subdivision structuring is already implicitly present in the semantic structuring of the relevant situation conventions and goal definitions and that the computation of the linguistic utterance, therefore, will be compositionally subdivided in accordance with, or with respect to, those semantic structures. In this case, the constituent subdivision of the transformation will have been implicit in the ontogenetic construction of the semantic organization of such representations.

Clearly, the second possibility is computationally more efficient: it avoids the intermediate consideration of the transformation to be subdivided and proceeds directly to the computation of the subdivided transformation. It approximates an algorithmic production of linguistic utterances. We might expect, then, at least in simple cases, that the second possibility is the one actually realized. It would have to be only in sufficiently simple cases (though those conceivably might include the majority of utterances), however, because semantic structuring cannot be sufficient, either microgenetically or ontogenetically, to fully specify those subdivisions and ultimate lexicalizations. Microgenetically, semantic structure constraints will generally leave open alternative decompositional possibilities, which, therefore, must be selected among more directly with respect to the transformation desired. Ontogenetically, semantic structures are never complete with respect to the representational transformations desired. Simply put, new semantic units and relationships are always potentially necessary and constructable: with great frequency early in the development of a linguistic system and with lower frequency later on. Such new constructions and the computations of the relevant utterances that require those new constructions must similarly be determined with respect to the transformation desired.

The two alternatives, however, are not mutually exclusive. It is quite plausible that the semantic structure provides a partial constraint on constituent structure within which a desired-transformation based constituent computation completes the construction of the utterances. Such a mixture is most likely the general case, and it raises two further questions (not to be addressed here): First, what is the nature of the boundaries of constraint between the two sources of constraint in such a composite computation? Second, how does such a mixed computation develop ontogenetically?

To summarize, a linguistic system functions as a goal-directed problem-solving servomechanism. The goal meaning constitutes the goal definition, the situation convention constitutes the task context, and the linguistic system per se defines the space of available actions in terms of its available differentiations, coordinations, recursions, and lexicalizations. [222] The problem is to derive a sequence of actions that accomplishes the operative goal in the given context. In these respects, a linguistic system does not differ from any other servomechanism. [223] It does differ, however, in that it operates on the world of conventions, constitutes a convention, and is able to productively define transformations on conventions. [224]

DISCUSSION: PERSPECTIVES ON COMMUNICATIVE ACTION SYSTEMS

Austin on Communication

The terminology and conceptualizations involved in the differentiations of communicative action types are clearly related to Austin's

(1962) analyses of speech acts. I would like to acknowledge those relationships and discuss them a little further.

The model presented has differentiated language within a general framework of action systems. General action systems constituted the initial focus and the pervasive conceptual foundation. Austin (1962) began with a focus on language acts per se and attempted to abstract various kinds of actions from them. Despite the opposite directions of these approaches, the results show striking similarities. There are serious differences between Austin's framework and the one developed here, but I would like to suggest that these derive primarily from Austin's attempting to make his abstractions within the scope of language acts and thus not realizing that his abstracted kinds of actions are of broader scope than language actions rather than contained within language. By thus entering the differentiation hierarchy at the wrong end, that is, within linguistic acts rather than the general class of system interactions, Austin missed the possibility that his action types could be organized as a sequence of progressive differentiations rather than as a package of abstractions (p. 147). I would like to offer the types of actions differentiated in the model above as explications of the forms of language actions which Austin partially identified. That is, I consider the objects of conceptual exploration, though not the definitions of those objects, to be convergent in the two approaches.

Austin defines perlocutions and illocutions in terms of their effects (pp. 115, 120), but locutions in terms of use (p. 94). It is inappropriate to designate an action system (though not necessarily an act) in terms of its effects, for these must be differentiated into the essential and the incidental, and, in one way or another, this differentiation must be in terms of the goals involved. Therefore, all differentiations of action systems in the text are consistently in terms of goals rather than effects (or in terms of other aspects of an action system).

Austin's perlocutionary act is essentially a fulfilled communication. Thus, the shift of definitional focus from consequences to goals is the fundamental difference between Austin's perlocutions and the prelocutions of this text. I had, in fact, wanted to use Austin's term "perlocutions" but was persuaded otherwise by two considerations: the definitional focus on consequences for perlocutions is powerfully embedded in the literature; and such a concern for consequences is itself embedded in the terms for actions that helped stimulate Austin's analysis, for example, persuade and humiliate. I chose "prelocutions" as being appropriately similar to "perlocutions" (a similar name for a similar concept) and also as indicating that prelocutions are logically, phylogenetically, and ontogenetically prior to illocutions and locutions.

Austin's illocutionary acts are defined in terms of the "force" they have on an interpersonal situation. This force is always of the symmetrically available nature characteristic of a convention (which is not necessarily to say symmetrically directed). For example, a warning is available as being a warning to all participants; it enters a warning as a part of the definition of the situation, even though directed at or meant for only one participant. I suggest that the critical distinction Austin attempted between perlocutionary and illocutionary acts (p. 109) is primarily one of perlocutionary acts taking minds as objects and illocutionary acts taking conventions as objects (which is indirectly to take minds as objects in the same sense that to take teacups as objects is also to take their constituent atoms as objects). Austin did not recognize the possibility of such a differentiation even though he recognized that perlocutionary acts can be accomplished without performing illocutionary acts (pp. 117-18) and thus that perlocutionary acts are of a broader scope. That is, Austin's perlocutionary effects on others' minds can be attempted (and accomplished) without necessarily involving illocutions (p. 118). Therefore, perlocutions form a different class of acts from illocutions, not just a different analytic aspect of "saying something" based on a different cut point of consequences (pp. 109-13). Furthermore, Austin seems not to have recognized that the aiming for effects of an illocutionary act (p. 115) makes an illocutionary act also a perlocutionary act, though of a special kind, and thus did not recognize that illocutionary acts could be subsumed under and differentiated within perlocutionary acts (though see his note on p. 108). I have attempted to capture these apparent underlying distinctions and relationships in my definitions of prelocutions and illocutions.

Austin also felt that illocutionary acts must be conventional (pp. 103, 105, 108) (though he seems slightly less certain on p. 118). This seems to me to have been part of Austin's analysis of illocutions rather than his definition of them, and thus I have taken it as a product of a confusion between conventions as objects of illocutions and conventional illocutions (that is, locutions), as well as a lack of appreciation of the possibility of nonconventional illocutions, for example, a warning strictly by pantomime (see p. 118; also Bennett 1973).

A locutionary act, according to Austin, is on the one hand generally equated to uttering a sentence or saying something in the full sense (pp. 94, 108). On the other hand, Austin claims that to perform an illocutionary act is necessarily to perform a locutionary act (p. 113) (thus denying the possibility of nonconventional pantomime) and that some illocutionary acts can be performed without saying anything (pp. 118-19). Austin's primary concept here seems to be that a locutionary act has meaning (p. 120), which I take to be conventional meaning, and therefore explicate locutionary acts in terms

of utterance types with conventional meanings. An example of a locutionary act that would not be a sentence would be clapping at a performance or, better, whistling at a performance, which has differing
conventional meanings in different cultures.

This leaves locutions which are generated by a productive system yet to be named. Austin's concepts of rhetic, phatic, and phonetic
acts are not appropriate here (pp. 92-93) (rhetic acts might seem to
be, but I don't wish to restrict the explications to verbal language),
so I have dubbed such locutions linguistic acts.

The Intuitive Appeal of Transmission Models

As with picture models of knowledge, transmission models of
communication have a strong intuitive appeal, and for good reasons.
Also as with picture models, those reasons derive from the transmission model approach being a simplified asymptotically limiting
case of the transformational model approach.

The asymptotic derivation of the transmission perspective from
the transformational perspective is somewhat simpler in form than
in the corresponding case with picture models because there is only
one characteristic that needs to be derived: the encoding rules. Encoding rules are an asymptotically limiting case of the differentiations
and transformations of linguistic utterances. The nature of the limiting relationship is that encoding rules arise in the limit from a progressive decontextualization of context-dependent differentiations and
transformations.

A linguistic utterance is essentially a complex indicator that
serves to context-dependently differentiate an illocution within the
space of possible or available illocutions. That illocution, in turn,
context-dependently transforms the current situation convention. The
function of reference is similarly accomplished within an illocution
through the context-dependent differentiation of a context-dependently
implicitly defining (differentiating) representation within the space
of possible or available representations. As those context-dependent
differentiations become more and more broadly and less situation-
specifically context-dependent—as those dependencies come to be on
more and more general and universal characteristics of the situation—
those differentiations correspondingly become more and more simple
and direct, more and more like idealized one-to-one naming or encoding relationships.

The idealized naming relationship has in fact been taken as paradigmatic for language (Dummett 1973), with sentences naming (structures of) fact and names naming entities. To the extent that the differentiations of illocutions and representations are in fact fully context-

independent, we have in effect simply encoded and transmitted the
goal meaning of the utterance rather than context-dependently transformed the situation convention toward that goal. To the extent that
the representations in that goal meaning are themselves encoded
knowledge, as in a picture model, then the goal meaning is transparent to the utterance encodings, and the utterance is itself a direct,
structurally isomorphic knowledge encoding. To take such an extremely decontestualized transmission and picture-encoding model
seriously leads to such conclusions as that the meaning of a word is
its referent (the encoding correspondence is direct and does not need
computing) or that the meaning of a sentence is the structure of potential facts that it represents (Wittgenstein 1961) or its representational truth conditions (Davidson 1971). That language involves something like sense and force as well as reference (Dummett 1973) attests to the inadequacy of extreme encoding models.

The most decontextualized languages available are formal languages, in which the differentiations involved depend on no contextual
characteristics narrower than the availability of the language itself.
This is also the closest possible approximation to the idealized encoding-transmission model. Certain proper nouns begin to approach
this level of decontextualized differentiation, such as "The Empire
State Building," but most language is filled with context dependencies,
with indexicality and deicticness.

Not only is it impossible for a language to become less context-dependent than a formal language, it is impossible at a practical level for natural
language to exhibit anything like that degree of decontextualization.
For one reason, possible illocutions and possible representations to
be differentiated are productively open-ended and thus could not in
principle be exhaustively anticipated and, thus, not assigned names.
Further, language must be learned within the framework of highly
context-dependent locutionary systems between infant and caregivers.
Decontextualization is a slow and progressive constructive process
through childhood and, in its extreme versions, into adulthood. At a
strictly pragmatic level of consideration, making use of the contextual
situation convention makes the required differentiations easier, not
harder. The contextual situation convention is a resource which a
relatively decontextualized utterance attempts to make as little use
of as possible. It would be impossibly cumbersome to try to carry
on natural communication with a strictly highly decontextualized language. Relatively decontextualized utterances and languages designed
for them are useful precisely for utterances that are desired to work
across as many and varied situation conventions as possible and thus
must be as independent of those contextual situation conventions as
possible.

The metaphor of the idealized encoding or naming relationship, thus, derives from taking the decontextualization of illocution and representation differentiations to an asymptotically unattainable limit. The metaphor has seemed desirable because one of the functions of language, the expression of thought, has often been taken as the essential function of language, and encoding and transmitting those thoughts seems like an obvious way to do that. The metaphor also has the powerful appeal of apparent simplicity. The metaphor has seemed possible because of a focus on seemingly paradigmatic cases and because apparent exceptions are often taken to mask a deeper level of greater decontextualization—the implicit full (decontextualized) level of greater decontextualization—the implicit full (decontextualized) meaning. In effect, by thus insisting on an ultimately decontextualized level of meaning, the context-dependent transformational conventional meaning of the utterance is being procrusteanly forced to have the same characteristics as, to be a possibly elliptical (and only in that sense context-dependent) encoding of, a picture model conceptualization of the representational goal meaning for the utterance: a fully decontextualized conventional meaning would simply be an encoding of the goal meaning. Such a conflation of conventional meaning with goal meaning (or occasional meaning) is intrinsic to the naming-encoding-transmission perspective. Backing away from the errors of this idealized metaphor and of its consequent conflation has been and continues to be a significant task in the study of language. [225]

That path back would seem to involve recognizing that (1) representational relationships must be interactively computed; (2) therefore representation must be by interactive implicit definition; (3) therefore there are no representational isomorphisms to be encoded; (4) therefore communication must be a form of interaction like everything else the organism does; (5) therefore communication must be fundamentally transformational; and (6) therefore the focus of study should be on the nature of those transformations and their objects and on the sensitivities and dependencies of those transformations on their contexts, objects, and goals.

Bennett

Bennett (1976) carries out an analysis that is in many ways parallel to and at least partly convergent with my own. He, too, begins with considerations of intrapersonal knowledge and action systems, moves to issues of meaning, and then goes on to language. His approach to these issues, however, is rather noticeably different from mine: my concern is to construct models within which the ontologies of these concepts may be explicated; Bennett's concern is to develop strategies and point out kinds of evidence by which hypotheses involving these concepts (usually hypotheses concerning presence or absence) might be empirically tested. Bennett uses a behavioristic approach, while I use a mentalistic approach.

The general parallelism of the structure of the discussions and the partial convergence and complementarity of some of the results, all in spite of the differences in approach, are suggestive and encouraging. The differences, however, are also noteworthy. Primary among these differences and the one I would like to discuss briefly is a difference concerning the basic concept of meaning. That difference, in turn, shows up most strongly with respect to the central focus of the linguistic systems secton: incomplete meanings.

Bennett's conceptualization of meaning is fundamentally Gricean in the sense that it is founded on the concept of an intention and focused on the case of someone meaning something by a particular utterance. Bennett does develop what he calls sub-Gricean conditions for meaning, which are weaker than Grice's though still in the same general framework. In particular, his sub-Gricean conditions eliminate the reflexivities of intentions required in Grice's proposal in such a way as to avoid falling prey to Grice's counterexamples that seemed to force those reflexivities.

Bennett's sub-Gricean conditions for meaning appear to succeed in being a weaker explication of non-natural meaning. In eliminating Grice's explicit reflexivities, they also become extensionally closer to my own explication (I have not previously mentioned the differences between Grice's explication and my own that are produced by Grice's requiring certain explicit reflexive intentions, only those more basic ones resulting from Grice's reliance on intentions at all). Bennett's explication, however, still does not provide an ontology for meaning and does not include inadvertent meaning. He has no concept corresponding to my occasion meaning (nor to situation convention in general), though he does to conventional meaning.

Bennett's lack of ontological concern is most striking with respect to his development of semantic structure in sentences. Basically, he discusses ways in which an observer of an unknown language community might come to make connections between certain sentence features (for example, words) and certain semantic features (for example, word meanings). His lack of ontological concern is evidenced by the fact that, although his discussion makes sense only insofar as the concept of semantic features makes sense, there is no attempt at all to explicate that concept. In contrast, much of the linguistic systems chapter is devoted precisely to an ontological explication of incomplete meaning—of meanings of (incomplete) parts of sentences.

Category Grammars

One formalism for describing decompositional categories and their compositional structuring is a category grammar (Ajdukiewicz 1967; Cresswell 1973; Geach 1972; Lewis 1972; Thomason 1974). Conventional meaning schemes yield not only the compositional categories per se but also the category structurings within which the constituent categories fit and upon which they operate, that is, the abstractions of the λ-operator (for example, Cresswell 1973). Thus, there is an initial compatibility between the formalisms of a category grammar and the constituent structurings generated by linguistic systems. Much of the conceptual foundation associated with a category grammar, however, would have to be altered to apply to linguistic system utterances. It is not clear whether such a program of alterations could succeed or what the result would look like if it did.

The categories in a standard category grammar are defined recursively from two fundamental categories. The two categories are versions of one category of constituents that have truth value, corresponding to declarative sentences, and another category of constituents that have direct reference to entities, corresponding to names.

The categories generated by a linguistic system neither have truth value nor constitute direct references: they are all forms of specification of aspects of a conventional meaning transformation. They are generated not by compositional recursion so much as by progressive differentiation, though the category structure so generated might then be formally definable by recursion. In such a formal definition, the two fundamental categories probably would likely be that of constituents with complete meanings and that of constituents that specified situation convention subject frames.

The meanings of linguistic acts are not definable in terms of truth conditions, as in usual category grammars, but rather in terms of functions on structures of truth conditions (functions on representations of the situation). It is not immediately clear how drastic a change this would force in the formalisms of intensional category grammars such as Montague grammars (Thomason 1974) (though it is clearly a fundamental change in the motivations for such a formalism) since the formal mechanisms for the introduction of such intensional entities as functions on truth conditions are already largely present. Clearly the specifics of the semantic interpretation rules would differ fundamentally, but much of their structure and that of the grammar might be transferrable.

Furthermore, the power of model theoretic possible world semantics (as in Montague grammars) for such problems as modals (for example, Hughes and Cresswell 1968), propositional attitudes (for example, Hintikka 1962, 1969), and tense (for example, Rescher and Urguhart 1971) would be potentially available in a formalization of linguistic systems, with three nonstandard constraints: (1) linguistic meanings must be represented in terms of transformations on possible world truth conditions; (2) possible world truth conditions must be in the form of partial descriptions of sets of possible worlds (as in Hintikka's model sets); and (3) such partial descriptions must be constituted as interactive characterizations.

Presupposition and Implicature

My primary concern with presupposition and implicature has been with explications of their nature and of the processes by which they function and occur. A typology for them is derived almost automatically from the differentiation hierarchy for linguistic action systems.

A more common linguistic focus is not on what presuppositions and implicatures are, or why they exist or how they work, but on how they and their internal relationships with respect to sentences and utterances can be described (for example, Karttunen and Peters 1979, p. 15). One basic problem for this descriptive task is the projection problem: How can the presuppositions and implicatures of an utterance be recovered from those of its constituents?

This is well illustrated by Gazdar's (1979) model. The heart of this model is a formally defined binary map called satisfiable incrementation. Essentially, satisfiable incrementation is a special way of incrementing a set (set union) of propositions with another set of propositions so that all potential inconsistencies arising from the second set are eliminated (p. 131). Gazdar considers the contexts of an utterance, the potential presuppositions of an utterance, and the potential implicatures of an utterance all to be sets of propositions. Thus, the operation of satisfiable incrementation provides a way of incrementing an utterance context with the potential utterance presuppositions and implicatures to yield a consequent utterance context (p. 132). This consequent context, in turn, is Gazdar's primary criterion for determining which of the potential presuppositions and implicatures actually obtain: inappropriate "potential" presuppositions and implicatures have been eliminated by satisfiable incrementation (p. 133). Satisfiable incrementation, then, is essentially Gazdar's answer to the projection problem.

There are at least three general questions to be asked of a model like Gazdar's: Is it adequate to the descriptive task it attempts? What is its relationship to psychological reality? Where do the potential presuppositions and implicatures come from and how do they work? Concerning the first, since satisfiable incrementation is always incrementation and never deletion it is difficult to see how Gazdar's formalism handles cases in which implicatures are explicitly (or inadvertently) used to contradict assumptions in the prior contextual situation convention. Concerning the second, Gazdar acknowledges (p. 124) that his potential presuppositions are purely technical, and it is clear that so also are the potential implicatures and the computations of satisfiable incrementation. This is not necessarily a point against Gazdar's task of formal description, but it does bear on the relationship of such a formal descriptive model to the sort that I have attempted to develop.

The most important question for current purposes is the third, concerning the nature and origins of potential presuppositions and implicatures. (This is, in effect, a special case of the second question.) At this point we find that potential presuppositions are given "mechanically" by a class of only partially specified subfunctions (p. 125) and that potential (scalar quantity) implicatures are defined in terms of "quantitative scales," which are intuitively "given to us" (p. 58). This does not necessarily have any bearing on Gazdar's primary task of formally solving the descriptive projection problem: his proposed solution to that is constructed around satisfiable incrementation, and for that solution he needs potential presuppositions and implicatures, wherever they might come from. It does, however, delimit and illuminate rather clearly the nature of Gazdar's primary task as being strictly descriptive. The nature and functioning of implicatures in his model is essentially Gricean (pp. 37-55), while that of presuppositions, though generally "pragmatic," is not further explicated.

Another problem of interest to linguists has been whether presuppositions are "semantic," "pragmatic," or both. A commonly accepted conclusion is that "semantic" presupposition is eliminable in favor of some combination of "pragmatic" presupposition, entailment, and conversational implicature (Boer and Lycan 1976; Kempson 1975). This issue, however, is posed in terms of an encoding truth condition conceptualization of semantics and a corresponding version of pragmatics; so its relationship to the model developed in this book is not immediately clear. In effect, I contend that presuppositions and implicatures are all functional and differ primarily in terms of the various functional levels that give rise to them. It is not surprising, therefore, that what might at first seem to be a "semantic" (encoding) phenomenon should turn out to be a "pragmatic" (functional) phenomenon.

Linguistic investigations, then, have tended to conclude that presuppositions are "pragmatic" in nature, in general agreement with my model, and to accept that implicatures are generally Gricean in nature. I would like to explore the nature of implicatures a little further.

Grice (1975) describes a set of maxims that together comprise a conversational cooperative principle. These maxims fall into four categories: quantity ("make your contribution as informative as is required"), quality ("do not say what you believe to be false"), relation ("be relevant"), and manner ("avoid ambiguity"). A conversational implicature occurs if a speaker appears to violate one of the maxims, but it is assumed that the speaker is in fact functioning within the conversational cooperative principle: the conversational implicature is the conclusion we must draw in order to retain the assumption of adherence to the maxims. An example would be: A: "Where does John live?" B: "Somewhere in the south of France." From this we conclude that B does not know exactly where John lives; otherwise he would have violated a maxim of quantity (Bach and Harnish 1979, p. 167). That B doesn't know exactly where John lives is the implicature.

Grice's conversational maxims comprise a situation convention of maximal communicative cooperation. Implicatures arise as necessary adjustments to the situation convention in order to maintain that cooperative definition of the situation. Grice (1975) also acknowledges that other implicatures can arise in a similar way from differing principles, such as "be polite," but he feels that the conversational maxims have a central place in the nature of talk. Situation conventions constituted in part by the conversational maxims, or by a politeness assumption, are essentially categories of definition of the situation about the linguistic interactions and interchanges that are to occur within that situation. That is, they constitute conventions about the forms and purposes of linguistic interaction, or language games. A conversational implicature, then, is a change in the situation convention that preserves the conversational cooperative language game; it arises as a conclusion about what must be the case in order for this utterance to be a move in a conversationally cooperative language game.

In effect, I have simply generalized this: an implicature is an adjustment to the situation convention in order to preserve the assumption of availability and appropriateness of an utterance; it arises as a conclusion about what must be the case in order for this utterance to be a move in the current language game. There are two aspects to this generalization. The first concerns its form: implicatures arise out of presumed availability and appropriateness. That is, implicatures arise out of presuppositions, deliberate or not, which become part of the situation convention by virtue of being recognized as presuppositions. This recognition may be a matter of explicit inference on the part of the participants, or some parts of it may have themselves become habitualized (generally as in Bach and Harnish 1979, though their model is based on communicative intentions in a fundamentally Gricean manner and thus differs in many respects from my own). Thus, any presupposition can potentially give rise to an implicature if it is not in fact included in the current situation convention, and, conversely, any potential implicature is such only by virtue of being a potentially discernible presupposition. (Note that word play, including jokes, can be appreciated for the elegance and craft of its implicatures even if the contents of those implicatures are generally known but that this is diminished if the implicatures are already part of the immediate situation convention—like giving away the punch line too soon. Most of the time, such metalinguistic perspectives are not salient, and a presupposition already included in the situation convention will not give rise to any sense of implicature.)

The second aspect of the generalization is that it is immaterial to generalize to language games if there are no other language games. In fact, there are a very large number of them and an unbounded number of potential language games, and many of them are inconsistent with the conversational cooperative principle. Hostile interrogation, for example, is not presumed to proceed in accordance with the cooperative maxims by anyone involved (though the interrogator might well conceal the hostile intent for as long as possible so as to get maximal benefit of the cooperative principles). Many if not most verbal games and contests involve changes in the maxims, such as playing the dozens, or one-upmanship contests. At a cultural level, Keenan (1976), as Gazdar states, "shows that Malagasy speakers make their conversational contributions as uninformative as possible" (Gazdar 1979, p. 54).

There are many language games, then, some including conversational cooperation, some inconsistent with it, and all capable of giving rise to implicatures. Furthermore, language games are hierarchically organized (as are situation conventions in general), perhaps as a lattice, in the sense that moves in some language games can change (transform) other language games, in the sense that the presuppositions and implicatures of some games take priority over others, and in the sense that many games are differentiations of others. Very little is known about these hierarchies or their relationships to each other. There is also a culturally and subculturally conventional default option structuring within the hierarchies in the sense that certain games and constraints on games, for example, conversational cooperation, will tend to be assumed unless otherwise indicated. [226] Finally, contra Wittgenstein, there is a highest inclusive game—illocutions. The fundamental question is, What illocution could this be? which becomes "What has to be the case in order for this to be an illocution in the current situation—with respect to the current situation convention?

Functional Grammar

From the perspective of the model developed in this book, language is a productive, conventional system for the manipulation of situation conventions. The nature of language, then, including grammar (including syntax), must necessarily be subsidiary to and derivative from this fundamental social function. The study of language, therefore, must acknowledge that functional nature and adopt a corresponding functional approach to its subject matter.

In this respect, the model presented here is closely compatible with functional approaches to grammar, which would include the Prague School and others. Silverstein, for example, argues against the "assumption of context-independent propositionality" in linguistics (1975, p. 159) and adopts the perspective that "speech is meaningful social behavior" (1976, p. 11). Halliday (1978) explores the social semiotic aspects of language, and Dik (1978), in a major contribution to a functional grammar, explicitly adopts a functional as opposed to a formal approach to language.

Yet, the full recognition of the transformational nature of language does not quite seem to be present in these functional approaches. A basic sense in which this can hold is that the proposition-encoding aspect of language can still be accepted as a primitive: social functional aspects must be added to and considered along with proposition encoding. In this respect, we again find the basic transmission-transformation hybrid of Wittgenstein and Austin. A second sense is that the special role and special properties of situation conventions as interactive objects can fail to be appreciated. Silverstein, for example, accepts pure reference and corresponding classical propositional analysis as valid for some (strictly symbolic) parts of language (1976, pp. 22-29). Dik (1978), on the other hand, suggests a basically differentiating (nonencoding) functional view of reference (p. 55) (although he also uses an unanalyzed concept of "designation" for both terms and predicates, p. 32), but he has nothing corresponding to a situation convention in his approach. Essentially, Dik (1978) seems to have a socially contextualized mind-as-object version of the transformational conception of language.

Thus, the classical home ground of the encoding-transmission perspective—reference, propositionality, and thought expression, in particular—has not yet been fully integrated into the functional approach. From the transformational perspective, reference and predication are accomplished through contextually differentiating organizations of indicators (or single indicators) of representations in situation conventions. Reference occurs when the differentiated representation is of entities (physical or more abstract) (see Linsky 1971; Strawson 1971, 1974). Reference itself can be differentiated in accordance with, for example:

Whether the implicitly defined extension of the representation is or
    is not a unit set (unique vs. collective);
Whether or not a representation of the indicated entities already exists
    (or can be easily presumed to exist) in the current situation
    convention (definite vs. indefinite);
Whether or not the representation differentiated has characteristics
    or components beyond those by which the differentiating indica-
    tions took place ("referential" vs. attributive) (Donnellan 1971);
    or
Whether or not the differentiating representation is at the first know-
    ing level (concrete vs. abstract).

Certain of these differentiating characteristics of reference may themselves at times and in certain languages be indicated as part of the differentiation of the representation. Predication is a further elaboration within and among representational schemes, which schemes must be organized and differentiated with respect to representations of relatively invariant patterns of interactive potentiality, that is, representations of entities, that is, through reference.

Propositional analysis, in this view, is the analysis of a given convention meaning-occasion meaning pair into a maximally decontextualized conventional meaning that would give the same occasion meaning. Often, propositional analysis is also concerned with a particularly perspicacious formalism for such maximally decontextualized conventional meanings, or with a formalism for the relationship between such decontextualized conventional meanings and the more natural conventional-occasion meanings to which they correspond. At times there is also a concern with, and assumption of, the psychological reality of such a natural-to-decontextualized correspondence.

In general, in the transformational view, the rules of usage in language games are constrained and given potential form at all levels of the hierarchy of communicative action systems. For example, the organization of the situation image with respect to actions and the entities that participate in them gives the basis for the categories of actor (of an intransitive action), agent (of a transitive action), and object (of a transitive action) from which the fundamental accusative-ergative distinction is derived (Dixon 1979), as well as other case categories such as recipient, location, and instrument (Fillmore 1968). The form of the apperceptive process as a transformation of the situation image gives us a basic subject-predicate differentiation, while the core role that invariances play in the organization of the situation image and in the manner of apperceptive differentiations ensures the centrality of reference. The fact that communication is with a context-sensitive agent requires means for regulating that context sensitivity of interaction, such as with respect to turn-taking. Various particularly important points or utilities of utterances can give specially marked forms such as questions and commands, and situation conventions in general allow subliminal decomposition, implicatures, conventional meanings, wider social involvements and constraints (for example, with respect to social class), and the possibility of metalinguistic perspectives and systems. The study of language, including grammar (including syntax), is properly the study of these and related constraints and possibilities and their consequences.

Phenomenological Approaches to Language

The phenomenon and phenomena of language are central to existential phenomenology. The essential participation of language in the fact and the process of living in a meaningful world assure that centrality. The concern of phenomenologists with language has tended to be with the nature of that participation and of language as such a participant. Though that concern is not identical to the one in this book, many of the relevant issues are the same. I will restrict myself to a few comments on a major point of comparison.

The primary concern of phenomenologists has been with language as it exhibits and creates meaning for the individual. The social nature of language is acknowledged, but it is derivative and not a major focus. My major point of comparison—and the source of my major criticism—is that the primacy of the social transformational nature of language is not sufficiently recognized.

The phenomenological concern with language as it exhibits individual meaning has similarities to the transmission concept of language as encoding and expressing thought, and those vestigial similarities contain the core of the error. In effect, phenomenologists recognize that the process of exhibiting (expressing) meaning is not some sort of passive, determinate, one-for-one encoding but rather an activity of exhibiting, showing, and pointing out and, furthermore, that this activity changes the meaning thus exhibited. Both the exhibiting and the changing (thus creating) are major foci.

But this is still a model of a (structure of) meaning(s) being exhibited (and perhaps changed in or by the exhibition). Unlike the encoding model, exhibiting is an activity that may change what is exhibited, but, like the encoding model, the fundamental activity is an exhibiting and not a transformation. In particular, there is no sense of a prior meaning or representational structure undergoing transformation into a consequent structure in the service of a goal, and, most particularly, there is no sense of those transformations being essentially operations on socially constituted realities (situation conventions) or derivative from such operations. From the transformational point of view, change in the meanings "exhibited" is not just an effect of a meaningful act; it is the point of the act. To consider just one underlying meaning structure as being exhibited and perhaps thereby changed is to collapse prior meaning with goal meaning with understood meaning with conventional meaning, not to mention occasion meaning. Such distinctions should help clarify the participation of language in meaning, but they are not available within a perspective on language as essentially "exhibiting."

Thoroughly developing this characterization of phenomenological approaches to language is a task far beyond the limitations of this discussion. So, as in several previous cases, I would like to offer illustrative support rather than thorough argument. Heidegger (1962) develops a thoroughly interactive conception of knowledge. "Being-in-the-world is essentially care," and care is "ahead-of-itself-Being-already-in-(the-world) as Being-alongside (entities encountered within-in-the-world)" (p. 237). To unpack this a bit in terms of my model, care is that aspect of interaction which is always a moving forward with respect to, concernful for, and solicitous of, interactive potentialities and goals. Drive or will, thus, "both turn out to be modifications of care" (p. 254). Furthermore, Heidegger's concern, for example, with the relationship between resistance to Being-out-for-something and the disclosedness of the world (p. 253) and with the sense in which "Reality is referred back to the phenomenon of care" (p. 255, Heidegger's emphasis) is at least partially convergent with the conception of reality as a structured field of interactive potentialities. In any case, the basic interactive flavor of Heidegger's conception of knowledge is clear and much more extensive than can be indicated here.

Heidegger's conception of language, however, is not primarily transformational. Meaning is articulated in discourse and "the way in which discourse gets expressed is language" (p. 204). To be sure, words accrue to meanings in the process of expression, as opposed to the encoding conception of representational meanings attached to words, and communication is never a transportation from the inside of one to the inside of another but rather a sharing of finding oneself in a situation (Mehta 1976, p. 166). But this sharing is through the articulation of meaning, an expression of oneself (Mehta 1976, p. 166), and, even though words accrue to meanings rather than the

other way around, there is no room in this view for the transformational distinction between, for example, conventional meanings and
goal meanings.

Similarly, Merleau-Ponty's conception of knowledge has an
interactive orientation, but his conception of language is not transformational. Regarding knowledge, Merleau-Ponty (1962) presents
a theory of perception in which "the thing and the world exist only
insofar as they are experienced by me or by subjects like me" (p.
333). This is still largely a sensory and intersensory conception (for
example, 1962, p. 327), but it develops a much deeper interactive
interpretation in which the world is a "pregnancy of possibles" (1968,
p. 250) for (and with) the body. Regarding language, Merleau-Ponty
early on has a concern with "the expression of thoughts in speech"
(1962, p. 183) in which "thought and expression are simultaneously
constituted" (p. 193) and the word is "the external existence of sense"
(p. 182). His conception of word meaning as gestural expression
(1962) is similar to, and becomes strongly infused with, Saussurean
conceptions (1973) of language and the linguistic sign, and continues
to develop within that framework (for example, 1968, p. 201).
Throughout this development, Merleau-Ponty views perception,
thought, and language as deeply similar. "The vision itself, the
thought itself, are structured as a language" (1968, p. 126). "The
structures of knowledge [are] those of language" (p. 239). Perception, and thus thought and language, are for Merleau-Ponty active
and differentiating rather than passive and encoding, but there is no
development of interactive transformation, no differentiations among
the various kinds of meanings, and nothing akin to a situation convention.

Another general manifestation of this exhibiting or expressive
view of language in phenomenological writings is a relative neglect
of the decomposition of utterances. Merleau-Ponty focuses almost
entirely on word meanings. Heidegger, though more concerned with
full acts, such as assertions, invitations, and warnings, gives little
attention to their structure. Husserl (for example, 1969) did develop
"the idea of a theory of syntactic forms and even of an a priori grammar for all possible languages" (Spiegelberg 1971, p. 97), but his
concern was with propositional logic, not with speech. Though it is
often inveighed against (for example, Merleau-Ponty 1968, p. 231),
the expressive view still contains vestiges of atomistic encoding, and
the focus of concern within that view with regard to meaning tends
to be on the expressive elements rather than the transformational
structure.

More recently, Kwant (1965) still writes of "the metamorphosis
of meaning into signification" (p. 75), and Lanigan (1977), though
adopting a much more social perspective than usual through a con-

sideration of speech acts and presenting a revealing explication and analysis of them, nevertheless adopts a view of speech acts as involving propositions in much the same sense as for Searle. The view of language as primarily exhibiting or expressing meaning intrinsically contains hidden encoding assumptions.

Gendlin (1962) examines the relationships between experiential meanings and words. A primary concern is with the manner in which the setting out of an experience in words can alter that experience. That is, there is an implicit view of language as exhibiting meaning here, but the focus is on the consequent changes, the alterations, the transformations of meaning rather than on the exhibitions per se. This theory of meaning change has given rise to major contributions to the theory and process of personality change (for example, 1970, 1978). Though deeply concerned with meaning change, however, this work was neither particularly interactive nor social in its view of language.

Nevertheless, there is a basic recognition in the analyses of these change processes that experiencing is not like a verbal scheme, and this poses a special problem: In what way is such nonverbally organized experience available to us, and how can we talk about it without imposing a verbal scheme? (Gendlin 1973, p. 282). The solution is to stop trying to statically, dissect meaning and language, to stop looking at the meaning-language relationship from inside one end or the other, in terms of how they fit one another, and instead to take a ninety-degree turn outside to look at the relationship between them from the side, as a whole (1973, p. 290). This relationship between meaning and language is one of transformational interaction.

In accordance with a commitment to a radical and consistent interactionism, Gendlin (1980) proposes a strictly process-based conception of the situation of the organism in its environment. One of his central concepts is a form of functional implication among processes that seems highly convergent with the implications among indices and index structures in the situation image, though developed in entirely different form. Furthermore, this functional "implying" is the foundation for symbolism, as is apperception for communication in my model. I do not know if this model develops a full social transformational view of language (the work is still in preparation), and Gendlin's concerns are not necessarily the same as mine, but the convergences at the points of contact are striking.

It is clear that in some sense language can and does express or exhibit meanings and changes that meaning in doing so. My claim is that this exhibiting and changing function is derivative from the social transformation character of language and cannot be properly understood without taking that character into account. Nevertheless, the personal-meaning exhibiting and changing function of language has not been a focus in this book, and that "taking into account" remains to be done.

Language Acquisition

In the last ten years, the study of language acquisition has acquired a major focus on the emergence of language out of pre-speech social and "pragmatic" precursors (for example, Bruner 1975a; Lock 1978; Bullowa 1979; Ochs and Schieffelin 1979; Lewis and Rosenblum 1977). In this focus it has come to have an orientation closely similar to and compatible with the transformational perspective. The theoretical orientations of this work still generally hold to a transmission-transformation hybrid in which propositions are encoded and everything else is social interaction (for example, Dore 1975), but basically the roots of language in interactive, socially meaningful communication have become clear and undeniable. An explicit consideration and exploration of the transformational perspective should help organize and integrate this work.

The acquisition of language is the acquisition of rule-governed language games. Language games are conventional (rule-governed) procedures and systems of procedure for carrying on socially meaningful interactions. (Language acquisition is at times taken to be, or at least to involve, speech act acquisition, for example, Bruner 1975b; Dore 1975. But a speech act is essentially a move in a language game, and it is the procedures that constitute the language games that are acquired, not the speech acts per se.) Language games do not form a simple unstructured set. They share aspects and components, procedures and rules, and this sharing induces relationships of intersection and inclusion among them. Language games, then, form an intersecting, hierarchically organized lattice structure. A number of questions about language and language acquisition turn out to be questions about the general organization of this lattice and of the child's developmental acquisition of it. Other issues are concerned with special language games and subgames within the lattice.

The general course of language acquisition is one of the differentiation, elaboration, and integration of the conventional procedures that constitute the language games. The lattice imposes constraints on this course of acquisition in that some games will be components of, and therefore precursors of, other games. Some precursor relationships will be among differing types of games, such as turn-taking as a precursor to many other games, while others will be between various stages of elaboration of a single type of game, such as increasing sophistication of requesting. Language games per se are characterized by the systems of procedures that constitute them. Types of language games are usefully characterized by the purpose or point for which those games are engaged in.

It is possible, of course, that points in the lattice that do not have any precursor relationship with each other will nevertheless generally be acquired in some particular temporal relationship. This could be a relationship of rough simultaneity if, for example, they each share an immediate precursor (this is a general point about precursor structures, for example, Bates et al. 1977), or it could be an ordering imposed by relative complexity rather than by a precursor relationship (see Brown 1973). Such relative complexities could be intrinsic to the types of games involved or could be dependent on the cultural specifics of the actual games available.

Differing paths and patterns of acquisition through the lattice will be possible (for example, Nelson 1973). The determinants of such differences in paths are generally unknown. Acquisition path differences will also occur between lattice points: there are in general many alternative interactive foundations for the acquisition of particular skills or procedures, for example, variations in adult-infant games. There may be modal paths between such points (or through the lattice in general), but there will also be individual variation based on predilection, situational accident, and the necessities of acquisition detours around such intrinsic obstacles as deafness or blindness.

Regardless of its course, the process of acquisition through the language game lattice will be a quasi-evolutionary progression of variation and selection, hypothesis generation and testing, concerning the procedures that constitute those games. One focus of investigatory concern is on the foundations for the hypotheses: genetic, temporal continuity, imitation, expansion, and so on. Results in this direction, however, seem to have been minimal. Far more productive have been explorations of the careful organization of selection pressures by the environment, especially by caregivers, that guide that quasi-evolution along useful paths. Such organizations of selection pressures generally take the form of a rich interpretive framework of adult assistance within which the infant can accomplish goals with minimal means and thus can experience and respond to selection pressures toward increasing sophistication of those means. This may also involve a metacognitive coordination of the infant's or child's activities—coordinative assistance, as well as physical and interpretive assistance—with corresponding developmental selection pressures (Wertsch 1977). This interpretive framework, implicit pedagogy, or "scaffolding" (Bruner 1975b) within the infant's social environment seems likely to ultimately explain much of the acquisition course selected by the quasi-evolutionary acquisition process: the law of effect is the ultimate external constraint on the construction of control structures (Dennett 1978). There are undoubtedly some genetic supports to this process, but they are also undoubtedly as little as possible (Bates 1979).

Such pedagogical frameworks can generate their own pedagogical language games, such as special intonation patterns for highlighting or emphasis (Gleason and Weintraub 1978) or other forms of hints (Bruner 1974a). Of course, most or all early language games are ultimately pedagogical in function, for example, early turn-taking games, but the focus here is not just on games that serve pedagogical functions but on interactive procedures that have general pedagogical points. These will most likely be implicitly developed between infant and caregiver as auxiliary aids in the course of the development of other language games and then carried over to the development of new games.

One interesting question concerning language game pedagogy is, How much does the implicit pedagogy of the adult-infant language game progression depend on implicit knowledge of the language game lattice on the part of the adult, and how much does it depend on backing up to appropriate levels and points in the lattice in response to feedback from the infant or child? Such implicit knowledge clearly will exist to some extent: we all learned language through the same general lattice, and, besides, its most basic organization is logically necessary and, thus, culturally and individually universal. Furthermore, "backing up" in response to feedback requires some sense of which way to back. On the other hand, such implicit knowledge is not necessarily functionally readily available, and the fine tuning, if not the general organization, of the adult's pedagogical skills certainly will require and make use of feedback. The development of the adult as language game pedagogue should be an interesting topic in itself. (Similar questions can be asked about the nature and consequences of child-infant and child-child pedagogy.)

Adult sensitivity, skill, and creativity in, above all, creating and maintaining interactive contact, providing an interpretive scaffolding for the infant's or child's means toward his goals, and imposing a gradual sophisticating selection pressure on those means and goals while maintaining that interactive contact and interpretive framework will be an important determinant of language acquisition. These processes must continuously accommodate such things as the infant's temperament and basic adaptive abilities, and particulars of the immediate situation. Some degree of such pedagogy is necessary for any child to acquire language. A great deal may be necessary for children with obstacles to normal acquisition.

The skill of the adult as language game pedagogue, however, may have interesting effects not only on the rate and paths of acquisition through the lattice but also, to some extent, on the structure of the (modal) lattice itself. Some of the precursor relationships in the lattice are logically necessary. Others, however, will be relative to the organization of selection pressures, the adult-implicit pedagogy, in the developmental environment. A sufficiently rich interpretive scaffolding, in other words, may allow a "normal" precursor to be skipped over or a new path to be taken. This ability to create new acquisition paths will be especially important for children for whom standard paths are blocked.

In general, procedures will develop with respect to one function (selection pressure) and then be available to serve a different function and, correspondingly, to serve as a beginning for quasi-evolutionary development with respect to the selection pressures of that new function. The new selection pressures may yield a progressive elaboration of the initial procedure, with that initial procedure always as a component, or it may yield a progressive transformation of that initial procedure such that it is eventually left behind or turned into something else. In either case, if that procedure is the only possible start for the quasi-evolution of the next point in the lattice, then it will be a logically necessary precursor and not subject to being skipped. The realm for creativity in sequencing (by adult or child or infant) is with respect to developments with more than one possible beginning. The normal precursor component procedure may be developed later rather than serve as the foundation, or the procedure that is normally left behind may be constructed later or not at all. In either case, a non-standard course of acquisition may be selected or made possible by the special organization of the quasi-evolutionary process of acquisition.

Whatever the specifics of the process of acquisition, the course of acquisition is constrained by the general organization of the language game lattice. The lattice, in turn, reflects basic characteristics of language as a conventional system for the manipulation of situation conventions. Those basic characteristics of language, then, serve as boundary conditions on and frameworks of possibility for the development of language. Understanding the nature of those constraints and possibilities is one of the major goals of the study of language acquisition.

The central constraint on the course of language acquisition is the sequence of differentiations of prelocutions, illocutions, and linguistic locutions out of general goal-directed systems. Within each of these levels, the sequencing of epiphenomenal presence, implicit instrumental presence, explicit instrumental presence, coordinated instrumental presence, and, finally, autonomous point should hold. That is, there should be a progression from epiphenomenal presence of one level in the procedures of a preceding level to an adaptation of certain procedures at the earlier level to critical characteristics of the next level, to a specialization of appropriate subprocedures to next-level characteristics, to a differentiation of those subprocedures into full coordinating and coordinatable servomechanism subroutines, and, finally, to the development of the potential for autonomous (noninstrumental) goal settings at the level of those new subroutines (see Nelson and Nelson 1978, for a related sequence). (As procedures become increasingly explicit and autonomous in their functional organization, they will also become increasingly explicit and autonomous in the inducement of hypotheses relevant to their further development.)

Thus, early infant distress crying is an epiphenomenal demand communication. As it becomes sensitive to the context sensitivity of the agents (adults) to whom it is addressed, it becomes condensed and stylized, more of a signal: it moves from Bruner's (1975a) demand mode to request mode. It has acquired an implicit instrumental presence. Later, procedures for request can be expected to become not just functionally adapted but functionally specialized. In acquiring such an explicit instrumental presence, the request procedure(s) become capable of separate execution and, thus, of participation in broader language games. The shift here is from Bruner's (1975a) request mode to his exchange mode. With the acquisition of full subroutine capabilities, coordinative instrumental request procedures become capable of subordination to and coordination with other task definitions: they become capable of Bruner's (1975a) reciprocal mode. Finally, requests as autonomous point would involve, for example, the ongoing relating of adult to child (for example, an attachment reassurance, Marvin 1977), and are probably at least implicitly illocutionary. This development from epiphenomenal to autonomous prelocutionary requests illustrates the development of language games within a particular type of game. Note the incorporation of other procedures during the course of the progression, such as turn-taking.

Such progressions from epiphenomenal to autonomous presence should be identifiable for most basic types of language games at each of the levels of prelocutions, illocutions, and linguistic locutions. The exceptions will be language games that are not possible in even an epiphenomenal sense at the level of general goal-directed systems. Metalinguistic games are likely examples. This structure of progressions of differentiation and elaboration, with their mutual integrations and coordinations, will constitute one of the basic organizational frameworks of the language game lattice and, thus, of language development.

The progression from epiphenomenal to autonomous is basically a constraint imposed by the nature of the quasi-evolutionary development of hierarchically modularized goal-directed systems (for example, Connolly and Bruner 1974). Other basic aspects of language impose their own constraints and possibilities. The organization and execution of hierarchical plans (for example, Sacerdoti 1977) must provide a constraining framework for syntax (for example, Greenfield 1978). The necessary organization of the situation image around actions with respect to entities (invariances) and the corresponding impositions on the organization of semantic structuring will yield the basic case relationships (Fillmore 1968; Brown 1973; Bruner 1975b). This same relationship of the situation image to semantic structuring will yield a two-part organization and development of (1) lexical category meanings on (2) a basis of functional and implicit definitional situation image representations (Nelson 1978, 1979). The levels of knowing impose such constraints as that explicit representations, and thus goal definitions, with respect to situation conventions are not possible until at least second-level knowing (around age four, Bickhard 1978, in press). It is also possible that explicit syntactic categories cannot be constructed on top of underlying semantic structurings until second-level knowing (Bowerman 1973). And so on. Constraints and possibilities arise from all aspects and at all levels of language as an action system, and ultimately all will need to be taken into account.

The study of language acquisition is concerned not only with such general properties of organization of the language game lattice and their consequences for the process and course of acquisition but also with particular types of games within the lattice. Reference and predication, propositionality, and subminimal decomposition, for example, are among the most important language game procedures in the lattice. Their acquisition and functioning, correspondingly, are among the most important concerns in the study of language and language acquisition. These functions, of course, form the paradigmatic home ground for the classical encoding-transmission approaches to language.

The boundary conditions for reference include the entity-anchored organization of the situation image, the functional subject-predicate organization of apperception, and the manner in which apperception must select subjects and predicates by differentiation. Differentiation must be with respect to available and salient characteristics; the entity anchoring of situation images ensures the saliency (and availability) of entity representations as principles of differentation; therefore, differentiations of entity representations will be a powerful and general means for differentiating general subjects and predicates of communications and utterances. Referencing, then, will be an essential aspect of both decomposition and propositionality. Eventually, of course, referencing also will make use of both decomposition and propositionality, such as in referentially descriptive phrases (decomposition) or quasi-referential assertions like "There's a book" (decomposition and propositionality).

Referencing is essentially the differentiation of entity representations within the situation images constituting the current social definition of the situation. Procedures for referencing begin with epiphenomenal indications of relevant objects (for example, from gaze or fussing and crying) and progress through such accomplishments as simple adapted procedures for joint focus of gaze and more explicit procedures, such as for pointing. Pointing, which undergoes its own development of explicitness and relative autonomy, functions initially and primarily as subsidiary to joint focus of gaze. A commonality among early referencing games is a calling attention to something in some way or another. Such insertion into the definition of the situation (quasi-reference in Lyons 1977; Atkinson 1979) is a language game type with many levels of sophistication and with functions in many other language games. Reference proper occurs when it is interleaved with subminimal decomposition.

The development of increasingly sophisticated referencing procedures is not only a development of increasingly flexible functioning with respect to other language games (subroutine modularization) but also a development of increasingly powerful functioning: a servomechanism organization requires that the available procedures be sufficiently powerful to attain the (referencing) goals from a variety of servomechanism "users" and in a variety of circumstances. An important aspect of such referencing power is the capability of differentiating representations at further and further remove from the immediate interactive foci in constituent situation images. That is, an important aspect of referencing power is the relative decontextualization of referencing procedures. Decontextualization, in turn, requires increasingly conventionalized procedures, since there are progressively fewer direct contextual indicators available. Conventionalized decontextualization also requires decomposition since the varieties and complexities of (referencing) tasks encountered will demand a productive task organization rather than an infinitude of single-step solutions. Finally, the development of decompositional conventionalized decontextualization will occur in conjunction with the development of corresponding semantic structuring and the progressive incorporation of the institutionalized resources of language proper. It should be noted that the chain of entailments from increasing modularization, to increasing functional power, to decompositional conventionalized decontextualization is not necessarily specific to referencing procedures.

Functional predication is the universal of communication. It is the transformation, the further elaboration, alteration, or interconnection, of representations. Predication is initially and most broadly a transformation of the entire situation convention (or a contextually clear aspect of it). As functional predication procedures increase in scope, autonomy, and power (for example, pre-speech "requests, offers, noticings, greetings, rejections, and denials" [Ochs 1979, p. 13]), they undergo their own decompositional conventionalized decontextualization and, it might be added, referentialization (as an aspect of decomposition). They also require increasingly explicit specification of the functional subject in the constituent situation images to which the transformation is to be applied.

Early communication tends to be strictly instrumental, in the service of body and physical situation goals. As the relevant procedures acquire explicit and coordination servomechanism differentiation, however, it becomes possible for the infant to engage in such communicative procedures with respect to relatively autonomous goals with no immediate physical instrumental point. Such a relatively autonomous insertion of representations into the definition of the situation, an insertion as distinct act, constitutes a comment or assertion. With this step, the development of propositional language games begins. (This will require at least some degree of specialization and differentiation of the illocutionary level.) Decontextualization with respect to propositionality will proceed from instrumental communications, to expressions such as of (dis)pleasure or surprise, to the paradigmatic insertions (assertions) of representations of completely external facts. (Both representations and communications are intrinsically interactively functional in nature. Propositionality arises as the decontextualization of that functionality.) Like its necessary adjunct, reference, propositionality can serve decomposition for other language games.

Productive decomposition is the defining characteristic of linguistic systems. It is involved in almost all adult language games and speech acts. Its boundary conditions include the functional subject-predicate organization of communications, the agent-action-object organization of situation images which constrains and provides available means of differentiation and specification, and the representational properties of situation conventions which allow subminimal decomposition with respect to that agent-action-object organization. Decontextualization of decomposition necessarily will involve the recursive interleaving of reference, predication, and propositionality. As such, it will also find boundary conditions in the nature of hierarchically modularized systems. Decomposition, in fact, will be formed and constrained at all levels and by all essential aspects of the differentiation hierarchy: a linguistic system is a productive locutionary, illocutionary, and prelocutionary hierarchically organized goal-directed servomechanism system. Decomposition is with respect to the basic properties of interactive representations and apperceptions, made possible by the properties of situation conventions, and in terms of the institutionalized power of semantic structuring and conventional meaning schemes. Its power and centrality to language games derive directly from the fact that decomposition is what provides productivity in the manipulation of situation conventions and constituent situation images, no matter what autonomous or instrumental point may be involved. Understanding the development and functioning of decomposition, then, is central to (though not exhaustive of) understanding the language game lattice.

Finally, the study of language acquisition must be concerned not only with the internal principles of organization and developmental consequences of the language game lattice and with particular games in that lattice but also with an external perspective on the relationship of language acquisition to other forms of development. All forms of development, for example, are constrained by the levels of knowing (Bickhard 1978, in press), and share a hierarchical goal-directed control structure organization. More fundamentally, just as the physical self is differentiated with respect to objects in the context of space (the potentialities of their motions), so is the social self differentiated with respect to situation conventions in the context of language games (the potentialities of their transformations) (Denzin 1977). Language development and social development are inextricably related: they are gradually and progressively differentiated out of the same interactive communicational foundation.

7
CONCLUDING COMMENTS:
FOUNDATIONS AND EXTENSIONS

The primary emphasis of this exploration has been on various aspects of communication and language, but the pivotal concept has been that of situation convention. Virtually all of the major aspects of communication depend on the conceptualization of situation conventions for their very definition, either in the sense of taking conventions as interactive objects or as constituting conventions themselves. Conversely, given the concept of situation convention, the exploration of communication and language yields a largely subsidiary structure of concepts and models.

The concept of situation convention itself is definable only from an intensional perspective and thus requires some degree of conceptual foundation concerning intensional structures and processes. The situation and world images together with the apperceptive and transformational structures and processes within them provide that foundation.

The model is open to further development of its foundations at all three of its levels: cognition, convention, and communication. At the level of cognition, the nature of goal definitions and goal computations, in particular, has not been fully specified with respect to situation and world images. [227] Correspondingly, the task definition aspect of situation conventions has been underdeveloped and, consequently, so also has the goal computation of linguistic utterances. The subject of particular cognitive structures in situation and world images (for example, objects) also has been touched upon only lightly and clearly is requisite to further understanding of the representational organization of situation conventions and linguistic situation conventions.

The convergence of situation images that constitutes a situation convention itself constitutes a foundational topic subject to further development at the level of conventions. The definition of situation convention provided would seem to be valid, but it is primarily in terms of functional relations among situation images, and ultimately it must be in terms of structural relationships. A first step toward greater structural specificity would be an explication in terms of the convergence of task definitions and representations of task environments, but to be more than suggestive such an explication requires a more structural understanding of general goal definitions at the level of cognition.

Similarly, the basic conceptualizations of incomplete meanings, linguistic situation conventions, semantic structuring, and conventional meaning schemes at the level of linguistic communication are subject to further structural specification and description and have similar requisites. [228]

Extensions of the model, however, do not necessarily require waiting for further development of its foundations. Thus, the conceptualizations of situation and world image provide an interesting perspective within which to view many general issues of cognition, while situation conventions constitute a similar perspective for sociology and anthropology.

The most obvious extensions, however, are in the area that has been given the most attention: communication. For example, fragmentary comments have been made concerning discourse and text-level analyses, some constraints and frameworks of analysis have been proposed for the ontogeny and phylogeny of communication, and the language function of meaning and thought expression has been sketched. All of these topics require much more attention. Similarly, perspectives on such conceptual issues as the natures of meaning, implicatures, and conventional meaning and their relationships to propositions, truth, and reality have been suggested but only partially developed, and, clearly, the analysis of linguistic systems is skeletal.

Essentially, the communication model claims to be a general framework within which the studies of communicational and linguistic interactions can be integrated and a foundation upon which they can be based. The destruction of those claims will, it is hoped, be a fruitful process.

More fundamentally, it is hoped that the overall model will make a contribution to the development of models of intensional and interactive processes in psychology, to the explication of social structures and processes, and to the understanding of the function of communication and language as the bridge between the two. The emergence of the social from the psychological is the true intersection of cognition, convention, and communication.

APPENDIX A:
Abstract Machine Theory

Mathematics consists, in part, of a structure of formal languages. The importance of such formal languages for my current purposes is that they create the possibility of a precision of thought concerning their respective subject matters that is difficult or impossible to obtain within ordinary languages. The most familiar mathematical language is that whose primary topic of discussion is quantity: arithmetic. Other mathematical languages have been motivated by topics and considerations ranging from the severely practical to the purely aesthetic. Abstract machine theory is a subcollection of formal languages within mathematics whose topics are in one way or another about processes: machine processes, computations, system processes, and so on. It turns out that there is a unity to the general concept of process in the sense that each of these languages, motivated by its own particular conception of process, can be applied and related to all of the other conceptualizations of process: they are all, in some sense, about the same thing. Abstract machine theory thus offers the possibility of a language or languages that could improve the precision of thought about psychological processes, and this is the way that theory is used in the text.

The primary area of machine theory to be used is that called automata theory. An automaton is a simple but powerful abstraction of the processes internal to a machine and of a machine's interactions with the environment. The basic simplification involved is to represent all of the complexities of all of the conditions of all of the components of a machine by a single unitary index of such a total machine condition. Such an index, representing the total internal condition, is called a <u>state</u> of the machine. A state, then, will capture all of the current information of relevance to the internal processes of the machine and, thus, to the machine's interactions with the environment. Note that, in constituting such a total index, a state loses all information about the internal structure of the machine: it's all summarized in a single index.

Accordingly, an automaton is conceived of as a collection of possible states together with three process rules: the rule for the automaton's internal responses to inputs, the rule for strictly internal processes, and the rule for outputs from the automaton. By a mathematical trick of considering "no input" to the automaton as, nevertheless, an input—a blank input—these rules can be reduced to

185

two: all internal machine processes are in response to some input, blank or explicit, and, thus, there is no need for a separate rule for strictly internal processes. It is to be noted that any internal machine process will be constituted by a change in the total condition, and, thus, will constitute a change of state. The internal processes of an automaton, therefore, are simply transitions among possible states.

In accordance with these considerations, the concept of an automaton is formalized as an ordered quintuple:

$\langle S, \Sigma, \Sigma', T, \Phi \rangle$ where

S = the set of possible states of the automaton

Σ = the set of possible inputs (including a blank input)

Σ'= the set of possible outputs (often $\Sigma = \Sigma'$)

T: $S \times \Sigma \rightarrow S$ is a function that maps ordered pairs of states with inputs into states. It thus describes the automaton's internal processes and responses to inputs. That is, each "next state" of the automaton is determined jointly by the current state and the current input, and T captures that dependency.

Φ: $S \rightarrow \Sigma'$ is a function from states to outputs that describes the output rules of the automaton. Each output is considered to be determined by the current state. (With such an output rule, an automaton is called a Moore machine.)

A useful way to conceptualize an automaton is in terms of what is known as a state transition diagram. If the states are considered as labeled points, then the transitions among them can be represented as arrows from one point (state) to another. The arrows can be labeled in accordance with the inputs that produce those particular transitions from those particular states. Note that more than one arrow can leave a single state, corresponding to the differing transition effects of differing inputs, and more than one arrow can enter a single state, corresponding simply to differing transitions into that state. With such point and arrow labeling, such a diagram of points and arrows will represent the process structure of the automaton. It will even represent the output rules insofar as the state labels determine the outputs.

It is to be noted that it is possible for there to be state-input combinations for which no transition is defined. This would correspond to the function T being undefined for some of the ordered pairs in its range, that is, to T being a partial function. An automaton receiving an input for which no transition is defined from its current state is considered simply to stop functioning.

It is of significance to consider an automaton's responses to strings of inputs. Clearly, an automaton will be traversing some path through its state transition diagram, possibly involving loops and cycles, in accordance with the inputs in the string. It should also be clear that the path traversed will depend not only on the string of inputs received but also on the initial state that the automaton was in when it started to receive the string: differing initial states might take the automaton into completely different parts of the diagram for the same input string. Finally, given the same initial state for all input strings, it is clear that different strings will, in general, traverse different diagram paths and, in particular, that differing strings with the same initial state may well leave the automaton in differing end states when the string is complete. Given the same initial state, then, the end state that an automaton is left in by a completed input string will contain information about that string. In particular, it will classify that string together with other strings that yield the same end state and differently from other strings that yield different end states.

In accordance with these considerations, a further definition is made in automata theory of something called a recognizer. A recognizer is an automaton together with two specifications: (1) a specification of a particular state $s_0 \in S$ as a fixed initial or start state, and (2) a specification of a particular subset of the states $F \subset S$ as the designated final states. An automaton with such a specified start state and set of final states is called a recognizer since it is said to recognize any input string that leaves the automaton in one of its final states when begun in its initial state. The recognizing capabilities of automata are a major focus of mathematical interest.

The potential outputs of a recognizer usually are not taken into account. If, however, they are explicitly considered as having potential influence on the inputs through their impact on the environment, then the "recognition" of an input string by an interactive recognizer can become equivalent to the testing for and detection of particular environmental circumstances or even the construction or creation of such environmental circumstances through those outputs. Once a recognizer is allowed to affect its environment then the attainment of an internal final state through the recognition (inducement) of an appropriate input string can become equivalent to many environmental tasks.

One of the primary deficiencies of automata theory is that the states of an automaton have no internal structure. They represent perhaps highly complex internal structure in an actual machine, but that structure is lost in the formalism of the simple index that represents a state in the theory. One approach to recapturing some of that structure in the formalism is to add to the definition of an automaton a further specification of how the states are constituted. One approach to such a further specification of the states is to consider the machine to be constituted by a collection {Ri} of memory or index registers, each containing at any particular time some one index out of some set of possible indices. In a computer, such registers are various memory and processing locations, and the indices are patterns of binary bits. The total conditions, or states, of the machine will thus be constituted by the configurations of indices in the registers. Correspondingly, state transitions will be constituted by changes in the configurations of register contents. That is, a change of an index will be a state transition, and vice versa. Since neither the registers themselves nor their index contents are specified as to their physical nature, this "register machine" approach allows a rather general treatment of internal structure and memory. Such an approach is of considerable importance in the text.

From the full register-machine perspective, any difference in the contents of any of the index registers constitutes a difference in the state of the total system. It can be useful, however, to consider state transition structures formed by proper subsets of the index registers. Such subsets of registers can correspond to functional (and perhaps physical) subcomponents of the total system, thus allowing analyses of the relationships among those components. It is also possible to differentiate a subset of registers as a strictly passive memory, not participating directly in the state constitution of any active functional components.

An important consequence of a functional component perspective is that it requires the simultaneous differentiation of passive memory registers. To consider the state transition structure of the functional component to be determined by only a subset of the existing registers requires that the effects of the excluded registers on the processes of the component be modeled in some way not yet defined; some additions are needed to account for registers not in a component to influence processes within the component. The difficulty is that, from a full register-machine perspective, an index in a register influences the system's processes by participating in the constitution of the system's state, but if the register under consideration is not within the functional component under consideration then its contents do not participate in the constitution of any of that component's states. Its influences, if any, on that component's processes, therefore, cannot be modeled within the framework thus far defined.

The necessary additions to complete such a component perspective model are to allow for the processes within a component to construct and to reference indices in registers outside of that component: specifically, to allow the state transitions within the component to set or construct indices in particular registers outside the component (as well as to determine the output from the system) and to allow state transitions within the component to depend on the current contents of particular external index registers as well as on the current state of the component and the current input. The relevant index rent state of the component and the current input. The relevant index registers not a direct part of the component thus become in effect a secondary environment for that component, receiving outputs (index constructions) and emitting inputs (index references) to the processes in the component. Such an index register secondary environment, however, differs critically from the overall system environment in that it is completely passive, strictly a store or memory, with no internal processes (transitions) of its own: the only way an index can be present in a register in order to be referenced by the system is to have been constructed in that register by that system at some prior time.

In principle, any arbitrary subset of registers could be taken as defining a subcomponent state transition structure, with all additional process dependencies modeled in terms of various rules of index construction and reference among the memory registers. However, such a random choice of registers constituting a functional component could require a completely unmanageable and uninterpretable set of rules of referencing and construction transactions with the external registers in order to model accurately the total system processes. An extreme example of this would be to take a single register as defining the only active component: the transaction rules between that component and the remaining registers would have, in effect, to capture the entire state transition diagram of the total system.

Clearly, it is meaningful to consider a subset of registers as defining a functional subcomponent only insofar as the transactions between that component and other registers are themselves functionally meaningful. A particularly important example of such a meaningful subcomponent is that of a state transition component that is embedded in the rest of the system in such a way that, whenever it is entered from elsewhere in the system, an index which is determined by the place (the state) from which the component is being entered is set in a particular register. This register, in turn, has the property that when the processing of the subcomponent is completed and it exits in a transition to some part of the system outside that subcomponent, the state to which it exits is dependent on the index that was set in that special register at the time of entrance. Thus, control can be passed to such a component so that the point of return from that component is determined by that part of the system that passed control to it in the first place. In particular, such a system subcomponent can be invoked, or called upon, to perform some particular (interactive) task, and then control returned to the point at which it was invoked. Thus, it can serve as a generalized performer of its task, available to be called upon from anywhere in the rest of the system. Such a functional subcomponent is called a subroutine. Registers that are set prior to calling a subroutine and referenced within it may be used to pass arguments or instructions to that subroutine, while registers that are set within a subroutine and referenced after its return can be used to pass results back to the calling component.

In general, indices are constructed by one system component in order to pass information to or at least make information available to other components. This information may be about strictly internal issues of functional organization, such as in the case of a subroutine, or it may in some sense be about the environment, such as an index representing the outcome of some interaction. In either case, however, the only effect an index can have is on the flow of control at various index referencing points in the system. That is, an index can have an effect only when it is referenced, and then only on (via) the transition flow. It is to be noted that the concept of passing on environmental information via an index is subsidiary to that of passing on information concerning functional organization: passing environmental information among components requires the conceptual differentiation of functional components, and the concept of a component requires functional organization information in the indices.

A special and important case of the transfer of information from one component to another is that in which an instruction to a component is taken as a goal definition by that component, that is, is taken as a representation of some environmental state of affairs which the component (if executed) then undertakes to bring about. A subroutine that accepts goal definitions as part of its instructions is called a servomechanism. The case of goal definitions is special in that it paradigmatically involves difficult issues of the nature of representation and of the relationships of representation and interactions. [228] The case of goal definitions is important, among other reasons, in that servomechanisms seem to be a ubiquitous feature of the organization of psychological systems. [229]

APPENDIX B:
Convention

David K. Lewis' (1969) explication of convention is essential to the development of the concepts in the text. In this appendix I wish to introduce the main outlines of that explication.

Preliminary to the concept of a convention is that of a coordination problem, and preliminary to that of a coordination problem is that of a game, as in game theory. The concept of a game, therefore, is where the discussion begins.

The basic idea of a game is that it involves two or more players facing a situation with the following characteristics: (1) each player has a number of alternative strategies of action among which he must choose say, strategies A and B for each of two players; (2) the outcome of the game is dependent on the joint pattern of choices among all the players, that is, in this case, on the patterns AA, AB, BA, and BB; (3) each player knows what all the possible strategy choices are for all the players, AA, AB, and so on; and (4) each player knows what all the preferences are for all the players among all the possible outcomes, thus, AA may be worth $100 to the first player and $25 to the second, while AB may cost player one $50 and be worth $75 to the second, and so on. Thus, basically, each player knows everything about the situation except what the actual choices in the game are going to be. One object of game theory is to find optimal decision rules for choosing strategies for different kinds of games.

One major category of games is that called zero-sum games. Zero-sum games are those in which whatever one player receives in a game must come out of or away from some other players. That is, there is a fixed amount of utility to go around, and the outcome of the game determines how it is to be distributed. The name "zero-sum game" comes from the pure case in which one player's gain is directly from other players' losses, that is, in which the net, or summed, utility for each outcome is zero. Zero-sum games, thus, are games of direct competition. They have been among the most studied of all.

A special kind of game has been defined by Schelling (1963) and called a coordination problem. The general idea of a coordination problem is that each of the players involved has a subset of possible strategy or action choices within which an exhaustive set of jointly preferred joint choice outcomes occur but among which they have no particular preferences as long as all the other players make the ap-

191

propriate choices so that one of those preferred outcomes does, in fact, occur. That is, there are two or more possible outcomes of the game which are equally preferred by each player in the game, and each of which is preferred over any other possible outcome in the game, also by each of the players. Thus, if I am to meet you for lunch, there may be a number of restaurants among which neither of us has any particular preferences just as long as we both end up at the same one. The problem, then, is not one of competition, as with zero-sum games, but, rather, coordination. All players have a common goal (reaching one of the preferred joint outcomes); the problem is to reach it. The communications and decisions involved in solving a coordination problem can be fully as complex as those for competitive problems, or even more so, especially when constraints occur on the cost or possibilities of communication. The general category of games involving coordination problems, however, has been much less studied.

Lewis' basic explication of a convention is, simply put, that a convention is a solution to a coordination problem. The simplicity of the explication masks a number of subtleties of distinction implicit in it. One of these distinctions is that between the existence of the coordination problem solution, or convention, and the origin of that solution. In particular, Lewis showed that the obvious origin of a convention in discussionaand agreement among the participants is not at all necessary. Thus, as one example of one alternative, you and I might accidently meet at a particular restaurant some Tuesday for lunch. We both enjoy the contact, and, for whatever reasons, end up there again the following Tuesday. After rather few Tuesdays of this, a convention of meeting on Tuesdays for lunch at that restaurant will be established between us without any mention of it ever needing to be made. This is very important to Lewis, for he wishes to analyze language as a convention, and the conventions of language, at least the first ones, can hardly have been established by discussion and agreement.

Other subtleties examined by Lewis involve, for example, the structures of beliefs that are necessary to constitute a convention, a solution to a coordination problem. One of the interesting results here is that there can be no doubts on any level about the existence of the convention or else the convention doesn't exist (rather, perhaps, some sort of decision problem with risk). Thus, if I doubt that you are going to show up at the restaurant for lunch, then meeting for lunch will not constitute a convention. Similarly, if I think that you doubt that I will show up for lunch, then, similarly, the convention does not exist. It turns out that, if at any level you think that I think that you think, and so forth, that there is uncertainty, then, while we might still end up meeting for lunch, we will not be doing so by convention.

An important aspect of Lewis' explication for my purposes is that, in detail, Lewis defines conventions in terms of patterns of regularities of behavior that constitute conventions. That is, for Lewis, conventions are things that are instantiated over time—that involve regularities over time. Certainly this is true of all of the easily conceived of conventions, such as driving on the right, luncheon conventions, fiscal, legal, protocol, politeness conventions, and so forth, and is likewise true of Lewis' examples. A major attempt I make in the text is to define a class of conventions that does not necessarily involve such temporal continuities.

APPENDIX C:
Speech Acts

Language has traditionally been conceptualized as an ideal structure of objects (for example, words, sentences, and propositions) and their relationships (for example, grammar). J. L. Austin (1968) made one of the most important breaks with this tradition when he began to consider the act of communicating linguistically, the speech act, as distinct from some object (the sentence) purportedly involved in that act. One point of origin for Austin was to explore the implications of the obvious fact that not all sentences are declarative. In particular, he noted that an utterance of a sentence may not necessarily assert a proposition. It might, for example, ask a question or give a command. Austin was interested, among other things, in what other kinds of acts besides assertions, questions, and commands might be performed by such speech acts and under what conditions such acts could be said to be successfully performed. Austin was, thus, an initiator of the study of language as a system of communicative acts rather than as an idealized abstract structure.

Three general categories that Austin pointed out of kinds of acts performed in linguistic communication are those of what he called locutionary acts, illocutionary acts, and perlocutionary acts. The intuitions behind these categories are, roughly, that a locutionary act is an act of performing a well-formed, or grammatical, utterance, such as saying, "The cat is on the mat"; an illocutionary act is an act of thereby producing in an audience some sort of understanding, such as to assert, question, warn, or command; and a perlocutionary act is one of producing some sort of effect by virtue of that understanding, such as to convince, alarm, or persuade. These concepts have been refined and developed by many people since Austin introduced them (for example, Searle 1969, 1971, 1975).

Both the general speech act approach to language and Austin's particular categories have strongly influenced the nature of the discussion in the text.

APPENDIX D:
Meaning

For the purpose of indicating one of the important motivations for my own explication and for contrast, I would like to sketch an outline of Grice's (1967) approach to the explication of meaning.

Grice makes an initial distinction between what he calls natural meaning and, correspondingly, non-natural meaning. The basic intuition of this distinction is that an event or thing has a natural meaning insofar as it serves to indicate something about the rest of the world through some natural connection, as in, "Those spots mean measles," while something has a non-natural meaning insofar as its indications about the rest of the world are given to it by the people who take it to have that meaning, as in, "Those three rings on the bell (of the bus) mean that the bus is full." Among other differentiating characteristics that Grice notes about these categories of meaning is that if "X meant P" is true in the natural sense, then that entails that P is true, while if "X meant P" is true in the non-natural sense, then the entailment does not follow. Grice then proposes the task of explicating non-natural meaning.

Grice first narrows his considerations from "X means P" in some timeless sense to "X means P" on some particular occasion, with X thus taken as some sort of event. Furthermore, Grice adopts the perspective that X is some action or, in a broad sense, utterance, of an individual, and the focus of explication shifts to an individual's meaning something by some action (or utterance). Grice suggests that the understanding of other cases of non-natural meaning can be developed out of an understanding of this basic case: that of an individual meaning something by a particular utterance.

Grice bases his program of explication on the intentions of the utterer. He begins with the tentative possibility that "X meant something" is true if X is intended by its utterer to induce a belief in some audience. Counterexamples can be presented, however, that meet this definition but do not seem to involve non-natural meaning, for example, leaving someone's handkerchief at the scene of a crime in order to implicate the owner. After a sequence of such counterexamples and revisions in the light of those counterexamples, Grice (1967) tentatively proposes that "A meant something by X" is equivalent to "A intended the utterance of X to produce some effect in an audience by means of the recognition of this intention." The critical development here is that the effect must not only be intended but that that intention must be recognized by the audience and that that recognition must be what yields the effects.

Grice's proposal served as the foundation for a great deal of further work on the explication of non-natural meaning, yielding progressive constructions of further counterexamples and still further revisions of the proposed explications. For my purposes, one of the most important consequences of this process was the construction within the explication of an infinite regress of intentions on the part of the utterer. Schiffer (1972), in particular, showed that the speaker must not only (first level) intend an effect by X, and (second level) intend that effect through recognition of that first intention but must also (third level) intend recognition of that second-level intention and also (fourth level) intend recognition of that third-level intention, and so on indefinitely. More specifically, Schiffer showed that if this regress is assumed to stop at any finite level then a counterexample is, in principle, constructable.

The apparent necessity of this regress of intentions was troublesome since it is clear that no one has ever thought through more than a few of its levels and that in ordinary circumstances we think through none of them at all in producing utterances with non-natural meanings. It has since become apparent, however, that the regress is avoidable by substituting for it a negative constraint on intentions that eliminates the whole class of potential counterexamples. In particular, the counterexamples have in common the property that, at some level, the speaker intends that some lower-level intention not be recognized by the audience. By excluding such intents to deceive from the explication (Grice 1969), the counterexamples are avoided without having to invoke an infinite regress of positive intentions.

The explication of "A meant something by X" in terms of A's intentions can, thus, proceed much more clearly. The question of whether A's intentions form the most satisfactory foundation for the explication of non-natural meaning in general, however, has been difficult to address, primarily because of a paucity of viable alternative foundations with which to compare it. The primary alternative has been meaning as conventional (Lewis 1969; Schiffer 1972), but it has seemed clear that not all meaningful utterances are conventionally meaningful utterances, thus the approach in terms of intentions has tended to dominate. In the text, an approach to the explication of meaning is suggested that would seem to be a third alternative.

NOTES

1. This and much of the following commentary on linguistics is derived from Yngve (1974, 1975, 1976).

2. A number of issues of the philosophy of science implicit in this paragraph are not pursued here, particularly those concerning the relationship between empirical content and falsifiability (Popper 1959), but the general point as made is, I think, sufficient for current purposes.

3. The entailments follow from the incompatibility if we assume that there are no additional fundamental kinds of knowledge or communication models: the incompatibility then leaves no other possibilities.

4. Several of these difficulties seem to derive as much from the general structuralist aspect of picture models as from the isomorphism aspect.

5. It might be possible to avoid a proliferation of types of elements if, for example, some hypothetical, very powerful type of element with, say, both propositional and value-oriented components was applied to all cases. But the ad hoc-ness would simply be compounded, and, in any case, the proliferation of elements, independent of how many types there are, would not thereby be avoided.

6. See Bickhard 1979, for a further discussion of such evolutionary difficulties.

7. The intrinsic value or motivational organization of knowledge is recognized by, for example, Heidegger (1962). Note that within picture models, with their static knowledge structures, the issue of action versus no action appears as quite a real one.

8. For an example of interactive modeling approaches to emotions and consciousness, see Bickhard (in press).

9. The hybrid models mentioned earlier between picture models and transformation models, with picture knowledge structures as objects of transformation, encounter the problems mentioned above concerning mind as the object of transformation. But these problems count as inadequacies of such hybrid models and not internal contradictions within them, and someone might want to contend that those inadequacies were only apparent or could be overcome. Thus, the tenuous compatibility between picture models and transformation models remains.

10. Partial realizations of this context dependency have at times yielded the conclusion that sentence forms per se do not have truth values, but only the particular utterances-in-context. This, of course, does not take into account the argument of the preceding paragraphs. Utterances-in-context may yield representations with truth values, but they are not themselves representations, and they do not have truth values.

11. There is nothing in the transformational model perspective to preclude the possibility of genetically based dispositions to certain kinds of hypothesis generation in learning language, but it does not

require it. Such a hypothesis of bias in language-learning hypothesis generation, in fact, encounters the interesting question of how the learning mechanism "knows" that it is engaged in "learning language" so that it can apply the bias(es) at appropriate times.

12. It should be clear that such an interactive perspective also constitutes a strictly intensional perspective: if any conceptual categories or distinctions are made from any perspective other than the intensional interactive perspective of the knowing system, for example, if any reference to states of affairs in the environment is made in any way except through representations in the system of those states of affairs, then the implication is that either the system has direct knowing access to the world, in violation of the basic definitional assumptions of interactive knowing, or those categories and distinctions have not been, and perhaps cannot be, explicated within the interactive knowing framework but must instead be provided from outside the interactive model by the human knower who is considering the model. Such categories and distinctions would constitute, therefore, challenges to the conceptual adequacy of interactive knowing to all and, particularly, human, knowing.

13. Formalizable as a Moore machine (Ginzburg 1968). See Appendix A for a general discussion of abstract machine theory.

14. Note that "well defined" in this context does not imply "predetermined."

15. The concept of an outcome can be formalized as a final state of a recognizer (Ginzburg 1968).

16. This concept of a register automaton is formalizable as in Brainerd and Landweber (1974, p. 86). Note that, since the state of the system is identical to the structure of indices, every interaction, no matter how "small," including a single state transition, is constituted by a change or changes in the indices.

17. Situation image as index structure and world image as control structure seem to integrate in one model both declarative and procedural forms of knowledge (Winograd 1975). Note that the virtual-real distinction of Bickhard (1978, and in press) applies to these senses of image.

18. Here and elsewhere in the text "redundant" is used in the information theoretic sense of "constraining possibilities" or "containing information about" rather than in the sense of "being superfluous."

19. In an efficient system, standard structures of the implicit situation image will be computed at the same time as the corresponding parts of the explicit situation image are generated. That is, commonly requested parts of the apperceptive process will be carried forward without necessarily waiting for explicit requests when time might be more limited. Such considerations of efficiency will be es-

pecially true if parallel processing capabilities are available. Standard structures of the situation image are often called frames (e.g. , Minsky 1975; Kuipers 1975).

20. The relationship between perceptual and transformational aspects of interactions is quite subtle. It would appear, for example, that there is no way for a system to make this distinction in other than a relative way within its own epistemological framework since it cannot know directly which characteristics the interaction assumed and which it created.

21. Note that, from the system perspective being developed here, the body, including at least parts of the peripheral nervous system, constitutes part of the environment to the central nervous system.

22. A sophisticated system will, of course, develop procedures for finding errors in its own control structures.

23. Procedures for such constructions ultimately must be based on principles of variation and selection (Campbell 1974). For further discussion and formalization, see Bickhard (in press).

24. Note that the construction of the ability to compute these implications is a construction of control structures, of the world image (possible situations), while the actual computation of such implications is a construction in the situation image (actual situation).

25. For a related philosophical position, see Rescher (1973).

26. Actually, such a second scan is likely to be much more cursory than the original—simply a check on and refinment of the implications of the original.

27. Consider as a contrasting example a blind individual constructing a representation of the positions of objects in a room: the available instantaneous redundancies are much limited, and temporal redundancies must suffice.

28. Hidden to prevent the generation of new explicit images, thus making knowledge of the current position of the object dependent on knowledge of the total past trajectory and preventing the direct construction of any simpler set of sufficient information. Note that physical translation is actually a logically rather simple form of trajectory in that, once spatial position is representable (itself nontrivial), the implications of a given translation are readily subsumed in the computation of a single next position, which is in itself sufficient information from which to compute the effects of any subsequent translation. Explicit recording of past translations, or even of original position, is not necessary. Far more complicated context dependencies in trajectory implications are conceivable, and, I will argue later, exist for other kinds of transformational trajectories. In general, in fact, indexing implications are not algorithmic and thus are not strict implications; they are, rather, frameworks for further hypothesis generation and testing.

29. Note that the world image ability to compute its way through such networks of locomotor and perceptual trajectories constitutes a system's knowledge of objects. Space is (in part) the transformational potential of objects. Space and objects are differentiated from one another, and neither is definable independently.

30. Much more can be said about goal-directed systems, motivation, and the relationship between them. These issues, however, are not a primary focus in this book.

31. A structure of indices is assumed to be internally connected by its relevances or else it would not form a functionally unitary structure at all.

32. Adopted and adapted from Minsky (1975), Kuipers (1975), and Winston (1974).

33. Under certain circumstances, this would be interpreted as a transformation of whatever the original index represented in the situation into whatever the resultant indices represent.

34. Note that a classificational category is a kind of degenerate form of a frame or network. As a frame, a category is a structure in which all the internal mutual indications are preclusive. As a network, a category is a point structure, with no mutual arrows (at least not with respect to the procedures that define the points, though possibly so with respect to others). A category is a contrastive set, such as the set of possible colors.

35. And, of course, categories can also serve as elements in frames, networks, and categories.

36. Adopted from Piaget (1954, 1971), Piaget and Inhelder (1969), Furth (1969), and Neisser (1976).

37. Related definitions might be attempted as follows: if the elements of an object scheme are defined to be the aspects of that object, then an object whose aspects are objects could be called a translatable object, and its aspects locations, and a translatable object whose aspects are translatable objects could be called a deformable object, and its aspects shapes.

These definitions (and that of object in the text) are presented only as illustrative suggestions: their deficiencies are clear, but they exemplify an approach. What is wanted is a structure of strictly (interactively) intensional definitions of cognitive elements and relations: object, property, location, part of, and so forth.

What is also wanted is a non-ad hoc explanation of why these representational structures are functional for a knowing system. To say that they are functional because they correspond to aspects of reality is to ignore the fact that all knowledge of that reality is constructed knowledge (Piaget 1954), constructed so as to be interactively maximally functional. Certainly reality is what it is, and representations must conform to that reality, but the differentiations, units, and structures by which we understand reality are not given by it but only allowed by it; and thus the question of "why that particular representational structure" must be answered at least in part in terms of intensional interactive functionality.

Realism at the level of the existence of the world is tautologically unavoidable (the world is what codetermines interactions), but simple realism at the level of particular structures in the world is a circular reification of one's own representational system.

38. The organization of time and space is primarily with respect to physical objects, though other kinds of objects may also participate.

One of the more difficult questions for an interactively intensional model is that of how time and temporal events can be represented. It might seem that procedures could only represent that which could be interacted with, and how could that be true of a past (or future) event?

39. Agents, of course, require greater specification than this, though it is not clear that preoperational children can differentiate much beyond this point. The relevant literature is voluminous, and includes Anscombe (1957), Bernstein (1971), Binkley, Bronaugh, and Marras (1971), Borger and Cioffi (1970), Brown (1974), Chihara and Fodor (1966), Fodor (1968), Goldman (1970), Rescher (1967), Shaffer (1968), Shwayder (1965), Taylor (1966), and White (1968). Discussion of agents and actions has been generally dominated by an extensionalist approach. I consider extensionalism intrinsically inadequate to the topic and would suggest that many of the most apparently intractable problems involved are consequences of its limitations.

40. The specifics of the representational form that constitutes a causal representation are unknown and a matter of controversy. See for relevant discussion Beauchamp (1974), Bunge (1963), Mackie (1974), Rescher (1973), Sosa (1975), and Von Wright (1974). I am convinced, as for agents and actions, that causality cannot be understood except from an intensional (and intentional) perspective.

41. That is, the basic categories of the sensory-motor period (Piaget 1954).

42. It is of interest to note that, among psychologists, concern for such principles of representational organization seems to be from either a semantic perspective (for example, Shank 1973) or a developmental perspective (for example, Piaget 1954) but rarely from a strictly cognitive perspective.

43. The situation image is a partial description whose elements are partial descriptions and, furthermore, whose elements are context dependent partial descriptions in the sense that their interactive implications will depend on the frame and network (scheme) contexts in which they occur.

44. As with interactions per se, specifications of the boundaries of action systems can be problematic. Roughly, I would claim that in both cases the boundary specifications are most appropriately made in terms of the servomechanism structure of the world image. This issue will not be dealt with directly in this text. The necessary differentiations will be in terms of focus rather than boundary.

45. This correspondence is not simple. The potentialities are functional potentialities of the world image, and thus a general analysis of the correspondence would require a framework for functional analysis. Wimsatt (1973) contains a relevant discussion. The general issues of functional analysis will not be focused on in this discussion.

46. This is broadened in the sense that it admits as objects many characteristics not usually so considered. What constraints need to be imposed in order to interactively characterize objects that are in some sense entities has been briefly discussed earlier. The particular properties that interactively characterize physical objects are further outlined in Piaget (1954).

47. The states and processes considered have broadened to a higher level of generality, for example, propositional attitudes, but have not in general received a great deal of analytic attention qua objects of language. See, for example, Grice (1969).

48. Insofar as this suggestion is valid, it points to a level in need of analysis between mind and the object of language (corresponding to the molecular level in the case of the teacup). I will not be focusing on this level of analysis in this discussion; the above argument simply has as its point that mind per se is not itself the object of language. With respect to the object of language that is developed later in the discussion, it will be seen that the participation of mind in that object is currently being addressed at least indirectly by sociolinguistics, symbolic interactionism, and, especially, ethnomethodology.

49. See Appendix B for a general discussion of convention.

50. Assuming even those cues are available, that is, that the person is physically present.

51. This argument holds with even greater force for knowledge of world images that might derive from more easily accessible type-of-person information, for example, demographics.

52. Note that a positive failure to characterize constitutes an undefined condition for the execution of the world image and thus yields interaction failure.

53. Though even in this latter case the structure of the situational characterization turns out to be more complex than might at first be appreciated. See Ryave and Schenkein (1974).

54. This is not to claim that all persons have the same goals in a situation but rather simply that all are in interaction with a situation constituted in part by other persons and therefore that all are

faced with an interpersonal-situation-characterization problem. The apparent exception of the case in which one or more persons are not aware of anyone else's participation is not of relevance to the existence of the characterization problem (or its mutuality), only to the participants' knowledge of that existence. Such issues of awareness are crucial to some points, but not to those being made in the text.

55. Note that this does not at all imply that the constituent situation images are complete in their characterizations, only that they are complete and valid relative to each other with respect to the salient aspects of the situation.

56. There are some issues not developed here that I would like to mention.

First, it would seem that interactively compatible situation images would not be interactively equivalent since each image, even if of the same situation, will be from a different perspective. This is true, but the ultimate perspective taken by each image is not itself a part of the image, and thus such perspectival dependency in situation images can be accommodated in the concept of interactive equivalence by, for example, translating each image to a common perspective for comparisons of equivalency.

It should be noted in this regard that another aspect of the issue of interactive equivalency is the motivational status of the individual. Situation images equivalent with respect to some goal settings may not be with respect to others. This is accommodated by including such goal settings as part of the image, and the equivalence of such goals across situation images is, at least in part, what constitutes a common problem.

Equivalence of control structures can be defined, for example, in terms of the functions they compute. But situation images are index structures, not control structures, and this raises an additional question about the concept of equivalence. Clearly, the equivalence of index structures must be derivative from the equivalence of control structures, but the nature of such derivations is not clear. One strategy might be to define equivalence in terms of some canonical form of situation and world images in which the interactive significance of particular indices would be comparable.

Further, even the equivalence of control structures, while definable, is not a solvable problem, that is, there is no algorithmic procedure that will evaluate with certainty two control structures as either equivalent or not equivalent (Rogers 1967, p. 33). Thus, even if the epistemological problem of acquiring knowledge of situation images were solvable, their equivalence would not necessarily be determinable.

The definitions, however, are in terms of the factual relationships, not an observer's knowledge of them. Any imputations of such relationships in given cases are, like all others, tentative and hypothetical (Popper 1965).

57. Note that it is the characterizations of the situation that must be equivalent, that is, of the same scope and interactively compatible. Again there is no claim that the characterizations are complete with respect to the actual situation.

58. This clause in McHugh (1968) stimulated my realization that definitions of situations are solutions to coordination problems, and, therefore, in that sense, conventions. This construal of definition of the situation required modifications of Lewis' (1969) explication, which provided the foundation for my understanding of convention. The nature of these changes in Lewis' explication of convention is developed in a later discussion.

59. This conceptualization of institutionalization is adopted from Berger and Luckmann (1966).

60. It might seem at first that interpersonal characterization problems are not necessarily problems of equivalence of interest, that is, not necessarily coordination problems. It might seem, for example, that the definition of the situation to be adopted can itself be a matter of conflict rather than coordination, as in the case of a negotiating session in which the topics to be negotiated are at issue. The point is valid but not as a counterexample to the basic existence of a coordination problem: conflicts can exist over subsidiary differentiations or transformations of the definition of the situation, but without some initial functioning situation convention there is no context within which the participants can even understand the existence of a conflict, much less resolve it. Such fundamental underlying definitions of situations may in most cases be arrived at readily and, in others, only with some difficulty. Nevertheless, a solution to this primary coordination problem is a prerequisite to any interaction at all.

One apparent class of exceptions to this point would be those situations in which one person intends to eliminate the necessity of interactively characterizing the other person at all, that is, to render the second person unconscious or dead without prior interaction with her or him. (Note that an intent simply to avoid another person requires some common characterization of the context within which the avoidance is to take place, even if the "outcome" of avoidance is not itself mutually desirable.) It is not clear to me whether instances of this case, for example, killing someone with a hidden sniper shot, are exceptions to the principle of interpersonal situations constituting coordination problems or exceptions to situations involving other persons constituting interpersonal situations (is the interaction in such a case with the other person at all or just with a material body?), or neither.

61. The core of this perspective is the claim that interpersonal situations and coordination problems are equivalent concepts. This claim imposes certain constraints on the concept of a person: in particular, a person must be something that can participate in the constitution of a coordination problem. This requirement would impose at least these constraints: (1) that a person have alternative action strategies available; (2) that it is meaningful to speak of a person selecting among such alternatives; (3) that such selections be sensitive to the situational context within which they occur; and (4) that it is meaningful to speak of interaction success or failure from the perspective of the person so that it becomes meaningful to evaluate the consequences of action strategy selections. The third constraint is not a simple dichotomy: sufficient interactive context sensitivity constitutes the existence of a situation image. I would argue that the fourth constraint requires goal directedness but will not pursue that argument at this time.

In this regard, it is interesting to ask if it is meaningful to consider the possibility of a person having conventions with himself, say, over time (see Lewis 1975, p. 26).

62. These logical steps are not necessarily temporally or computationally distinct, depending on the particular case.

63. Whether potential in the world image or actually apperceived in the situation image.

64. Supra-individual, not extra-individual. Conventions are not simply external to individuals but rather encompass them.

65. They are available as plan but not as image in the terminology of Bickhard (1978).

66. The example is adapted from Schiffer (1972).

67. Egocentrism is most commonly recognized in young children in whose situation images no (zero) levels of perspective are accommodated, but this is clearly a special case of the more general incompleteness (see Bickhard 1978).

68. This complexity can become especially fierce if some levels of representation contradict other levels, as in deceptions. This hierarchical facet of human encounter is among those addressed particularly by Goffman (1969, 1974).

The ramifications of perspective-level egocentrism must also ultimately be taken into account in an explication of what constitutes "sufficient" compatibility among situation images for a convention to exist. The criterion in the text (interactively equivalent characterizations) would seem to be a necessary and sufficient functional constraint on the situation images, but its explication in terms of the structural properties of situation images remains to be attempted.

69. This epistemological reflexivity, and corresponding uncertainty, is not logically different from knowledge about any other as-

pect of reality, but it is more striking in the case of conventions, especially situation conventions, in the developmental sense in that the presuppositions of interaction with the material world are usually established once and for life in early childhood, while those of interactions with persons must in some sense be established at each encounter. Such establishment is not necessarily explicitly problematic at each encounter, but it is subject to being so. Realities of (situation) conventions are more fragile than realities of material objects. The assumption of interactive constancy is less tenable in the case of socially constituted objects than in the case of material objects.

70. These epistemological limitation characteristics of conventions and of interactions based on conventions are a major focus of interest in ethnomethodology, for example, Turner (1974) and Mehan and Wood (1975).

71. Note that a presumed definition of the situation might conceivably be false yet not falsified, as long as the actual course of interaction did not involve direct disconfirmations of expectations.

72. Many levels of presupposition will not be tested or established explicitly unless an interaction failure at higher levels does, in fact, occur. In case of failure, such levels of implicit presupposition can then be tested in the search for a level of recovery of definition of the situation. Such dynamics occur primarily in terms of situation conventions.

Note that if the ground for a particular interaction is one of doubt rather than presumption then the individual has engaged in a decision with risk (Luce and Raiffa 1957) rather than acted in accordance with a convention. Lewis' (1969) "common knowledge" functions to eliminate such cases, though a negative constraint (Grice 1969; Lewis 1975) would seem to serve more parsimoniously.

73. Such temporal context dependencies of definitions of situations are of interest in both sociolinguistics (for example, Gumperz and Hymes 1972) and ethnomethodology (for example, Turner, ed., 1974).

74. See Appendices C and D for general discussions of speech acts and meaning.

75. I have not defined intentions. I take them to be conscious goal settings. See Bickhard (in press) for a definition of consciousness in a systems framework. For purposes of the discussion here, however, I will not need more specificity than that of goals, whether conscious or not.

76. It will be assumed that current goal definitions are included in the situation image.

77. The concepts in this section are strongly influenced by Grice's explication of meaning (Grice 1967, 1969; Schiffer 1972). The basic approach is allied to Bennett's meaning-nominalist strategy

(Bennett 1973). It will become clear, however, that the differences are fundamental.

78. Clearly, any attribution of a convention will characterize some other persons and therefore be part of a significance. Thus, any interaction with meaning will be a communication. The definition of meaning and utterance in terms of significance and communication is therefore not arbitrarily restrictive but rather intrinsically restricted.

79. Note that one way, perhaps the easiest way, to have a symmetry of indexing in a significance with respect to the participants is to have no participant perspective indexing. No indexing is necessarily symmetric. It is also highly egocentric, but that is not the point. Such egocentrism, however, is necessarily the case among young children, and thus Grice's formulation of meaning in terms of intentions (about recognition of intentions) would seem to exclude them from meaning anything (intentions require more than one perspective level).

80. Perhaps they might be named according to their perspective structuring, as, for example, an intended-to-be-understood meaning.

81. There would seem, however, to be the possibility of a correct attribution, therefore convention, with respect to one coordination problem, and a simultaneous incorrect attribution with respect to some other. In such a case, only the correct attribution in fact participates in a convention; therefore, the argument in the text holds.

82. Hopcroft and Ullman (1969). Note that such classifications by formal grammars are not necessarily the only relevant ones.

83. I have, however, made the differentiation between quasi-language and language in order to accommodate the known computational complexity of language. It seems plausible, however, that language is effectively defined as quasi-language and that its computational complexity is a manifestation of the general potential complexity of apperceptive computations.

84. There would not seem to be much question about such instances constituting definitions of the situation: they constitute symmetric and equivalent definitions of what was just said, if nothing else. Such possibilities are indicated by the non-anomalousness of such sentences as "that (didn't mean what/meant more than) you thought it was going to."

85. A version of inadvertant meaning could be constructed within the Gricean program in terms of someone forgetfully or inadvertently using a phrase or clause that has a different conventional meaning than that intended. This would fit within the Gricean program through an explication of conventional meaning in terms of intentions (for example, Grice 1971). Not all cases of inadvertant meanings involve conventional meanings, however, such as the earlier example of an incorrect warning shout, and thus do not provide an indirect path by which they can be traced back to intentions.

86. Grice's third criterion is not met, but this criterion is directly a constraint on intentions and is, without additional supporting arguments, dismissable as an artifact of the fact that Grice's examples are all of intended meaning. Similarly, it is not clear if Grice's second criterion is met, but this uncertainty turns directly on whether or not "what is meant" is being used in such a way as to presuppose intentions.

87. Note that an utterance in conformance with Gricean criteria concerning intentions would seem to be an instance of an utterance with a goal meaning and, if the Gricean intentions are met, would seem to be an instance of a fulfilled utterance. Thus, the explication above appears as a generalization of Grice's explication, a generalization just broad enough to include the cases of unintended meanings. This, clearly, assumes the basic equivalence of Gricean explications with the above explications in respects other than that of intentions (goals) versus apperceptions.

As pointed out earlier, Grice, in effect, assumes that utterer understood meanings must be derived from and equivalent to utterer goal meanings. Meanings not derived from intentions, according to Grice, cannot occur (except, perhaps, through a misuse of conventional meanings). I claim, in contrast, that understood meanings, utterer's or audience's, can occur independent of goal meanings and, in some cases, without there being any relevant goal meaning at all. Occasion meaning, then, must be derived primarily from understood meaning and not goal meaning.

It is of interest to note that occasion meaning must be supraindividual (and, thus, mind as object of language is not adequate) in order to account for the various relationships that obtain among utterer understood meaning and audience understood meanings. For example, in an earlier discussion it was argued that mind cannot be the proximate object of language since that would imply that a command could not be successfully uttered unless it were obeyed. A possible counterargument to that might seem to be that the command need only be understood, not necessarily obeyed, in order for its utterance to be successful. But the content that is understood must be so understood by all concerned, and understood mutually and with symmetry, in order for that success to obtain. In other words, the utterance must accomplish a situation convention in order to have social meaning. Situation conventions, therefore, must be the proximate objects of meaningful communications, however much it may be true that mind is indirectly involved and may even be an indirect object.

88. Note that if the apperceptions based on the outcomes of the interactions are primarily perceptual, that is, if the interaction tests and detects more than it transforms, then the overall subsystem of

procedure together with goal space will tend to be called a perceptual system rather than an action system. Systems with primarily perceptual apperceptions but whose interactions involve the skeletal musculature tend to be called cognitive systems and tend to involve spaces of relatively abstract goal representations. Any sophisticated detection system, such as qualitative analysis in chemistry, would be an example. Both action and perceptual systems manifest complex subroutine (servomechanism) structures and are organized in turn under higher-level cognitive and goal-determining systems. As remarked earlier, all interactions involve in principle both perceptual and transformational apperceptions.

89. The relationship of this nomenclature for actions to that of J. L. Austin (1962) will be discussed later.

90. As well as for the sense in which language can serve as its own metalanguage.

91. The convergence with Austin's concepts with such an opposite approach, however, would suggest otherwise. See the discussion of Austin.

92. The situation is interesting in which such deception is seen through, thus restoring a measure of symmetry to the situation. Such a situation is not relevant to the discussion because such an inadvertent restoration of symmetry is by definition not possible as a goal and thus cannot be part of an action system.

It is possible, however, to plan an apparent slip and thus an attributed "seeing through" on the part of the "victim," all of which simply introduces some new level of asymmetry. It is questionable, however, whether such acts could be said to have been either produced or taken as conventional, though it is clear that their significance would be in some sense parasitic upon (derivative from) their conventional significance. Goffman (1974) contains relevant discussions.

93. Productive systems of locutionary acts <u>are</u> linguistic systems.

94. Just as maximum possible cognitive capacity in an individual is strongly culture-dependent (you are not likely to invent calculus in a culture that doesn't have a number system), so also is communication and situation convention capacity in general (you are not likely to invent a bureaucracy in a culture that defines institutional interpersonal relationships strictly in terms of kinship). The evolution of social technology is as important as the evolution of physical technology.

95. Or, for that matter, everyone knows that everyone knows but no one knows that everyone knows that everyone knows, or any other level of failure of full mutuality of knowledge.

96. Locutions are not the only transformations on situation con-

ventions that leave them as situation conventions: it is interesting and useful to consider body language metacommunications and the visual and musical arts (among others) largely as nonconventional illocutions.

97. Note that an equivalent point applies to physical objects.

98. I don't mean to imply that all strict prelocutions are manipulations in the pejorative sense—there are clear exceptions in young children and in special circumstances among adults—but rather that manipulations frequently require strict prelocutions and prelocutions parasitic upon illocutions.

99. Such definitions are, of course, ultimately renderable and functional in terms of their effects on more physically and biologically primary interactions, but they are clearly not epiphenomenal relative to physics and biology—they create possibilities, via information savings and specialization (perhaps a form of information savings), that would not exist otherwise.

100. I find it useful, in fact, to define mathematics as the study of formal languages, with differing kinds of mathematics (for example, arithmetic, algebra, topology, computation theory) being differentiated as involving languages about differing topics (for example, quantity, structure, continuous structure, systems).

Note that this view of mathematics does not make any necessary commitment to any particular philosophy of mathematics since it does not prejudge the issue of the nature and source of the constraints and possibilities involved in a formal locutionary structure.

101. Almost any lower species' caretaking or mating or conflict ritual would be an example. See Hinde (1970) or Marler and Hamilton (1966) for many specifics.

102. The issue of the evolution of development of that cognitive capacity prior to its assimilation to prelocutionary systems is a separate consideration.

103. Consider a warning call among herd animals. Note that such signals are, from an evolutionary perspective, locutions as well as illocutions.

104. I argue in Bickhard (in press), in fact, that the evolution of language, as distinct from its development, requires cognitive capabilities qualitatively beyond this.

105. Note that the analogical motivation by which a pantomime can be understood, and thus serve as a potential locutionary precedent, can itself be based upon the forms of underlying genetic prelocutions.

106. Such a delay of vocal capability beyond the corresponding locutionary cognitive capability would, if it exists, undoubtedly have adaptive significance—perhaps to strengthen mother-infant ties through dyadic institutionalization or (inclusive) perhaps to ensure the maximal assimilation of vocal locutions to the later development of illocu-

tionary systems organized with respect to temporal trajectories of situation conventions.

107. There is, of course, also the possibility that the production and comprehension of linguistic locutions requires special cognitive skills beyond those of other productive action systems and that the timing of the onset of these skills is genetically controlled. The model as developed gives no a priori support to such a possibility, but it is compatible with it and thus, at this point of development, is neutral with respect to such innateness hypotheses as McNeill's (1970).

108. This is not in either case necessarily to say a formal metalanguage, though I would contend that it serves as the cultural and individual foundation for language and metalanguage formalization.

109. This does not preclude the construction of an action system subordinate to one superordinate system, which later becomes subordinate to some other action system constructed later than the original system.

110. A possible exception to the general statement might be an action system that is functionally autonomous but whose goal space only allows a finite action space: such a system could not be productive in the usual sense of the word.

111. To attempt to explain those interactions in terms of input-output regularities of the system without reference to its interior processes is merely a highly degenerate version of the second approach mentioned above, and one of severely limited power. It is potentially successful only for a system with no memory (no temporal context dependency) and is thus absurd for human beings.

112. It might seem that prediction is an alternate criterion of usefulness for descriptions, and so it is. But although prediction is differentiable from explanation in a strict utilitarian sense, conceptually it is simply an approximation to one aspect of an explanatory model.

113. This point has been made many times but seems continuously to need repeating. For some interesting versions of the point, see Fodor (1968), Popper (1959), or Rescher (1973).

114. The force of this point becomes most apparent with the realization that capacities can be infinite.

115. This point is actually just another manifestation of the fact that science is concerned with the counterfactual as well as the factual: the counterfactual must be dealt with in terms of such characterizations (see Rescher 1973).

116. There is an assumption here of sufficient speaker homogeneity that the capacity described is more language specific than speaker specific. There is also an assumption that acceptability is not highly situation specific in the fact that judgments are made of language act types rather than context-embedded tokens.

Note that judgments of unacceptability are not necessarily taken at face value: the judgment must be for "the right reason" (and not simply because the sentence is difficult to process, for example). This introduction of secondary criteria for the acceptability of judgments is undoubtably necessary, but it introduces conceptual difficulties into the specification of the capacity being considered and raises the possibility of circularity in that specification (Peters 1972 contains relevant discussions).

117. These conceptualizations of competence and performance seem to me to be as close as can be obtained to Chomsky's (1965) concepts within this more precise framework.

118. Performance as a capacity and performance as explanatory are greatly confused in the literature, and this confusion visits itself indirectly on competence, producing a conceptualization which is somehow supposed to be both descriptive and explanatory. But to be simultaneously descriptive and explanatory is incoherent: a representation of a class of potential interactions contains no process concepts and thus cannot be a process explanation of those interactions. This is obscured by the fact that a finite representation of an infinite set will (likely) be a procedure by which that set can be recursively enumerated, and procedure sounds like process. But the fact remains that an enumeration of an event type cannot provide an explanation for an occurrence of an instance of that type (for example, what are the prior conditions and by what laws and processes do they yield that event?).

119. See, for example, the definition of "pragmatics" in Morris (1970, 1964).

120. Another possibility would be that semantics involves constraints that do not participate in acceptability judgments and, thus, would not be involved in syntactics, but then it would also not be a part of grammar.

121. An equivalent contention is made in Lightner (1976).

122. Note that there is no a priori guarantee that observationally differentiable characteristics of a system's interactions correspond to ontologically differentiable mechanisms or processes inside the system. A single mechanism can manifest multiple characteristics simultaneously. Such descriptive characteristics generally will have little usefulness in an explanatory model because they will not capture any unitary interactive capacity of the system. They may (or may not), nevertheless, be useful for other purposes, such as prediction.

123. It is also clearly true that underlying system structure is partly inferred from and tested against such error criteria definitions and descriptions of capacity. But this is not a circularity; it is a dialectic. It is an instance of the metaphor of science as a ship being constantly rebuilt while always at sea.

124. I ignore phonology as a capacity corresponding to action structures not discussed in the text.

125. The distinction between algorithms and heuristics is usually based on an evaluation of the logical or mathematical certainty of success. The relevant consideration in the above context is the presence or absence of an apperceptive presumption of success.

126. It is also plausible that such modes might differ from time to time in a given servomechanism, depending on such factors as time demand, error cost, and currently available processing capacity. This would seem more likely with the error-reponsiveness trichotomy than the heuristic-algorithmic distinction since, if an algorithm exists that is efficient enough to be of use at all, it will commonly be efficient enough to be optimal relative to heuristic approaches under virtually all conditions, while error-processing costs and benefits will be subject to more varied relative advantages.

127. Actually, translatability from goal definitions to situation images probably suffices. It is not clear if the unidirectionality of the translatability requirement has any important consequences. It would imply, however, that the representational capacities of goal spaces might, in particular systems, be a proper subset of the capacity of that system's situation images.

128. Goal definitions are subject to the constraint of being referenceable by procedure executions in addition to the constraint of being translatable into situation images.

129. Goal definitions will also depend on apperceptive implications. A goal will, in general, be selected as (part of) a means toward the end of some higher goal on the basis of the selected goal's having (part of, or steps toward) the higher goal as part of its apperceptive implications. Thus, decompositions of particular interaction computations will reflect corresponding decomposability within the agent-world relationship and, thus, within the corresponding apperceptive implications.

130. It is assumed here that the construction of procedures, either phylogenetically or ontogenetically, is an evolutionary or quasi-evolutionary (variation and selection) procedure, with success feedback required for relatively "small" steps of variation in order for those steps to be selectively retained. Thus, if too high a complexity is required before success feedback is attainable, the construction path will be unstable and unlikely to be successfully traversed.

131. This is essentially a brief particularization of an argument concerning the relationships among decomposability, hierarchy, and systems found in Simon (1969).

132. Material objects considered as patterns of potential interactions which remain invariant under physical transformations. It should be noted that the hierarchicalization of servomechanisms, and

thus the decomposability of interactive potentialities, extends far below the level of objects (Piaget 1954).

133. The basic model is highly compatible with a correspondence theory of truth and an evolutionary theory of growth of knowledge (Popper 1965, Campbell 1974). The correspondence, however,
is not with the world-in-itself but rather with the structure of potential interactions (Rescher 1973, but with a distinctly different conclusion with respect to the nature of truth).

134. Clearly, this has been the case in the past, and it would
seem that many conceptualizations of the relationships between language and truth (and language and reality) have been and are influenced by this error (for example, a general tendency to confuse
memory for words with representations of the world, exemplified in
Tulving [1972], for example, in spite of the critical distinction drawn
there). I contend that the conceptualization of language as fundamentally representational (for example, Wittgenstein 1961) is in error.

135. The situation and world image characterizations are thus
close "in spirit" to the model set formalizations of Hintikka (for example, 1969). The interactive and potential apperceptive structuring
within the world image would relate to "trans-world identifications"
(for example, Kripke 1972), except that individuals are not taken as
primitive (Scott 1970). Such structuring would certainly correspond
to accessability relations (Hughes and Creswell 1968) and would
recur at each level of knowing (Bickhard, in press), thus creating a
hierarchy of accessability structures.

136. General goal-directed systems also encounter "situation
memory" (past dependencies) in rudimentary form, as in the fact
that objects of themselves tend to stay in one place. Such memory,
however, is frequently directly apperceivable and, thus, need not be
explicitly computed as a trajectory. Exceptions would be, for example, the consequences of hidden or unperceived translations of an object, whose computations require (constitute) representations of the
corresponding trajectories.

It is suggestive, in fact, that memory in a child seems to develop in direct correspondence to the child's ability to represent the
memory (past dependency) of the environment. It provides a potential
for integrating event memory with the fundamental "memory" (storage) for procedures.

It is also suggestive that a child's "animism" might be seen as
a lack of differentiation of the kinds and degrees of context sensitivity
to be found in the environment. The differentiation of causal from
intentional past sensitivities, for example, might well be impossible
until a later developmental stage is attained.

137. The point here is about potential complexity, not common
complexity. It is not often that such extended past sensitivities are

relevant in our daily lives (and, even then, they are frequently short-
ened by more recent apperceptive foundations), but their very possibility affects the organization of prelocutionary systems. Even one
level of sensitivity recursion is sufficient to strongly differentiate
prelocutionary systems from most other action systems.

138. Such actions as the direct infliction of pain might seem to
be exceptions to this path of effects through the situation image, but
I suggest elsewhere (Bickhard, in press) that pain and other motivational states are themselves subsumable under general computational,
and thus apperceptive, models. The point, then, is that effects on an
agent's interactive character are obtainable only through effects on
that agent's situation image.

139. Such consonance need only be in structure, not necessarily
qua apperceptions and goals. Thus, people interact with physical objects quite well without knowledge of the inter- and intra-molecular
forces with which those interactions are consonant. Similarly, effective communication is constrained by the logics of apperceptions and
goals, and might even be maximally efficient if based on explicit
knowledge of such logics, but is not dependent upon such explicit
knowledge in order to have consonance with such constraints.

140. Note that such communications need not necessarily be
understood as goal communications; they might be taken as natural
aspects of the situation. Some goal communications, in fact, will fail
if understood as communications by their recipients. Their success
depends on their being taken as natural parts of the environment.
That is, some goal communications are unsuccessful if understood
as such.

141. As examples, consider constraints on information capacity
or intermediate storage capacities for various computations.

142. Note that a non-decomposed communication will be trivi-
ally closed. Note also that a communication might be computationally
decomposed in the servomechanisms that execute the interaction without that decomposition bearing any particular relationship to the goal
significance. In other words, it is perfectly possible for a communication to be interactively decomposed without thereby being communi-
cationally decomposed.

143. A significance is a modification or an updating of an already existing situation image. Thus, some aspects or components
of a significance may be derived from the prior situation image within
which the communication apperception occurs rather than from the
communication interaction per se. Thus, the full structure of a significance must be recoverable from any closed communication decomposition, but it is not necessarily the case that each such component of a significance be explicit in the communication.

144. In order to break the natural structuring and sequencing of

specification and characterization, the computation of an apperceptive significance would have to be excised from the standard temporal flow of interaction and taken as an interactive goal in its own right. That is, significances would have to be taken as goal objects of interaction as well as aspects or components of interaction. This would involve an interaction with the internal situation image as its "environment" and thus could conceivably be done only with higher-level interactive (knowing) systems (Bickhard 1978) but would still be "unnatural." Such a process, however, will underlie many higher-order cognitions (apperceptions) and, perhaps, certain sophisticated communications as well.

145. Clearly, these notions of subject and predicate are not directly syntactic.

146. There is no reverse implication that illocutions must be or be capable of such decomposition within minimal units.

147. Decompositions of significances, nevertheless, can still occur within strictly prelocutionary systems. The constraint, as mentioned earlier, is that the constituents of such decomposed significances must themselves be significances. That is, prelocutionary systems can decompose significances but not minimal significances.

148. That is, the communications and the fact of their being communications are, in general, mutually available in a dyadic interaction. There is thus little ground for attributing any asymmetry to the relationships among the respective situation images, and precisely such a lack of asymmetrical attribution constitutes a situation convention attribution which, if mutually valid, constitutes a situation convention. The level of construction of such a situation convention with respect to its intrinsic layering of ontological reflexivity will, of course, be constrained by the cognitive capabilities of the organism(s) involved.

149. Most commonly, in fact, they will be parasitic on illocutions in the sense that they will require some minimal situation convention framework of interaction within which the appearance—but not the actuality—of the mutuality and symmetry of other situation conventions will be manipulated. That is, strict prelocutions frequently involve manipulative deception about and within the framework of situation conventions.

150. The implicit construction of such epiphenomal situation conventions, however, clearly puts the species, or the individual, in contact with a gradient of evolutionary, or developmental, pressure toward the construction of such illocutionary systems.

151. In fact, the exploration of the potentialities of illocutions and situation conventions, on both personal and social levels, constitutes a major pattern of history and one that has perhaps just begun. Such exploration, however, has been almost entirely of a strict

trial-and-error form, since only recently have the conceptual tools begun to be available for the preliminary consideration and criticism of such potentialities before actually trying them out.

The discussions that follow in the text focus primarily on illustrative properties of illocutionary systems per se. The discussion of the constructive properties of situation conventions would move in the direction of sociology and history, such as the historical development of bureaucracy. It is evident, however, that situation conventions and illocutions are intrinsically bound and reciprocally generative.

152. That is, issues of mutuality, symmetry, and interactive compatibility among situation images are issues of the relationships among the representational contents of those images and thus partake of that content.

153. Requiring, in fact, higher-level knowing systems (Bickhard 1978).

154. This illustrates rather clearly that apperceptions as well as interaction computations can potentially be nonalgorithmic problem-solving procedures.

155. If the conventional situation convention is, in part, that of a conversational interchange, then utterance implicatures should partially correspond to (and were clearly motivated by) Grice's conversational implicatures (Grice 1975). Utterance implicatures, however, should apply in principle for any contextual situation convention. An example might be a perfectly innocuous utterance that takes on amusing indirect meaning within a particular humorous situation convention. Another example might be provided by a violation of sidewalk walking conventions (Ryave and Schenkein 1974), say, by one individual forcing his way in between two others carrying on a conversation. The particular implicature meaning of such an act will generally be resolved by other elements of the situation (for example, whether the first individual is an acquaintance or stranger, whether his expression is angry or pleasant, and whether the pair were blocking the sidewalk), but will not necessarily require any conversational aspects. Note that utterance implicatures are part of utterance meanings.

156. Inadvertent implicatures, incidentally, provide excellent examples of inadvertent meanings, for example, "How many people are coming to your party tomorrow night?" to someone who was to be given a surprise birthday party.

157. Clearly motivated by Searle's indirect speech acts (Searle 1975), though, as with implicatures, intended to be a broader context. Thus, if two men are members of an audience for a speech which they are obligated to hear, and one of them, catching the attention of the other, smiles and makes an intention movement as if to leave, this may well count as an indirect utterance (illocution) with the indirect (goal) meaning that the speech is bad. It would not seem to qualify for Searle's indirect speech acts.

158. For a general discussion of communication through stylized movement and intention gesture, see Spiegel and Machotka (1974).

159. Classification by decomposition is also possible for prelocutions, though not decomposition within minimal units.

160. As when an utterance is directed primarily at a particular individual but changes the definitions of the situation for all participants. This, in at least some cases, is actually a special case of topic specification.

161. A distinction must be made between the relationship of instantiation between adjacent levels of action systems and the relationship of instrumentality between adjacent systems. General action systems, prelocutionary systems, illocutionary systems, and so on, are general categories of action-system types, each one of which is a particularization of the one above. Thus, any actual action system that instantiates any one of these levels also instantiates each of the higher levels. An actual illocutionary system, however, may also function as an instrumental means for an actual prelocutionary system (through instrumental points) in addition to being itself an instantiation of the prelocutionary system type. The sequence of differentiations, thus, provides both a hierarchy of instantiation levels of action system types and a hierarchy of subsystem component levels of actual action systems.

162. Searle (1975) presents such an analysis, which has been very useful in the generation of the taxonomic framework presented in the text, though he does not develop it in these terms.

163. Such acts, of course, must be taken as illocutions in order to be understood as such. That is, they must be taken as having significances with the mutuality and commonality of situation conventions in order to affect situation conventions. In some cases, understanding an action as being an illocution will precede the understanding of the rest of the meaning of that illocution. Such would be the case, for example, if an action is intended to be an illocution, as with Grice (1967); such an intention is recognized and the meaning then understood through implicature. This is probably the most common pattern, but neither the intention nor its recognition is necessary, only the recognition that the act can be and is being taken as an illocution. Such inadvertent illocutions may occur where the inadvertence is at the level of the significance per se, for example, saying something that turns out to have a meaning neither considered nor intended before saying it or, interestingly, when the inadvertance is at the level of the meaning but not of the significance, that is, when a significance is intended but the mutuality and commonality of a meaning is not, yet a meaning is what is generated. An example would be someone who makes a face of distaste, intending it as a purely private gesture, but who is observed and commonly understood by all participants.

164. The typifications and transformational effects of a locution must be available jointly and reciprocally to all participants prior to the performance of that locution. Otherwise those effects will not be determined conventionally but will be inferred either naturally or through implicature, and the action will not be a locution. Conventional meanings, therefore, must be institutionalized.

This is, in effect, a version of the reason why Lewis' original explication of convention (Lewis 1969) is intrinsically institutional: it is extensional and, therefore, meaningful only with respect to (potential) repetition and intrinsically of an institutional temporal duration. In the case of conventional meaning this becomes: conventional meanings are properties of action types, that is, are regularities of effect of those types, and the potentials of those regularities must have the person and temporal scope (however small) of an institution.

165. It is not sufficient simply that such cultural familiarity exist among the participants. The fact of such common knowledge among the participants must itself be common knowledge. That is, such common knowledge must be (a presupposed) part of the prior situation convention. A similar argument would hold for any other superficially nonconventional constraint on the potentiality of a locution: it must not only be present, it must be common knowledge that it is present. Conventional presuppositions, therefore, are always presuppositions concerning the prior situation convention and, therefore, are always a species of indexical presuppositions.

166. Or ironic versions of these, depending on how evident such "deservingness" is. Note that the transition to irony, at least in this case, is thus a continuum with possibilities of ambiguity.

167. Searle's (1969) example of an American soldier reciting a line of rote-memorized German to his Italian captors in order to convince them that he is a German soldier would thus seem to be an example of an indirect utterance based on a conventional presupposition implicature. This example will be classified more finely in the discussion of linguistic systems.

168. It would seem that this conceptualization of conventional implicature is inclusive of but broader than Grice's concept of the same name (Grice 1975), though the boundaries of Grice's concept are not at all clear to me. For example, would Grice's conventional implicature include a case of participant status implicature through the use of certain status registers?

169. It should be noted that the relationships of these differentiations at the level of locutions to those at the level of illocutions are different from those at the level of illocutions to those at the level of prelocutions. In particular, from prelocutions to illocutions is a differentiation of objects of interaction with concomitant consequences for all other aspects of the action system, while from illocutions to

locutions the interactive object remains the same, only the means change, and therefore the differences are not as great. Thus, for example, goal meanings are intrinsically (cognitively) different from goal significances; they must attribute the mutuality and commonality of conventions as well as whatever other content they contain. "Indirect goal significances" might be generalized from indirect goal meanings as a kind of indirect point of a prelocution, but such a concept basically would introduce no new distinction. The goal meanings of locutions, however, are just like the goal meanings of illocutions: there need not be any cognitive difference whatsoever. The same is true with respect to indirect goal meanings and conventional indirect goal meanings.

The differentiations from illocutions to locutions are analytic and are cognitively representable only from a metalevel, while those from prelocutions to illocutions are cognitively represented at an implicit level whenever an illocutionary action system is differentially developed. In other words, the only way a locutionary action system can be differentially developed is if the construction of the locution is itself taken as a goal for some system, which constitutes a shift to a metalevel, while a new goal space for the differentiation of illocutions from prelocutions is already present in the nature of the corresponding objects of interaction. Again, the differentiation of locutions from illocutions is one at the level of means, not ends.

170. There is a hint here of the possibility of dichotomous distinction between the availability of a locution within a particular situation convention and the applicability of that locution to that situation convention. Extreme cases of inapplicability, however, would seem to constitute unavailability as well, and, thus, the distinction would have to form at least a continuum of potentiality. Furthermore, consideration of the many forms of possible constraints on potentiality would seem to yield the conclusion that such a continuum, if coherent at all, would be best conceived of as a strictly analytic aspect of a complexly structured space of possible presuppositions rather than a cognitively explicit ordering.

171. Two possible distinctions would seem to appear within this framework. First, there is the distinction between that part of the posterior situation convention that is different from the prior situation convention, the occasion meaning and that part which is the same. Formal explication of this distinction might be more difficult than would at first appear: it rests on a more precise explication of the structure and content of situation convention, which, in turn, rests on a similar further explication of situation image.

Second, there would seem to be a distinction between some sort of a "direct" or "conventional" occasion meaning of a locution and whatever implicatures it gives rise to. It is not clear to me that a dichotomous distinction of this sort would survive careful scrutiny. In particular, it seems plausible that the distinction would yield a continuum of implicature "distances."

172. It is of interest to ask whether the conventional meanings of locutions are defined intensionally or extensionally. Extensional definition would require explicit extensional definition of situation conventions, which is neither present nor possible. Conventional meanings must, therefore, have the status of intensionally defined procedures, and, among other questions to which that gives rise, that of their algorithmic status (or lack of it) looms interestingly. Further explication of intensional conventional meanings, thus, also rests upon further explication of situation conventions, situation images, and apperceptions.

173. It may vary in degree, however. A minimally deictic locution would be akin to a constant function (though it seems doubtful that any locution is that insensitive to its context), but even that would be deictic by virtue of the fact that any conventional meaning is only a partial function. For it to be a total function would imply its potentiality in any and all situation conventions, which would make it no longer conventional.

174. To attribute truth value to a locutionary type is akin to attributing primeness, or lack of it, to a function on the integers. This point is similar to, but broader than, one drawn by Searle (1971).

175. The assumption in such a definition would be that the concept of functional power imposes a partial ordering on candidate systems (probably true), and that there is some set of greatest elements with respect to that ordering (Birkhoff 1967) (potentially false). Such would appear to be the case with respect to computational power, with a Universal Turing machine being an instance of a greatest element.

It could be the case, however, that every such system is necessarily limited, but that each system has limitations not shared by some other system. Thus, there would be systems of (locally) maximal functional power but no system of greatest power (though one might be derived indirectly through some method of weighting the limitations). Such a state of affairs might be the case, for example, among formal logics relative to the avoidance of Russell-type paradoxes.

Furthermore, even if such a definition of greatest power were coherent, a claim of such power for any particular candidate system might well be falsifiable, if false, but not demonstrable if true (as with the claim of greatest computational power for Universal Turing machines and their computational equivalents, Boolos and Jeffry 1974).

176. An implicit assumption is that locutions must have in some sense distinct conventional meanings in order to be considered distinct locutions. The point here is simply that computational power of

the linguistic system be a locutionary power and not, for example, an ability to introduce an indefinite number of variations on a single locution.

177. Two implicit assumptions here are that contextual situation convention and goal meaning pairs themselves form a "productive" set and that that productivity is itself recursively compositional. These assumptions seem quite plausible in the light of the earlier discussions on situation conventions and goal meanings.

178. This is basically a special case of the point that interactions will be structured in accordance with the structure of agent-world interaction possibilities. It has a slightly different flavor from the extra ingredient of the potentiality for arbitrariness in conventions.

179. The possibility that is eliminated by such compositional dependence is that the variations in computational power have relevance only to the size of the set of possible locutions and that that set nevertheless spans only a limited range of functional capability. That is, the compositional dependence of computational power eliminates another conceivable level of irrelevant variations on a theme. To assert relevance, however, is not to specify how much or what kind of relevance.

180. It seems plausible, in fact, though I do not have a strong argument, that decompositional constructive systems that did not decompose within minimal significances would be of limited computational power. The basic idea is that decomposition only with respect to full significances would be on the order of propositional logic compared to more powerful logics. Insofar as some such reasoning holds, then linguistic systems must necessarily decompose within minimal units.

181. Not all utterance action constituents will have constituent meanings. Decomposition with respect to meaning will only proceed to some finite point below which action decomposition will be with respect to strictly identificatory (action typificational) or strictly physical aspects.

182. Otherwise meaning would have to be a (possibly multidimensional) continuum, in which case the concept of constituent composition would have little relevance.

183. There is an ambiguity or vagueness in the use of the word "minimal" in this definition that would seem to correspond to something like a continuum of "lexicality" in natural language. "Minimal" could be taken in the sense that any further decomposition would yield subconstituents with no constituent meanings, corresponding generally to the level of morphemes; or "minimal" could be taken in the sense that any further decomposition would yield subconstituents whose constituent meanings were not sufficient to determine compositionally the meaning of the given constituent, corresponding generally to words.

The distinction stems from the fact that some constituents will have constituent meanings by direct typification but will occur in structures whose overall constituent meanings cannot be recovered solely from the contributions of the constituents: an additional typification of constituent meaning at the level of the structure itself will be required to resolve ambiguities or vaguenesses remaining from the strict composition of the component constituent meanings. Thus, we have decompositional minimality in the sense of a minimal typified unit below which there is no (typified) constituent meaning and decompositional minimality in the sense of a minimal typified unit below which the constituent meaning is not (strictly) compositionally recoverable, or, equivalently, in the sense of a maximally typified unit above which all constituent meanings are recovered purely compositionally and not typificationally. The basic distinction, therefore, is between (minimal units of) typified contributions to conventional meaning and (minimal units of) compositional contributions to conventional meaning.

This distinction would appear to define a continuum of usage, rather than a dichotomization of levels. That is, on the one hand, the minimally typified unit would appear to correspond to morphemes, but the definitiveness of typified lexical meaning will vary widely among morphemes and contexts, and some can even occur "independently" as words, for example, "full" alone and in "youthful" or "awful." On the other hand, the maximally typified constituent would appear to correspond to words, but words overlap with morphemes as action constituents (above with "full"), and they participate as constituents in higher-level typifications, ranging from idioms to compound nouns (for example, Carroll and Tanehaus 1975), to restricted idioms (Chafe 1970).

It seems likely to me that this typification-composition continuum of lexical meaning is a strong component of the field of diachronic (especially typificational) language processes, both historical and ontogenetic, but, though it may affect synchronic processes, does not derive from synchronic aspects of language. Note that the relative structure of typifications and compositions can vary from one individual to another within a linguistic community and within the same individual or community from time to time (for example, McCawley 1976). Note also the absence of such a typification-composition continuum in formal languages.

184. The statement "The king of France is bald" could also be used to implicate that France does, in fact, exist and has a king, if the existence of France were somehow not already a part of the situation convention. Clearly, in most circumstances, the existence of France is common knowledge, and thus its presupposition does not give rise to an implicature because it is already there.

185. And these facts are not necessarily themselves represented (indexed) in the situation image. That is, the fact of a particular perceptual experience being of an object, or of a particular object being an agent, or of a particular inter-agent situation being a situation convention may be cognitively epiphenomenal for a given individual and invariably will be if the individual is young enough.

186. Their social reality is constituted by the cross-typification of such procedures. Such typifications must be extensionally (functionally) equivalent (or "nearly" so) and must be intensional in form (or else the situation conventions involved would also have to be extensionally defined) but are not likely to be equal in all possible respects of procedures (for example, as stated in some canonical procedure language). This leaves open the interesting question of just what aspects of procedures are cross-typified.

187. Note that, as long as agents are similarly epiphenomenally represented, causality, intentionality, and convention all will be conflated in a reified way. I would suggest that explicit (virtual) representation of agenthood requires second-level knowing (as a property of real representations of certain objects) and that explicit (virtual) representation of situation conventions requires third-level knowing (as properties of real representations of agents). Thus, these conflations would be disentangled progressively as a child developed. See, for example, Bickhard (1978) for the concepts involved.

188. Contextualization with respect to such physical cues will successfully mimic a valid situation convention contextualization only insofar as the relevant situation convention is not subject to complex temporal trajectories.

189. Imitation requires an interesting version of such cofunctional representations. In particular, the representations involved must be of a sufficient level of abstraction to incorporate the differences in perspective, in agent, and in modality that are involved in the shift from perception to creation.

190. Cofunctionality is the form of world image representation out of which all others are differentiated. The ability to produce what is received and to receive what is produced comes to be hierarchically organized in complex cofunctional schemes developed through circular reactions in early childhood (Piaget 1954). Only slowly do reception and production become differentiated as systems; only slowly are transformational apperceptions differentiated from perceptual apperceptions and, thus, self from world.

191. Such individuation and selection is, in fact, an observational frame and is only indirectly definable in terms of system structures. A system will, in fact, be organized in accordance with the structure of agent-world interaction possibilities and will, therefore, have definable boundaries and structures of servomechanisms, and

so on, but the definitions of those definable boundaries and structures can be made only from a metaperspective on the system.

192. Pure illocutions can function only with respect to conventional prior conditions with little or no conventional arbitrariness in form for, insofar as the form of a prior characterization must be learned as a convention (as opposed to having a nonconventional form but simply constituting a conventional attribution in the current situation), that conventional form will be appropriate only to a similarly conventionalized transformation, that is, to a locution. It is conceivable that a pure illocution could operate on an arbitrary conventional form by some kind of implicature (though I do not offhand have any examples), but that would have to be an implicature based on an initial effect on less arbitrary forms.

193. Most arbitrary of all, of course, is when the content of the attribution is itself a convention.

194. This sounds something like a Whorfian possibility (for example, Dale 1976), but there are at least two differences: (1) Whorf would need to assume a very large degree of such underlying arbitrariness together with a very large degree of cultural constraint, and both issues are open; and (2) Whorf would need to assume that those cultural constraints make a difference in something other than the conventional meaning appropriateness with respect to which they were defined. It might conceivably make a difference in (correspond to?) constructions of culturally institutionalized conventions, in which the arbitrary structures are culturally self-fulfilling, but it could not possibly override in any general sense the basic hypothesis-testing constraints on representations of natural world phenomena.

195. Semantic structuring, clearly, will be present only with respect to those structures in situation images which can be operated on by conventional meanings—for which conventional meanings have developed, both historically and ontogenetically.

Clearly, strict locutions also will have corresponding semantic structurings, but those structurings are not likely to be nearly as complex as the structuring appropriate to a linguistic system.

196. Such processes assume and require that the "containers" or "labels" have independent properties by which they can be identified. Indices and index structures, however, have only functional properties, and functional properties are intrinsically relational. Thus differentiations with relational structures are the only possibilities.

Lenneberg (1967) is correct that (most) words "tag" the cognitive processes by which we deal with the environment, but the only "tags" available are those constituted by functional relationships.

197. Formal languages generally push as close as possible to this limit and, with a little blinking at the facts, might appear to

reach it. What they in fact do, however, is either assume a one-element-type differentiation (one-to-one reference relationships) for every possible representational component, if the ontology is assumed to be infinite, or directly define such a differentiation, if the ontology is finite. In addition, they "flatten" and broaden the context dependencies to the point that the "only" aspect of the contextual situation convention that anything depends on is the potentiality of the (entire) language system.

It is clear that the context dependency is not eliminated, but it might appear that, at least within those contexts, the characterization of the naming relationship as a differentiation is a mere quibble, that if all differentiators differentiate uniquely then it is only vacuously true to call them differentiators. This is true up to a point, but the critical failure of such a system to be what it appears to be is contained in the condition "within those contexts," for it is within the context of the assumptions or definitions of such a language that the naming function of the symbols is assumed, and it is precisely my point that that naming function cannot be computed as an effective procedure except through interactively functional intensions, which can only be specified in terms of functional relations and which, therefore, can only be specified by differentiation and not by direct labeling. There are no strings tied from names to things, and, even if there were, some procedure would have to follow the strings. Reference can only be accomplished by an interactive agent.

In a language in which an infinity of names is defined recursively in terms of finite procedures, for example, numerals or well-formed formulas, it might seem that the naming relationship would be taken care of implicitly. Clearly, however, if the names are taken to reference something external, then again there must be an agent as interpreter. If the names are taken to reference by implicit definition, then the forms of the implicit definitions must themselves be procedures (or interpreted by procedures), and, again, the names have only functional relationships to each other. (Implicit interactive definition is precisely how procedures do define characteristics of the world. The problem of learning is to find functionally useful interactive implicit definitions and relations.)

Finally, if the "names" are taken not as referring to the world but rather as constituting it, as in an uninterpreted formal logic, then they would need no interpretation. But then they themselves become the objects of interaction, and the same problem is simply posed in a more formal framework: symbols and types of symbols must be interactively recognized in their own right. The general point, in fact, first occurred to me when I realized that a Post production rule (Minsky 1967) required a procedure to interpret it and thus to interactively recognize the symbol strings, string types, and contexts with respect to which it is defined. An algorithm presumes an algorist (Shaw and McIntyre 1974).

198. Any transformational scheme must be cofunctional at least in the sense that it apperceives its own effects.

199. Thus, specifications constitute transformations of focus, while updates constitute transformations of structure. Focus, however, is "simply" structure relative to (relevant to) current task definitions, and thus all (incomplete) meanings are fundamentally transformational in a structural sense.

200. Conventional meaning schemes are the only kind of meaning schemes that will be discussed in this book; therefore, "conventional meaning scheme" and "meaning scheme" will be used interchangeably.

201. Such recursiveness cannot yield such trivial computational powers as, for example, unbounded iterations of "very," since it is a recursion of decompositions of complete meanings. The functionality of such recursions is simply that some of the functional relevancies with respect to which a scheme is to be specified could, in isolation, themselves correspond to complete meanings.

202. Selections of subject focus in the situation convention are, in such cases, often in terms of the external manifestations of that which determines such selections nonconventionally, for example, gaze direction can pick out the focus (subject) of comment. As before, note that some such conventions are, in effect, at the level of phylogenesis, and not ontogenesis, and also that such meaning understandings are, strictly, generally computed by implicature by the adult, if with respect to a child.

203. Note that any such element of conventional arbitrariness, no matter how small (and any habitualization will introduce some), will, of necessity, involve a corresponding semantic structuring of appropriate situations.

204. This does not preclude the possibility of ontogenetic reorganization of already constructed meaning schemes; nor does it preclude the false starts and approximations of the hypothesis-testing search procedure by which the linguistic system approaches a fit with the wider linguistic community.

205. Functional linguistic differentiations in ontogeny, for example, Brown (1973), thus provide evidence concerning the progressive development and hierarchical structuring of meaning schemes.

206. Selection and alteration of interactive focus is a functional and fallible aspect of any interactive procedure: it is part of the implicit classification of a situation that is constituted by engaging in one interaction rather than another. Thus, the point made in the text is not specific to meaning schemes. A general scheme for differentiation of focus might be functionally distinguishable within the total sys-

tem but probably not structurally distinguishable. Some schemes, however, may be more specialized with respect to focus than others.

207. Thus, I would contend that the basic sensory-motor organization of language actions is partly a result of ontogenetic origins but is fundamentally a commonality of organization resulting from a commonality of logical constraints on interactive representations. Semiotic extensions (McNeill 1974) are useful precisely because representations of invariant patterns of interaction are useful.

208. Exploration of such semantic organization is the focal concern of, for example, Kintsch (1974), Miller and Johnson-Laird (1976), Shank (1973, 1975), Tulving and Donaldson (1972), and Woods (1975).

209. As Shank (1975) points out, logical adequacy of representations is only a general constraint: functional efficiency is a much more restrictive constraint. The problem, however, is not only to define systems that are logically adequate and functionally efficient but also to understand the constraints of adequacy and efficiency to which those systems must conform. In part, such constraints are contingent upon the particular interaction patterns that the world allows, but, more fundamentally, adequacy and efficiency are both defined and constrained by the underlying tasks of interactive knowing and quasi-evolutionary learning. The organization of world images ultimately must be understood on both levels.

210. As has been argued, the organizational basis for the world and situation images is likely to be the categories of action, object, and actor, with action primary. To this extent, a basic structural constraint is imposed on linguistic systems. An action might conceivably be specified as to abstract type in isolation (for example, "a walk happened"), but in order to be located in a situation image it must be connected with some component with a more stable temporal trajectory, that is, the actor or the affected object of interaction. Thus, there would be two basic meaning-scheme strategies available for the specification of an instance of action: actor-located, exemplified in accusative languages, and object-located, exemplified in ergative languages (Halliday 1970).

Barber (1975) has argued that voice distinctions correspond to differing categories of the possible relationships between actor and affected object, with active-passive and active-middle distinctions constituting two alternative strategies for categorizing the underlying semantic possibilities. His arguments are restricted to accusative languages, but the general point is easily extendable to ergative languages: it would be interesting to see how well it holds up in broader investigations.

211. Within such a tree of constituent meanings, there will be no particular barrier to overlap at the level of lexical items other

than the structurings of available meaning schemes. For example,
if a single representational component of the situation convention
occupies positions in differing constituents of linguistic sequential
decomposition, that component may well not be (fully) specified
lexically in all such constituents, assuming the underlying structure
is nevertheless recoverable by the meaning-scheme apperceptions.
Cases in which sequential specifications intersect themselves seem
to provide much of the complexity of linguistic systems.

Actually, the most relevant intersections seem not to be so
much at the level of the aspects of the situation specified but rather
at the level of the representational procedures by which they are
specified, that is, at the level of types of constituent meanings, and,
considered in those terms, it clearly must be so: constituent semantic meanings are the frameworks for decomposition and lexicalization and not the raw structures-with-the-world which those meanings
represent. For example, if we consider that pronouns activate a contextually (meaning-scheme) identifiable specification procedure, but
that that invoked procedure may or may not function in the same context of specification in which it is initially identified and thus may or
may not result in a representational specification of the same component or aspect of the external situation, then the examples in Partee (1972) do not appear so troublesome. (For example, "John gave
his paycheck to his wife, and Harry gave it to his mistress.")

212. It should be noted that the structuring of a linguistic act
yielded by such a meaning-scheme constituent structuring involves
both part-whole relationships and meaning-dependency relationships.
It thus crosses the boundary between constituent grammars and dependency grammars, thereby lending support, at least in principle,
to similarly integrative grammar attempts, such as that by Hudson
(1976). On the other hand, it is not clear but what any procedural approach to grammar will involve intrinsically both constituent and dependency considerations (for example, Lakoff and Thompson 1975b).

213. Such implicitly defined categories constitute an implicit
structural (semantic) characteristic of the linguistic situation convention. Such implicit characteristics can only become explicit for the
system insofar as that system can represent the situation from a
higher level of ontological reflexivity. Within such an encompassing
perspective, characteristics that can only be implicit in the lower
level of egocentrism can become explicitly represented as characteristics of that lower level and thus, perhaps, serve to reorganize the
lower-level structures in terms of their implicit characteristics.
Implicit semantic categories of differentiations of conventional meaning might, for example, become organized as explicit categories of
positional (syntactic) function (Bowerman 1973). Such a movement
up the levels of ontological reflexivity would constitute a corresponding
movement up the levels of knowing (Bickhard 1978, in press).

214. Such decompositional structuring and coordination clearly must extend downward to the minimal level of incomplete meanings, but it must also extend upward to the decomposition and coordination of complex meanings into component but nevertheless complete meanings. Coordination within complete meanings yields sentential cohesion; coordination of complete meanings within complex meanings yields textual cohesion (Halliday and Hasan 1976).

Textual cohesion and discourse cohesion are clearly related, but discourse cohesion can be approached in a more piece-wise fashion, with the situation convention at the end of each discourse turn serving as the context for the text of the next turn. Textual cohesion could be similarly analyzed with respect to the situation conventions yielded by each utterance as contexts for the next (and at the end of each lexical item as contexts for the next, in the case of sentential cohesion), but the sequencing of such acts of situation convention updating must, to some extent, be planned as a whole, and, to that extent, is not adequately piece-wise analyzable. It is clear that, even at the level of discourse, there will be preplanned constraints within the goal definitions of (some) participants upon the potential contents and sequencings of discourse, and thus a strictly piece-wise analysis must be modified in these cases as well. Fundamentally, a piece-wise analysis is in terms of alternating sequences of situation conventions and acts, while a thorough analysis must be in terms of situation convention trajectories and strategies.

215. Such coordinations are themselves characteristics of meaning scheme constituent structurings and thus may themselves yield constituent categories, that is, may yield categories more dependent on the particular decompositional coordination involved than on the constituent within which the decomposition is taking place. Constituent categories, therefore, may be specified with respect to position relations in the linguistic act as well as with respect to incomplete meaning specification.

216. Limitations of computational practice would include absolute limitations on computational potentiality as well as limitations on computational time and efficiency within real-time situations.

217. The existence of parallel channels implies that the structuring of linguistic acts is not necessarily strictly sequential. The utilization of parallel channels would probably be most informative and least likely to be redundant with respect to indications of higher-level meaning-scheme corrdination choices rather than lower-level lexical meanings or with respect to metacommunications that are not strictly part of the linguistic utterance at all.

218. The relevances of such coordination alternatives will be in terms of the structures, likelihoods, and desirabilities of particular apperceptive derivations that might be made from them. Poten-

tially relevant characteristics will include indirect indication of utterer's prior knowledge, presupposition, task orientation, or valuation, and so forth (whether truly or falsely) as well as potential effects on similar characteristics of the states of the audience.

219. The existence of felt meanings (Gendlin 1962) with respect to which or out of which utterances are produced essentially indicates that, whether or not goal meanings are semantically structured, they are not in general lexically structured.

220. Just as there may at times be choices among alternative constituent structurings, so may there also be choices between direct lexicalization and further subdivision.

221. Note that this model involves a consistent conceptualization of knowledge as procedural (for example, Hewitt 1971, Winograd 1972, 1973): the basic knowledge of the world image is procedural, as are that part of the world image specialized for situation conventions and that part of the world image specialized for linguistic situation conventions.

222. It should be noted that both the productions of such constituent structurings and their understandings are products of the context-dependent executions of procedures. In particular, meaning-scheme coordinations and lexical specifications both function in terms of context-dependent partial descriptions of the structures and processes to be coordinated and specified. Thus, they may yield usefully context-dependent consequences, even if with some variation across contexts, and, by virtue of their applicability across those contexts, may serve to functionally organize them.

Such functional context generalizability seems to underlie metaphor at the level of specifications (Bobrow and Norman 1975) and squishes at the level of constituent coordinations (Ross 1972, Lakoff 1973). (The basic orientation of Ross' squishes from verb to noun may correspond to a basic gradient of constituent categories from predicate specifications to subject specifications. Such kinds of specification will become mixed as iterations of subdifferentiations proceed.) Hedges (Lakoff 1972b) would seem to be subspecifications within standard representational procedures of the salient aspects of the procedures in a given context. Such phenomena should provide constraints on the functioning of such context-dependent descriptions.

223. It is clear from the existence of false starts that linguistic systems do not function algorithmically. It is not clear whether or not the general linguistic system problem is capable of algorithmic solution. Grammars, however, traditionally have implicitly assumed that the relationship between sound and meaning was in principle algorithmically computable. Exceptions have appeared recently in approaches to grammar that acknowledge the necessity of procedural considerations and thus, implicitly at least, acknowledge the possi-

bility of relationships computable only heuristically (Lakoff and Thompson 1975a, 1975b). Thus far, however, the question of algorithmicness has not been addressed directly.

224. An ultimate logical source of the functional productivity of linguistic systems may be the ontological reflexivity of situation conventions. It is because of this reflexivity that a language can serve as its own metalanguage and thus can, in principle, modify and improve itself with respect to new functional requirements.

225. Dummett (1976), for example, traces a structure of arguments that lead from a simple encoding conceptualization of meaning (direct reference as meaning) to a truth condition conceptualization, to a verificationist approach, to a falsificationist approach, each step coming closer to interactive implicit definitions. But the entire discussion proceeds within an assumption that the meaning of an utterance is somehow its representational power. No distinction such as that between conventional meaning and an occasion meaning is made.

226. What is sometimes discussed as "what a person says in a favored sense" (Grice 1975), to be distinguished from implicatures "proper," would seem to correspond to the occasion meaning appropriate to the highest-level language game in which it can occur, to the most decontextualized occasion meaning. Grice's generalized conversational implicatures perhaps correspond to the additions to the occasion meaning obtained from moving to the highest-level de-fault language game, to the corresponding decontextualized occasion meaning.

227. An explication of goal definitions within the perspective of interactive knowing involves quite a number of fundamental issues. For example, it must be clarified how indices that influence processing control flow can constitute situational representations, especially when the state of affairs represented does not (yet) exist; the relationship between goal representations and representations of already existing situational states of affairs must be established; and the difference between goal instructions and other kinds of instructions must be understood. In general, goal definitions constitute an intersection of many issues of interactive knowing.

228. Increased structural specification through increased functional specification, that is, the approach to structure through function, is inevitable in any black box systems analysis. In this regard, it should be noted that abstract machine theory is itself a (set of) formalism(s) for functional structures.

229. Note that (homeostatic) goal maintenance can be taken as a special (continuous) case of goal attainment.

BIBLIOGRAPHY

Ajdukiewicz, K. 1967. "Syntactic Connexion." In Polish Logic, edited by S. McCall. London: Oxford University Press.

Anscombe, B.E.M. 1957. Intention. Ithaca, N.Y.: Cornell University Press.

Atkinson, M. 1979. "Prerequisites for Reference." In Developmental Pragmatics, edited by E. Ochs and B. Schieffelin. New York: Academic Press.

Austin, J.L. 1962. How to Do Things with Words. New York: Oxford University Press.

Bach, K., and Harnish, R.M. 1979. Linguistic Communication and Speech Acts. Cambridge, Mass.: M.I.T. Press.

Barber, E. 1975. "Voice: Beyond the Passive." In Proceedings of the First Annual Meeting of the Berkeley Linguistics Society, edited by C. Cogen et al. Berkeley, Calif.: Berkeley Linguistics Society.

Bates, E. 1979. "The Emergence of Symbols: Ontogeny and Phylogeny." In Children's Language and Communication, edited by W.A. Collins. Hillsdale, N.J.: Erlbaum.

_____. 1976. Language and Context. New York: Academic Press.

_____. et al. 1977. "From Gesture to First Word: On Cognitive and Social Prerequisites." In Interaction, Conversation, and the Development of Language. Edited by M. Lewis and L. Rosenblum. New York: Wiley.

Bateson, G. 1972. Steps to an Ecology of Mind. New York: Ballantine.

Beauchamp, T.C. 1974. Philosophical Problems of Causation. Encino, Calif.: Dickenson.

Bennett, J. 1976. Linguistic Behavior. London: Cambridge University Press.

_____ 1973. "The Meaning-Nominalist Strategy." Foundations of Language 10; 141-68.

Berger, P.L., and Luckmann, T. 1966. The Social Construction of Reality. New York: Doubleday.

Bernstein, R.J. 1971. Praxis and Action. Philadelphia: University of Pennsylvania Press.

Bickhard, M.H. (in press). "A Model of Developmental and Psychological Processes." Genetic Psychology Monographs.

_____. 1978. "The Nature of Developmental Stages." Human Development 21; 217-33.

_____. 1979. "On Necessary and Specific Capabilities in Evolution and Development." Human Development, 22; 217-24.

Binkley, R.; Bronaugh, R.; and Marras, A., eds., 1971. Agent, Action, and Reason. Toronto: University of Toronto Press.

Birkhoff, G. 1967. Lattice Theory. Providence, R.I.: American Mathematical Society.

Bobrow, D.G., and Norman, D. 1975. "Some Principles of Memory Schemata." In Representation and Understanding, edited by D.G. Bobrow and A. Collins. New York: Academic Press.

Boer, S., and Lycan, W. 1976. The Myth of Semantic Presupposition. Bloomington: Indiana University Linguistics Club.

Boolos, G.S., and Jeffry, R.C. 1974. Computability and Logic. London: Cambridge University Press.

Borger, R., and Cioffi, F., eds. 1970. Explanation in the Behavioral Sciences. London: Cambridge University Press.

Bowerman, M. 1973. "Structural Relationships in Children's Utterances: Syntactic or Semantic?" In Cognitive Development and the Acquisition of Language, edited by T.E. Moore. New York: Academic Press.

Brainerd, W.S., and Landweber, L.H. 1974. Theory of Computation. New York: Wiley.

Brown, R. 1973. A First Language. Cambridge: Harvard University Press.

Brown, S.C., ed. 1974. Philosophy of Psychology. New York: Barnes.

Bruner, J.S. 1975a. "From Communication to Language: A Psychological Perspective." Cognition 3(3); 255-87.

_____. 1975b. "The Ontogenesis of Speech Acts." Journal of Child Language 2; 1-19.

_____. Jolly, A.; and Sylva, K. 1976. Play: Its Role in Evolution and Development. New York: Basic Books.

_____. et al. 1966. Studies in Cognitive Growth. New York: Wiley.

Bullowa, M., ed. 1979. Before Speech. London: Cambridge University Press.

Bunge, M. 1963. Causality. New York: World.

Campbell, D.T. 1974. "Evolutionary Epistemology. In The Philosophy of Karl Popper, edited by P.A. Schilpp. LaSalle, Ill.: Open Court.

Carroll, J.M., and Tanenhaus, M.K. 1975. "Prolegomena to a Functional Theory of Word Formation." In Papers from the Parasession on Functionalism, edited by R. Grossman; J. San; and T. Vance. Chicago: Chicago Linguistic Society.

Chafe, W.L. 1970. Meaning and the Structure of Language. Chicago: University of Chicago Press.

Chihars, C.S., and Fodor, J.A. 1966. "Operationalism and Ordinary Language." In Wittgenstein: The Philosophical Investigations, edited by G. Pitcher. Garden City, N.Y.: Doubleday.

Chomsky, N. 1965. Aspects of the Theory of Syntax. Cambridge, Mass.: M.I.T. Press.

Cicourel, A. 1974. Cognitive Sociology. New York: Macmillan.

Connolly, K.J., and Bruner, J.S., eds. 1974. The Growth of Competence. New York: Academic Press.

Copleston, F. 1962. A History of Philosophy. New York: Doubleday.

Cresswell, M.J. 1973. Logic and Languages. London: Methuen.

Dale, P. S. 1976. Language Development: Structure and Function. 2nd ed. New York: Holt, Rinehart and Winston.

Davidson, D. 1971. "Truth and Meaning." In Readings in the Philosophy of Language, edited by J.F. Rosenberg and C. Travis. Englewood Cliffs, N.J.: Prentice-Hall.

Dennett, D. 1978. "Why the Law of Effect Will Not Go Away." In Brainstorms, edited by D. Dennett. Bradford Books.

Denzin, N.K. 1977. Childhood Socialization. San Francisco: Jossey-Bass.

Derwing, B.L. 1973. Transformational Grammar as a Theory of Language Acquisition. London: Cambridge University Press.

Dik, S.C. 1978. Functional Grammar. Amsterdam: North Holland.

Dixon, R. 1979. "Ergativity." Language 55(1); 59–138.

Donnellan, K. 1971. "Reference and Definite Descriptions." In Semantics, edited by D. Steinberg and L. Jakobovits. London: Cambridge University Press.

Dore, J. 1975. "Holophrases, Speech Acts and Language Universals." Journal of Child Language 2; 21–40.

Dummett, M. 1976. "What is a Theory of Meaning? (II)." In Truth and Meaning, edited by G. Evans and J. McDowell. London: Oxford University Press.

_____. 1973. Frege: Philosophy of Language. New York: Harper & Row.

Ervin-Tripps, S., and Mitchell-Kernan, C. 1977. Child Discourse. New York: Academic Press.

Evans, G., and McDowell, J., eds. 1976. Truth and Meaning. London: Oxford University Press.

Ferguson, T.S. 1967. Mathematical Statistics. New York: Academic Press.

Fillmore, C.J. 1968. "The Case for Case." In Universals in Linguistic Theory, edited by E. Bach and E. Harmes. New York: Holt, Rinehart and Winston.

Fodor, J.A. 1968. Psychological Explanation. New York: Random House.

Freedman, D.G. 1974. Human Infancy. New York: Wiley.

Freud, S. 1963. "Instincts and Their Vicissitudes (1915)." In General Psychological Theory, edited by P. Rieff. New York: Collier.

Furth, H.G. 1969. Piaget and Knowledge. Englewood Cliffs, N.J.: Prentice-Hall.

Gazdar, G. 1979. Pragmatics. New York: Academic Press.

Geach, P. 1972. "A Program for Syntax." In Semantics of Natural Language, edited by D. Davidson and G. Harman. Dordrecht, Holland: Reidel.

Gendlin, E.T. 1980. "A Process Model." Unpublished.

____. 1962. Experiencing and the Creation of Meaning. New York: Free Press.

____. 1978. Focusing. New York: Everest House.

____. 1970. "A Theory of Personality Change." In New Directions in Client-Centered Therapy, edited by J.T. Hart and T.M. Tomlinson. Boston: Houghton Mifflin.

____. 1973. "Experiential Phenomenology." In Phenomenology and the Social Sciences, edited by M. Natanson. Evanston, Ill.: Northwestern University Press.

Gibson, J.J. 1979. The Ecological Approach to Visual Perception. Boston: Houghton Mifflin.

____. 1966. The Senses Considered as Perceptual Systems. Boston: Houghton Mifflin.

Ginzburg, A. 1968. Algebraic Theory of Automata. New York: Academic Press.

Gleason, J., and Weintraub, S. 1978. "Input Language and the Acquisition of Communicative Competence." In Children's Language, edited by K.E. Nelson. vol. 1. New York: Gardner Press.

Goffman, E. 1974. Frame Analysis. Cambridge: Harvard University Press.

_____. 1959. The Presentation of the Self in Everyday Life. New York: Doubleday.

_____. 1969. Strategic Interaction. New York: Ballantine.

Goldman, A.I. 1970. Human Action. Englewood Cliffs, N.J.: Prentice-Hall.

Graeser, A. 1978. "The Stoic Theory of Meaning." In The Stoics, edited by J. M. Rist. Berkeley: University of California Press.

Greenfield, P.M. 1978. "Structural Parallels Between Language and Action in Development." In Action, Gesture and Symbol, edited by A. Lock. New York: Academic Press.

Grice, H.P. 1975. "Logic and Conversation." In Syntax and Semantics. Vol. III: Speech Acts, edited by P. Cole and J.L. Morgan. New York: Academic Press.

_____. 1967. "Meaning." In Philosophical Logic, edited by P.F. Strawson. London: Oxford University Press.

_____. 1971. "Utterer's Meaning, Sentence Meaning, and Word Meaning." In The Philosophy of Language, edited by J.R. Searle. London: Oxford University Press.

_____. 1969. "Utterer's Meaning and Intentions." Philosophical Review 78; 147-77.

Gumperz, J.J., and Hymes, D. 1972. Directions in Sociolinguistics. New York: Holt.

Halliday, M. 1978. Language as Social Semiotic. Baltimore, Md.: University Park Press.

_____. 1970. "Language Structure and Language Function." In New Hori-
  zons in Linguistics, edited by J. Lyons. Baltimore, Md.: Penguin.

Halliday, M. and Hason, R. 1976. Cohesion in English. London: Longman.

Harman, G.H. 1971. "Three Levels of Meaning." In Semantics,
  edited by D.D. Steinberg and L.A. Jakobovits. London:
  Cambridge University Press.

Heidegger, M. 1962. Being and Time. New York: Harper & Row.

Hewitt, C. 1971. "Procedural Embedding of Knowledge in Planner.
  International Joint Conference on Artificial Intelligence (IJCAI2).

Hinde, R.A. 1970. Animal Behavior. New York: McGraw-Hill.

Hintikka, J. 1969. Models for Modalities. Dordrecht, Holland:
  Reidel.

_____. 1962. Knowledge and Belief. Ithaca, N.Y.: Cornell University
  Press.

Hopcroft, J.E., and Ullman, J.D. 1969. Formal Languages and
  Their Relation to Automata. Reading, Mass.: Addison-Wesley.

Hudson, R.A. 1976. Arguments for a Non-Transformational
  Grammar. Chicago: University of Chicago Press.

Hughes, G.E., and Cresswell, M.J. 1968. An Introduction to
  Modal Logic. London: Methuen.

Husserl, E. 1969. Formal and Transcendental Logic. The Hague:
  Martinus Nijhoff.

Kant, I. 1965. Critique of Pure Reason. New York: St. Martin's
  Press.

Karttunen, L., and Peters, S. 1979. "Conventional Implicature."
  In Syntax and Semantics. Vol. II: Presupposition, edited by
  C. Oh and D. Dinneen. New York: Academic Press.

Katz, J.J., and Fodor, J.A. 1971. "The Structure of a Semantic
  Theory." In Readings in the Philosophy of Language, edited by
  J.F. Rosenberg and C. Travis. Englewood Cliffs, N.J.:
  Prentice-Hall.

Keenan, E.O. 1979. "On the Universality of Conversational Implicatures." Language in Society 5 (1976): 67-80, as cited in

G. Gazdar. Pragmatics. New York: Academic Press.

Kempson, R.M. 1975. Presupposition and the Delimitation of Semantics. London: Cambridge University Press.

Kenny, A. 1973. Wittgenstein. Cambridge: Harvard University Press.

Kintsch, W. 1974. The Representation of Meaning in Memory. New York: Wiley.

Knapp, M.L. 1972. Nonverbal Communication in Human Interaction. New York: Holt.

Kripke, S.A. 1972. "Naming and Necessity." In Semantics of Natural Language, edited by D. Davidson and G. Harman. Dordrecht, Holland: Reidel.

Kuipers, B.J. 1975. "A Frame for Frames." In Representation and Understanding, edited by D.G. Bobrow and A. Collins. New York: Academic Press.

Kwant, R.C. 1965. Phenomenology of Language. Pittsburgh: Duquesne University Press.

Lakoff, G. 1973. "Fuzzy Grammar and the Performance/Competence Terminology Game." In Papers from the Ninth Regional Meeting of the Chicago Linguistic Society, edited by C. Corum et al. Chicago: Chicago Linguistic Society.

_____. 1972a. "Linguistics and Natural Logic." In Semantics of Natural Language, edited by D. Davidson and G. Harman. Dordrecht, Holland: Reidel.

_____. 1972b. "Hedges." In Papers from the Eighth Regional Meeting of the Chicago Linguistic Society, edited by P. Peranteau et al. Chicago: Chicago Linguistic Society.

_____. and Thompson, H. 1975a. "Dative Questions in Cognitive Grammar." In Functionalism, edited by R. Grossman; L. San; and T. Vance. Chicago: Chicago Linguistic Society.

_____. 1975b. "Introducing Cognitive Grammar." In Proceedings of the First Annual Meeting of the Berkeley Linguistics Society, edited by C. Cogen et al. Berkeley, Calif: Berkeley Linguistics Society.

Lanigan, R. L. 1977. Speech Act Phenomenology. The Hague: Martinus Nijhoff.

Lenneberg, E.H. 1967. Biological Foundations of Language. New York: Wiley.

Lewis, D. 1975. "Languages and Language." In Language, Mind, and Knowledge, edited by K. Gunderson. Minneapolis: University of Minnesota Press.

____. 1972. "General Semantics." In Semantics of Natural Language, edited by D. Davidson and G. Harman. Dordrecht, Holland: Reidel.

____. 1969. Convention: A Philosophical Study. Cambridge: Harvard University Press.

Lewis, M., and Rosenblum, L., eds. 1977. Interaction, Conversation, and the Development of Language. New York: Wiley.

Lightner, T.M. 1976. Review of Goals of Linguistic Theory, edited by S. Peters. Language 52; 179-220

Linsky, L. 1971. "Reference and Referents." In Semantics, edited by D. Steinberg and L. Jakobovits. London: Cambridge University Press.

Lock, A., ed. 1978. Action, Gesture and Symbol. New York: Academic Press.

Luce, R.D., and Raiffa, H. 1957. Games and Decisions. New York: Wiley.

Lyons, J. 1977. Semantics. London: Cambridge University Press.

Mackie, J.L. 1974. The Cement of the Universe. London: Oxford University Press.

Marler, P., and Hamilton, W.J. 1966. Mechanisms of Animal Behavior. New York: Wiley.

Marvin, R.S. 1977. "An Ethological-Cognitive Model for the

Attenuation of Mother-Child Attachment Behavior." In <u>Attach-ment Behavior</u>, edited by T.Alloway, P. Pliner, and L. K. Rames. New York: Plenum.

McCawley, J.D. 1976. "Some Ideas Not to Live By." <u>Die Neueren Sprachen</u>. Vol. 2. Frankfurt am Main; Verlag Moritz Diesterweg.

____. 1974. "James McCawley." In <u>Discussing Language</u>, edited by H. Parret. The Hague: Mouton.

____. 1972. "A Program for Logic." In <u>Semantics of Natural Language</u>, edited by D. Davidson and G. Harman. Dordrecht, Holland: Reidel.

____. 1971. "Where Do Noun Phrases Come From?" In <u>Semantics</u>, edited by D. D. Steinberg and L. A. Jakobovits. London: Cambridge University Press.

McHugh, P. 1968. <u>Defining the Situation</u>. New York: Bobbs-Merrill.

McNeill, D. 1974. "Semiotic Extension." Paper presented at the Loyola Symposium on Cognition, Chicago.

____. 1970. <u>The Acquisition of Language</u>. New York: Harper & Row.

Mehan, H., and Wood, H. 1975. <u>The Reality of Ethnomethodology</u>. New York: Wiley.

Mehta, J. L. 1976. <u>Martin Heidegger: The Way and the Vision</u>. Honolulu: University of Hawaii Press.

Merleau-Ponty, M. 1973. <u>Consciousness and the Acquisition of Language</u>. Evanston, Ill.: Northwestern University Press.

____. 1962. <u>Phenomenology of Perception</u>. New York: Humanities Press.

____. 1968. <u>The Visible and the Invisible</u>. Evanston, Ill.: Northwestern University Press.

Miller, G.A.; Galanter, E.; and Pribram, K.H. 1960. <u>Plans and the Structure of Behavior</u>. New York: Holt, Rinehart and Winston.

Miller, G. A., and Johnson-Laird, P. N. 1976. Language and Perception. Cambridge: Harvard University Press.

Minsky, M. 1975. "A Framework for Representing Knowledge." In The Psychology of Computer Vision, edited by P. Winston. New York: McGraw-Hill.

____. 1967. Computation. Englewood Cliffs, N.J.: Prentice-Hall.

Montague, R. 1972. "Pragmatics and Intensional Logic." In Semantics of Natural Language, edited by D. Davidson and G. Harman. Dordrecht, Holland: Reidel.

Morris, G. 1970. Foundations of the Theory of Signs. Chicago: University of Chicago Press.

____. 1964. Signification and Significance. Cambridge, Mass.: M.I.T. Press.

Neisser, U. 1976. Cognition and Reality. San Francisco: Freeman.

____. 1967. Cognitive Psychology. New York: Appleton-Century-Crofts.

Nelson, K. 1979. "Explorations in the Development of a Functional Semantic System." In Children's Language and Communication, edited by W.A. Collins. Hillsdale, N.J.: Erlbaum.

____. 1973. "Structure and Strategy in Learning to Talk." Society for Research in Child Development Monographs, serial no. 149, 38(1-2).

____. 1978. "Semantic Development and the Development of Semantic Memory." In Children's Language, edited by K.E. Nelson. vol. 1. New York: Gardner Press.

Nelson, K.E., and Nelson, K. 1978. "Cognitive Pendulums and Their Linguistic Realization." In Children's Language, edited by K.E. Nelson. vol. 1. New York: Gardner Press.

Ochs, E. 1979. "Introduction: What Child Language Can Contribute to Pragmatics." In Developmental Pragmatics, edited by E. Ochs and B. Schieffelin. New York: Academic Press.

____. and Schieffelin, B., eds. 1979. Developmental Pragmatics.

New York: Academic Press.

Partee, B. 1972. "Opacity, Coreference, and Pronouns." In Semantics of Natural Language, edited by D. Davidson and G. Harman. Dordrecht, Holland: Reidel.

Peirce, C.S. 1972. Charles S. Peirce: The Essential Writings, edited by E.C. Moore. New York: Harper & Row.

Peters, S., ed. 1972. Goals of Linguistic Theory. Englewood Cliffs, N.J.: Prentice-Hall.

Piaget, J. 1978. Success and Understanding. Cambridge: Harvard University Press.

____. 1954. The Construction of Reality in the Child. New York: Basic.

____. 1962. Play, Dreams, and Imitation in Childhood. New York: Norton.

____. 1969. The Mechanisms of Perception. New York: Basic.

____. 1971. Biology and Knowledge. Chicago: University of Chicago Press.

____. 1976. The Grasp of Consciousness. Cambridge: Harvard University Press.

____. and Inhelder, B. 1971. Mental Imagery in the Child. New York: Basic.

____. 1967. The Child's Conception of Space. New York: Norton.

____. 1969. The Psychology of the Child. New York: Basic.

Popper, K.R. 1965. Conjectures and Refutations. New York: Harper & Row.

____. 1959. The Logic of Scientific Discovery. New York: Harper & Row.

Rescher, N. 1973. Conceptual Idealism. Oxford: Blackwell.

____, ed. 1967. The Logic of Decision and Action. Pittsburgh: University of Pittsburgh Press.

___ and Urquhart, A. 1971. Temporal Logic. New York: Springer.

Richie, D.M. et al. 1980. "Gibson's Theory and Metatheory: An Appreciation and Critique." Unpublished.

Rogers, H., Jr. 1967. Theory of Recursive Functions and Effective Computability. New York: McGraw-Hill.

Ross, J.R. 1972. "The Category Squish." In Papers from the Eighth Regional Meeting of the Chicago Linguistic Society, edited by P. Peranteau et al. Chicago: Chicago Linguistic Society.

Ryvave, A.L., and Schenkein, J.N. 1974. "Notes on the Art of Walking." In Ethnomethodology, edited by R. Turner. Baltimore, Md.: Penguin.

Sacerdoti, E.D. 1977. A Structure for Plans and Behavior. New York: Elsevier.

Scheffler, I. 1974. Four Pragmatists. New York: Humanities Press.

Scheflen, A.E. 1974. How Behavior Means. Garden City, N.Y.: Doubleday/Anchor.

Schelling, T.C. 1963. The Strategy of Conflict. New York: Oxford University Press.

Schiffer, S.R. 1972. Meaning. London: Oxford University Press.

Scott, D. 1970. "Advice on Modal Logic." In Philosophical Problems in Logic, edited by K. Lambert. New York: Humanities Press.

Searle, J.R. 1975a. "Indirect Speech Acts." In Syntax and Semantics. Vol. III: Speech Acts, edited by P. Cole and J.L. Morgan. New York: Academic Press.

___ 1975b. "A Taxonomy of Illocutionary Acts." In Language, Mind, and Knowledge, edited by K. Gunderson. Minneapolis: University of Minnesota Press.

___. 1969. Speech Acts. London: Cambridge University Press.

_____. 1971. "Austin on Locutionary and Illocutionary Acts." In Readings in the Philosophy of Language, edited by J. Rosenberg and C. Travis. Englewood Cliffs, N.J.: Prentice-Hall.

_____. 1972. "What Is a Speech Act?" In Language and Social Context, edited by P. Giglioli. New York: Penguin.

Shaffer, J.A. 1968. Philosophy of Mind. Englewood Cliffs, N.J.: Prentice-Hall.

Shank, R.C. 1975. "The Structure of Episodes in Memory." In Representation and Understanding, edited by D.G. Bobrow and A. Collins. New York: Academic Press.

_____. 1973. "Identification of Conceptualizations Underlying Natural Language." In Computer Models of Thought and Language, edited by R.C. Shank and K.M. Colby. San Francisco: Freeman.

Shaw, R., and McIntyre, M. 1974. "Algoristic Foundations to Cognitive Psychology." In Cognition and the Symbolic Processes, edited by W. Weimer and P. Palermo. New York: Wiley.

Shwayder, D.S. 1965. The Stratification of Behavior. New York: Routledge.

Silverstein, M. 1976. "Shifters, Linguistic Categories, and Cultural Description." In Meaning in Anthropology, edited by K. Basso and H. Selby. Albuquerque: University of New Mexico Press.

_____. 1975. "Linguistics and Anthropology." In Linguistics and Neighboring Disciplines, edited by R. Bartsch and T. Venneman. Amsterdam: North Holland.

Simon, H.A. 1969. The Sciences of the Artificial. Cambridge, Mass: M.I.T. Press.

Sosa, E. 1975. Causation and Conditionals. London: Oxford University Press.

Spiegel, J.P., and Machotka, P. 1974. Messages of the Body. New York: Free Press.

Spiegelberg, H. 1971. The Phenomenological Movement. Vol. 1. The Hague: Martinus Nijhoff.

Strawson, P.F. 1974. Subject and Predicate in Logic and Grammar. London: Methuen.

____. 1971. "On Referring." In Logico-Linguistic Papers, edited by P. F. Strawson. London: Methuen.

Taylor, R. 1966. Action and Purpose. Englewood Cliffs, N.J.: Prentice-Hall.

Thomas, W. I. 1967. "The Definition of the Situation." In Symbolic Interaction, edited by J. G. Manis and B. N. Meltzer. Boston: Allyn & Bacon.

Thomason, R. 1974. Formal Philosophy. New Haven: Yale University Press.

Tulving, E. 1972. "Episodic and Semantic Memory." In Organization of Memory, edited by E. Tulving and W. Donaldson. New York: Academic Press.

____. and Donaldson, W., eds. 1972. Organization of Memory. New York: Academic Press.

Turner, J.H. 1974. The Structure of Sociological Theory. Homewood, Ill.: Dorsey.

Turner, R. 1974. "Words, Utterances and Activities." In Ethnomethodology, edited by R. Turner. Baltimore, Md.: Penguin.

____, ed. 1974. Ethnomethodology. Baltimore, Md.: Penguin.

Von Neumann, J., and Morgenstern, O. 1944. Theory of Games and Economic Behavior. New York: Wiley.

Von Wright, G. 1974. Causality and Determinism. New York: Columbia University Press.

Wertsch, J.V. 1977. "Metacognition and Adult-Child Interaction." Unpublished.

White, A.R. 1968. The Philosophy of Action. London: Oxford University Press.

Wiggins, D. 1967. Identity and Spatio-Temporal Continuity. Oxford: Basil Blackwell.

Wimsatt, W. 1972. "Teleology and the Logical Structure of Function Statements." Studies of the History of Philosophy and Science 3; 1-80.

Winograd, T. 1975. "Frame Representations and the Declarative-Procedural Controversy." In Representation and Understanding, edited by D.G. Bobrow and A. Collins.

_____. 1973. "A Procedural Model of Language Understanding." In Computer Models of Thought and Language, edited by R.C. Shank and K.M. Colby. San Francisco: Freeman.

_____. 1972. Understanding Natural Language. New York: Academic Press.

Winston, P. 1974. New Progress in Artificial Intelligence. AI-TR-310. Cambridge, Mass.: M.I.T. Artificial Intelligence Laboratory.

Wittgenstein, L. 1961. Tractatus Logico-Philosophicus. New York: Routledge and Kegan Paul.

_____. 1958. Philosophical Investigations. New York: Macmillan.

Woods, W.A. 1975. "What's in a Link: Foundations for Semantic Networks." In Representation and Understanding, edited by D.G. Bobrow and A. Collins. New York: Academic Press.

Yngve, V.H. 1976. Personal Communication.

_____.1974. "The Dilemma of Contemporary Linguistics." In The First Lacus Forum, edited by A. Makkai and Y.B. Makkai. Columbia, S.C.: Hornbeam.

_____. 1975. "Human Linguistics and Face-to-Face Interaction." In Organization of Face-to-Face Interaction, edited by A. Kendon, R. Harris, and M. Key. The Hague: Mouton.

Yu, P. 1979. "On the Gricean Program about Meaning." Linguistics and Philosophy 3(2); 273-88.

INDEX

NAME INDEX

77
VonWright (1974), 201

Wertsch (1977), 175
White (1968), 201
Whorf, 225
Wiggins (1967), 60
Wimsatt (1973), 202
Winograd (1972), 13, 231
Winograd (1973), 13, 231
Winograd (1975), 12, 198

Winston (1974), 200
Wittgenstein, 41, 42, 167, 168
Wittgenstein (1958), 12, 41, 42
Wittgenstein (1961), 10, 41, 160, 214
Woods (1975), 228

Yngve (1976), 196
Yngve (1974), 11, 196
Yngve (1975), 11, 196
Yu (1979), 87

apperceptive procedure(s), 138, 139, 141-42, 144; convention-alized, 143, 144; transformation of a situation image by, 144

apperceptive process(es), 45, 49-50, 109, 137, 138, 155, 169, 198(fn 19); construction of the situation image, 48; as transformation of a situation image, 169-70

apperceptive products, 139, 140, 141

apperceptive selection, 150, 155

apperceptive semantic structural types, 151

apperceptive significance, 81, 91, 115, 116, 117, 118, 215(fn 144)

apperceptive structures, 66, 67, 69, 71, 82, 111, 117, 121, 142, 183

apperceptive transformation, 140, 150

artificial intelligence, 12, 13

audience, 80, 81, 87, 90, 127, 130, 194, 195, 196, 217(fn 157); specification, 127

automata theory, 135; deficiency of, 187

automaton(a), 45, 185, 186; end (final) state(s) of, 186, 187, 188, 198(fn 16); formalization, 186; initial (start) state(s) of, 187; process rules, 185-86; process structure, 186

autonomous point, 177, 178

autonomy, levels of, 102-3

behavioristic approach, Bennett, 162

British Empiricism, 10

boundary condition(s), 177, 179, 181; of productive decomposition, 181; for reference, 179

care, 171

category(ies), 200(fn 34, 35)

category grammar, 163

causality, 201(fn 40)

characterization(s), 79, 116, 117, 121, 125, 127, 146, 147; problems, 67, 68, 69, 75, 203(fn 54) (interpersonal, 203[fn 54], 204 [fn 60]); situation image component, 147

causal potentialities, 139

cofunctional(ity), 56, 57, 140, 153, 140(fn 190); of conventional meanings, 140

cognition, 12, 32, 33, 37, 63, 88, 98, 112, 183, 184

cognitive capability(ies), 98, 99, 216(fn 148)

cognitive systems, 209(fn 88)

cognitive development, 32

communication, 3, 4, 5, 9, 13, 14, 15, 37, 79, 89, 90, 98, 102, 113, 114, 115, 116, 117, 118, 119, 121, 123, 137, 142, 156, 161, 179, 182, 183, 184, 192, 207(fn 78), 209(fn 94), 216(fn 139, 140, 142, 143), 216(fn 148), 218(fn 158); act, 38, 98; action types, 157-58; apparent impossibility of decomposition of, 121; closed, 116; complete, 116; computation of significance of, 114; and constituents of the significance, 116; constraints on nature and form of, 116; decompositions of, 115, 116, 117, 118, 119, 121; early, 181; effective, 114; as encoded transmission, 13; epiphenomenal demand, 178; as form of interaction, 161; fulfilled, 79, 80, 157; goal, 79, 80, 115, 215(fn 140); Heidegger's conception of, 171; and illocutions, 120; interactively functional, 181; models of, 7-42,

254

197(fn 3); perception of as an utterance, 123; potential for decomposition, 113; as prelocutionary act, 89; significance of, 113-14, 115, 116; systems, 64; successful, 115; transformation models of, 5, 9, 12, 13, 14, 15, 17, 21, 22, 28, 29, 30, 31, 32, 39, 41, 42, 86, 87, 159, 197(fn 9, 11); transformation models: criticism of, 28-29; logical consequences of, 34-39; and Witt - genstein, 41-42; from transformation perspective, 34, 35, 36, 37, 38, 39, 42, 159; transmission models of, 5, 9, 10, 11, 13, 14, 15, 16, 17, 21, 22, 28, 29, 30, 31, 35, 39, 42, 86, 87, 159, 160, 161, 168, 179 (criticism of, 17, 21-22; description, 10-11; intuitive appeal of, 159; and Wittengenstein, 41); types of, 79

communication action systems, 82, 157, 168-69

complete communication, 79, 80

competence, 212(fn 117, 118)

complete meaning (see meaning)

complete utterance, 82, 84, 85, 131, 132, 153

compositional structuring, 151, 163

computational dependence, 133-34

computational power, 132, 134, 221(fn 175), 222(fn 179, 180)

computation, apperceptive (see apperceptive computation)

computer-to-computer "Communication", 11

conceptual foundation studies, relevance of, 2

conceptual grounds, nature of, 2

constituent(s), category(ies), 163, 230(fn 215) (structures of,

152); of communication, 116; composition, 222(fn 182); and illocution(s), 120; sub-action structures, 135; structurings, 155, 156, 163, 231(fn 220, 222)

contextual situation convention, 123, 124, 129, 130, 133, 137, 138, 139, 143, 147, 150, 154, 160, 217(fn 155), 222(fn 177)

context dependence, 98, 137, 138, 139, 160, 161

context dependency(ies), 76, 83, 98, 138, 139, 160, 161, 197(fn 10), 199(fn 28), 226(fn 197); temporal, 211(fn 111)

context sensitivity, 51, 91, 98, 113, 114, 119, 130, 154, 161, 170, 178, 205(fn 61), 214(fn 136)

control, concept of, 8

control structure, 2, 3, 8, 11, 12, 16, 22, 23, 24, 26, 27, 33, 40, 46, 47, 48, 52, 55, 56, 59, 64, 89, 94, 102, 182, 198(fn 17, 22), 199(fn 24); and action system, 89; equivalence of, 203(fn 56); location of internal error, 199(fn 22); microgenesis, 102; process, 8

convention(s), 29, 30, 38, 66, 69, 70, 71, 72, 73, 74, 75, 76, 77, 78, 81, 82, 83, 84, 85, 88, 90, 91, 92, 96, 97, 98, 99, 115, 126, 127, 128, 129, 138, 139, 140, 144, 145, 156, 158, 166, 183, 184, 191-92, 204(fn 58), 205(fn 61, 64), 217(fn 155), 219(fn 164), 220(fn 169), 224(fn 187), 225(fn 192, 193); apperception of, 76; communicational apperception of, 115; coordination of, 127; established by agreement, 29; established by habitualization, 30; explicated by Lewis, 76-77; goal, 81; hierarchies of, 72; implicit existence of, 73; implicit participation in, 88; institutionalized, 69, 70, 71, 72,

255

74, 76, 78, 83, 90 (and coordination problems, 78; hierarchy of potentiality, 71; and
society, 90); and interaction,
74-75; and language, 72; linguistic, 154; linguistic system,
156; as object, 158, 183; as
objects of conventional illocutions (locutions), 158; as objects of illocutions, 158; and
occasion meaning, 82; posterior, 143; prior, 143; reflexivity of, 73; situation convention inclusions, 126; and
social structure, 78; supra-
individual level of, 132, 140,
143; transformations on, 156
conventional acts, 91, 92
conventional meaning, 83, 89,
112, 128, 129, 130, 131, 132,
133, 135, 137, 138, 139, 140,
142, 144, 145, 146, 147, 148,
149, 153, 158, 161, 162, 170,
171, 172, 207(fn 85), 208(fn
87), 219(fn 164), 224(fn 172,
173), 221(fn 176); apperceptions, 141, 146; complete, 132,
137, 138, 139, 142, 145, 152-
53, 155; computation of, 140,
149; conflation of, 161; decontextualized meaning, 161; differentiation within, 153; incomplete, 132, 137, 139, 145,
153; linguistic situation convention, 146; nature of, 138;
potential-situation-image
aspects of, 149; procedure,
139, 140, 144, 146, 149; semantic structuring definition
of, 146; specifications of, 147,
151; subdivision of, 155; transformation, 145, 163
conventional meaning scheme(s),
132, 148, 149, 150, 151, 152,
153, 154, 168, 181-82, 184, 227

(fn 205, 206), 230(fn 215), 231
(fn 222); linguistic, 146, 149, 152,
154; linguistic system, 150;
strategies, 228(fn 210); structures,
152, 154
conventionality, 100; supra-individual, 144
conventionalization, 143
conventionalized structures, 144
conventionalized structuring, 146
conversational cooperation principle,
166; and language games, 167
conversational maxim, 166
coordination alternatives, 230 (fn 218)
coordination problem, 66, 69, 71,
72, 73, 75, 77, 78, 83, 96, 98,
120, 191, 192, 204(fn 58, 60),
207(fn 81); interpersonal, 145,
205(fn 61)
constructivism, 39
correspondence theory of truth, 214
(fn 133)
cross-typified "gesture," 150

deception, 91, 209(fn 92), 216(fn 149)
decomposition, 120, 121, 122, 126,
131, 150, 153, 154, 179, 180, 181,
213(fn 129), 215(fn 142), 216(fn
146, 147), 218(fn 159), 222(fn 180,
181), 222-23(fn 183), 227(fn 201);
decontextualization of, 181; into
incomplete meanings, 143-44;
linguistic, 150, 153; of meaning,
222(fn 181); of minimal significances into constituents, 120,
122; productive, 181; structure,
135, 230(fn 214); subminimal,
170, 179, 180, 181; types of, 150
decontextualization, 160, 161, 180,
181; of context-dependent differentiations, 159; of context-dependent transformations, 159; conventionalized, 180; decompositional conventionalized, 180, 181;

256

of illocution differentiations,
161; of referencing procedures,
180; of representation differentiation, 161
deicticness, 160
deictic locution, 221(fn 173)
definition of the situation, 31, 42,
69, 70, 73, 76, 84, 92, 94,
96, 120, 121, 123, 127, 144,
158, 166, 179-80, 181, 204
(fn 58, 60), 206(fn 71), 206
(fn 72), 207(fn 84), 218(fn 160);
cooperative, 166
demand mode, 178
description(s), 103, 104, 105,
106, 107, 118, 143, 144, 164,
165, 184; and explanation,
103-4; partial, 164, 201(fn 43)
descriptivism, 3
development(al)(ly), 98, 99, 100,
101, 201(fn 42); constraints
on, 182; language (see language); social, 182; stages,
32, 33, 40
developmental psycholinguistics,
14, 34, 37-38, 39
differentiation(s), 146-48, 151,
156, 160, 179, 181, 225(fn
196), 226(fn 197); apperceptive, 155; context-dependent,
147, 159, 160; decontextualized, 160; functional, 145,
146; of functional position,
147-48; functional relational,
148; relational, 147; of the
representation, 168-69; structural, 147
distress call system, 98

effect, categorization by, 124,
125; transformational, 135,
219(fn 164)
egocentrism, 74, 205(fn 67), 207
(fn 79); perspective-level, 206

(fn 68), 207(fn 79)
emotion(s), 27; interactive model
approach to, 197(fn 8)
encoding models, 159-60
encoding rules, 159
epiphenomenal presence, 177, 178
error, -corrected, 109, 110; criteria of, 104, 105, 106, 107;
-sensitive, 109, 110
ethnomethodology, 86, 202(fn 48),
206(fn 70, 73)
evolution(ary), 98, 99, 100, 122,
210(fn 103); cultural, 100
exchange mode, 178
explanation, 103, 104, 106, 211(fn
112), 212(fn 118); and description,
103, 104
explicit instrumental presence, 177-
78
existential phenomenology, 170
expression, internal private, 87
extensionalism, 201(fn 39)

falsification, 106
floor apportionment, 127
focus, 227(fn 199)
force, 158, 160
formal logic, 117, 118, 226(fn 197)
formal operations, 101
frame(s), 54, 55, 56, 146, 199(fn 19),
200(fn 34, 35), 201(fn 43); apperceptive, 132; consequent, 140;
observational, 224(fn 191); posterior situation convention, 140;
subject, 140, 146, 149, 154; situation convention, 163; transformation of, 150
functional autonomy 96, 97, 102
functional efficiency, 151-52
functional position, 147-48
functional power, 132-33, 134, 150,
180, 221(fn 175); computational
surrogate, 134
functional predication, 180

functional type(s), 147
functionally autonomous (system), 103, 211(fn 110)
functionally relevant context(s), 149

game, concept of, 191; coordination problem, 191; zero-sum, 191
game theory, 77, 191
genetic evolution, 100
goal, attainment of, 232(fn 229); categorization by, 124-25; computation, 183; differentiations of action systems, 156-57; image, 103; of prelocution, 125-26; proximal, 124, 125
goal communication (see communication)
goal convention (see convention)
goal definition(s), 89, 90, 97, 101, 103, 109, 110, 113, 124, 148, 155, 156, 179, 183, 184, 190, 206(fn 76), 213(fn 127, 128, 129), 232(fn 227); ontological level of, 97; and prelocutionary systems, 113; and situation image, 110
goal-directed systems, 108-10, 154, 177, 178, 200(fn 30), 214 (fn 136); aspects of, 109; modes of, 110
goal meaning (see meaning)
goal representation, 209(fn 88)
goal significance (see significance)
goal space(s), 99, 101, 102, 103, 107-8, 110, 111, 208-9(fn 88), 211(fn 110), 213(fn 127), 220 (fn 169)
goal structure(s), 135
grammar(s), 105, 106, 109, 168, 170, 194, 207(fn 82), 229(fn 212), 231(fn 223); and action

systems, 108; category, 163; functional, 168; Montague, 163; phonological component of, 105; semantic component of, 105; study of, 170; syntactic component of, 105, 212(fn 120)

habitualization, 30, 38, 69, 70, 72, 100, 151, 227(fn 203); original, 150-51; and situation convention, 69-70
habitualized, 100, 167
heuristic-algorithm distinction, 213 (fn 125, 126)
hypothesis generation, 104, 175, 197-98(fn 11), 199(fn 28)
hypothesis testing, 33-34, 38, 104, 151, 175, 199(fn 28), 227(fn 204)

iconic resemblance, 126
idealization, 3-4
identity(ies), 97
illocution(s), 90, 91, 92, 93, 94, 95, 96, 97, 98, 99, 100, 101, 113, 119, 120, 121, 122, 123, 124, 125, 126, 128, 129, 137, 150, 157, 158, 159, 160, 168, 177, 178, 210 (fn 98, 103), 216(fn 146, 149, 151), 218(fn 163), 219-20(fn 169), 225 (fn 192); categorization of, 124-25, 128; conventional, 101; epiphenomenal, 120; indirect, 124, 217(fn 157); and linguistic acts, 101; nonconventional, 158, 210 (fn 96), properties of, 119-20; strict (pure), 120, 128, 131, 150; transformations, 126
illocutionary act, 89, 90, 91, 93, 158, 194; Austin's, 158
illocutionary capability, 98
illocutionary goals, 97, 99, 101, 127; internal structuring of, 127-28; point of an, 127
illocutionary implicatures, 124

action system, 89, 103, 157; analysis of, 102, 103, 106, 112; as basis of communication, 28; coding rules, criticism of, 21; coordination problems, 78; decontextualized, 160; definition of, 6, 83, 134, 168; development of, 38, 179, 182, 210(fn 104); emergence of, 174; evolution of, 210 (fn 104); and expression of thought, 86, 87, 161, 168, 170; formal, 8, 160, 185, 223 (fn 183), 225-26(fn 197); formalization(s) of, 101, 211(fn 108); foundation of, 98-99; function of, 87; functional approach to, 168; games, 166-67, 169, 174-76, 178, 180, 181, 182, 232(fn 226) (lattice structure, 174, 175, 176, 177, 178, 179, 182; pedagogical, 175-76; procedures, 179; productive decomposition, 181; propositional, 181; transformational view of, 169; Wittgenstein and, 41, 42, 167); Gendlin's view of, 173; genesis, 98; grammar, 105; Heidegger's conception of, 171-72; institutional perspective on, 90, 106; instrumental function of, 41, 42; learning, 197-98(fn 11); locutionary systems, 101; mathematical, 185; and meaning, 4, 173-74; Merleau-Ponty's conception of, 172; and mind, 65; and model theoretic semantics, 112; nature of, 168; object of, 64, 65, 66, 90, 94, 202(fn 48); and object permanence, 99; phenomenological approach to, 170; philosophy of, 34-35; and pro-

ductivity, 93; quasi-, 83, 100, 207 (fn 83); relationship between truth and, 214(fn 134); rule-governed games and Wittgenstein, 42; Saussurean conception of, 172; situation conventions, 111; social communication-based models, 87; social transformation nature of, 171; and society, 90; study of, 170; syntax, 105; systems, 108 (construction of, 98; productive, 93); thought expression model of, 86-87, 168; thought-expressive function of, 41, 42, 86, 168; truth and falsity of, 112

lattice, 182; and language acquisition, 174, 179; and language games, 176; structure of, 176-77

law of effect, 176-77

learning, 33, 34, 38, 48, 151, 226 (fn 197)

lexical items, 135, 138, 147, 151, 153, 154

lexical types, 147

"lexicality", 222(fn 183)

lexicalization(s), 153, 156

linguistic act(s), 89, 90, 92-93, 98, 99, 100, 101, 102, 133, 134, 135, 137, 138, 146, 149, 153, 154, 155, 163, 229(fn 212), 230(fn 217); constituent meaning structuring of a, 153-54; conventional meaning of, 138; indirect, 135, 137; locution, 159; meaning of, 163; structure of, 155

linguistic capacity, 106-7

linguistic competence, 104, 105

linguistic computational ability, 149

linguistic computations, 148-49

linguistic performance, 105

linguistic productivity, 132

linguistic system(s), 64, 91, 97, 98, 100, 101, 109, 128, 131-56, 163, 164, 181, 184, 209(fn 93),

219(fn 166), 222(fn 176), 225(fn 195), 227(fn 204), 228(fn 210), 231(fn 223), 232(fn 224); as action system(s), 135; category grammar, 163; constituents of, 149; decomposition of, 222(fn 180); development of, 150-51; form of, 108; functional organization of, 151; goal-directed, 154; and hierarchical meaning scheme, 150; institutionalized, 101, 108; nature of functioning of, 156; ontogenesis of, 151; productive, 132-33; productivity of, 137, 146

linguistics, 3, 34, 35, 37, 39, 168, 196(fn 1); basic assumptions of, 11; definition of, 3; developmental psycholinguistics, 14; essential subject matter of, 37; prescriptive approaches, 3; problem of circularity in definition of, 4

locution(s), 90, 91, 92, 95, 97, 99, 100, 101, 102, 113, 120, 128, 129, 130, 138, 140, 148, 150-51, 152, 157, 177, 209 (fn 96), 210(fn 103), 219(fn 164, 165), 219-20(fn 169), 220 (fn 170), 221(fn 172), 221-22 (fn 176), 225(fn 195); action system, 99; apperception of, 148; construction of, 101; conventional meaning of, 130-31, 138; and illocutionary systems, 97; indirect, 130; institutionalized, 100; and language, 102; linguistic, 177, 178 (utterance, 152); possible, 222(fn 179); and situation conventions, 95; strict (or pure), 131, 144, 146, 149; vocal, 210(fn 106)

locutionary act(s), 89, 90, 93, 133, 158-59, 194; linguistic, 133

locutionary cognitive capability, 210 (fn 106)

locutionary implicatures, 130

locutionary systems, 97, 101, 129, 133; context-dependent, 160; productive, 101, 209(fn 93)

locutionary type, 131, 138, 221(fn 174)

logical positivism, 10

machine configurations, 131, 141

machine theoretic structures, 140

machine theory, 2, 6, 8, 45, 140, 185-90

meaning(s), 4, 6, 41-42, 79-86, 108, 119, 121, 122, 123, 126, 128-29, 130-31, 133, 134-35, 137-38, 149-50, 158-59, 161-62, 171-73, 184, 195-96, 207(fn 78), 208 (fn 87), 218(fn 163), 222(fn 182), 232(fn 225); and apperceptive representation, 84; Bennett's conceptualization of, 161-62; change theory of, 173; complete, 131, 138-39, 140, 149, 150, 151, 153, 155, 163, 227(fn 201), 230(fn 214) (linguistic, 155); complex, 230(fn 214); constituent, 135, 137, 139, 153-54, 222(fn 181, 183), 228-29 (fn 211) (lexicalized, 155); constraints on, 82-83; conventional, 83, 223(fn 183), 225(fn 194, 195), 229(fn 213) (instantiation of, 150; invoked, 146); decomposition of, 120-21, 135; decontextualized level of, 161; experiential, 173; felt, 231(fn 219); goal, 80-82, 84-85, 87, 89, 123, 124, 126, 132, 133, 134, 135, 137, 154, 156, 160, 161, 171-72, 208(fn 87), 220(fn 169), 222(fn 177) (conventional indirect, definition of, 130; indirect, definition of, 124; external structuring, 126; indirect, 124, 130, 217[fn 157], 220[fn 169], [conventional, 130, 220[fn 169]];

linguistic presupposition, 135; and linguistic transformations, 132; representational, 161; utterer, 208[fn 87]); Grice's model of, 195; implicit full (decontextualized), 161; inadvertent, 162, 217(fn 156); incomplete, 131, 132, 137, 139, 140, 141, 142, 143-44, 145, 149, 151, 153, 162, 184, 227 (fn 199), 230(fn 214) (conventionalized structurings, 145; double context dependence, 138-39; linguistic situation conventions, 143, 144; possibility of, 143; procedures, 142, 143; specification of, 153); indexical presupposition, 123; institutionalized, 153; intended, 131, 208(fn 86); intended-to-be-understood, 207(fn 80); irrelevant, 207(fn 85); lexical, 134, 135, 137, 138, 139, 151, 153, 154 (differentiation of, 151); lexical category, 179; linguistic, 164; maximally decontextualized, 169; natural, 85, 195; non-natural, 85, 195, 196 (differentiation between natural and, 85); occasion, 82, 83, 85, 111-12, 122, 130-31, 133, 161, 162, 169, 171, 208 (fn 87), 220(fn 171), 232(fn 226) (conventionality of, 143; locutionary, 130; relationship between conventional meanings and, 131); ontology of, 161-62; potential, 85; prior, 171; structure, 170; sub-Gricean conditions for, 162; sub-minimal, 137; transformational, 139; utterance, 217(fn 155); utterer understood, 208(fn 87); word, 172

meaning-language relationship, 173
meaning scheme (see "conventional meaning scheme")
memory, 62, 113, 188, 189, 211(fn 111), 214(fn 134, 136); context with, 113; passive, 188; situation, 214(fn 136); warehouse model of, 62
meta communicational systems, 122
metalanguage, 101, 209(fn 90), 211 (fn 108)
metasystem, 101
microgenesis, 98, 102, 132, 134
mind, 5, 7, 8, 9, 11, 30, 31, 65-66, 86, 93, 94, 202(fn 48), 208(fn 87); changes in underlying assumptions, 7-8; characteristics of, 8; classical approaches to, 7; control structure process and, 8; and language, 65; as object, 65, 93, 158, 168, 197(fn 9), 208(fn 87)
modal(s), 163
Moore machine, 186, 198(fn 13)
morpheme, 222(fn 183)
motivation, 26-27, 33, 53, 200(fn 30); and knowledge, 26-27; and trajectories, 52
motivational selections, 52

networks, 54, 55, 56, 57, 137, 146, 200(fn 29, 34, 35), 201(fn 43); transformational, 137, 149
nonconventional (natural) structures, 150
nonpreparatory processing, 62-63

object(s), 25, 35, 36, 37, 57-58, 59-61, 65-66, 93, 94-95, 97, 101, 102, 117, 118, 121, 124-25, 150, 152, 169, 200(fn 37), 202(fn 46), 224(fn 185), 228(fn 210); and action systems, 65; aspects of an, 200 (fn 37); categories of, 124; complexity, 93; deformable, 200(fn 37)

263

(shapes of a, 200[fn 37]); external structuring of, 125, 126, 128; interactive model of, 25; internal structuring of, 125, 127, 128; permanence of, 40, 50, 99; physical, 48, 57, 60, 65, 70, 94, 95, 125, 145, 201 (fn 38), 202(fn 46), 210(fn 97), 215(fn 139); proximal, 65, 119, 124-25, 208(fn 87); schemes, 57-58 (elements of, 200[fn 37]); of transformation, 13-14, 15, 29, 30, 31, 35, 36, 37, 38, 94, 95, 161, 197(fn 9); translatable, 200(fn 37) (locations of a, 200[fn 37])

observation(s), 103, 104, 106

ontogenesis, 98, 102, 132, 134, 149

ontology, 3, 81, 84, 161, 162

output(s), 185-87, 189

parallel channels, 230(fn 217)

partial descriptions of sets of possible worlds, 164

partial ordering, 153, 221(fn 175)

pedagogy, 175, 176

perception, 40, 62, 63, 172; and apperception, 62; differentiation of, 224(fn 190); Merleau-Ponty's view of, 172

perceptual, 48, 76, 79, 118, 199 (fn 20)

perceptual apperceptions, 79, 118, 208-9(fn 88)

perceptual relevancies, 152

perceptual system, 208-9(fn 88)

performance, 212(fn 117, 118)

perlocution, 157-58

perlocutionary act, 157-58; as fulfilled communication, 157

person, concept of a, 205 (fn 61)

perspective level, 81

phatic acts, 159

phenomenological sociology, 13

phenomenology, existential, 170

philosophy of language, 34-35, 39

phonetic acts, 159

phonology, 213(fn 124)

phylogenesis, 98, 102, 134

picture models (see "knowledge")

play, 87, 122

pragmatics, 14, 36, 86, 105, 106, 107, 108, 165, 212(fn 119); and semantics, 108

pragmatism, 11

predicate(s), 117, 122, 146, 147-49, 150, 168, 179, 216(fn 145); specification of, 149, 150

predication, 168, 169, 179, 180, 181; functional, 180; from transformational perspective, 168-69

prediction, 211(fn 112), 212(fn 122)

prelocution(s), 90, 91, 93, 94, 95, 96-97, 98, 99, 100, 118, 119-20, 122, 125-26, 127, 128, 137, 157, 158, 177, 178, 210(fn 98), 218 (fn 159), 219-20(fn 169); cognitive, 98; conventional, 92; and decomposition, 122; genetic, 210(fn 105); innate, 98, 99; points of, 125-26; strict, 120, 210(fn 98), 216(fn 149)

prelocutionary act(s), 89-91, 93, 96, 98, 120

prelocutionary action system(s), 90, 91, 93, 95, 98, 99, 100-1, 107, 108, 113, 118, 119, 210(fn 102), 215(fn 137), 216(fn 147), 218 (fn 161)

prelocutionary capability, 98

prelocutionary communication, 114

prelocutionary goal, 126, 127, 128

prelocutionary system, 118; properties of, 113

preparatory processing, 62

prescriptivism, 3

presupposition(s), 75, 123, 129,

147, 155, 156, 159, 160, 161, 169, 181, 190, 197(fn 10), 198 (fn 12); apperceptive, 84, 85, 116; aspects of interactive knowing systems, 132; assimilation to control structure, 22; assimilation to (structural) isomorphism, 17-18, 19, 59, 161; context, 146; by interactive implicit definition, 161; of context, 116; epiphenomenal, 139-40; functionally valid, 142; genetic, 98; interactive, 22-23, 25, 181; interactively functional, 181; and isomorphism, 17-18, 19; linguistic situation conventions, 131; logical adequacy of, 228(fn 209); natural conventional form, 145; non-conventionalized, 145; representations of, 143; of a situation, 121-22

representational categories, basic, 58; derivative, 6

representational organization, 50, 51, 201(fn 42)

representational structural types, 145

representational structure (or element), 145, 146, 149, 152, 153, 171, 200-1(fn 37); principles of, 149

request mode, 178

rhetic acts, 159

role(s), 97

rule, of construction transaction, 189; post production, 226(fn 197)

satisfiable incrementation, 164-65; computations of, 165

scaffolding, 175

scheme(s), 45, 55, 56, 57, 58, 59, 62, 132, 137-38, 140, 141, 143, 144, 146, 147, 148,

149, 151, 152, 169; cofunctional, 224(fn 190); conventional meaning, 132, 149-50, 227(fn 200); object (see "object scheme"); procedural, 131, 149; representational, 145, 169; transformational, 227(fn 198)

selection pressures, 175, 176, 177

self(selves), 97, 127, 182

semantic(s), 13, 35, 36, 86, 105, 106, 107, 108, 112, 165, 212(fn 120); encoding truth condition concept, utilization of, 165; lexical, 36-37; and pragmatics, 108

semantic features, 162

semantic structure(s), 132, 146, 149, 150, 151, 152, 153, 154, 155, 156, 162; and conventional meaning scheme(s), 149

semantic structural categories, development of, 152

semantic structuring, 131, 144, 146, 149, 150, 151, 152, 153, 155, 156, 179, 180, 181, 184; of representations, 153

semiotic extension, 228(fn 207)

sense, 160

sensory-motor period, 40, 201(fn 41)

sentence(s), 164; organization of, 37; truth value of, 34-35

servomechanism(s), 45, 52, 56, 93, 99, 101, 109, 110, 111, 117, 156, 180, 181, 190, 209(fn 88), 213 (fn 126, 132), 215(fn 141), 225 (fn 191); goal-directed problem-solving, 156

significance(s), 79-80, 81, 83, 91, 92, 114, 115, 116, 117, 118, 119, 120-21, 123, 127, 128, 131, 134, 137-38, 139, 207(fn 78, 79), 209 (fn 92), 215(fn 143), 216(fn 147), 218(fn 163); apperceptive, structure of, 81; constituents of, 116; conventional, 91, 209(fn 92); decomposition of, 118, 120-21;

goal, 79, 80, 84, 89, 114, 115, 126, 215(fn 141), 220(fn 169); as meaning, 128; minimal decomposition into constituents, 120; pragmatic presuppositions of the, 114

situation(s), 67, 68, 69, 70, 71-72, 73, 75, 76, 77, 81, 87, 89, 91, 93, 96, 103, 109, 110, 113, 114, 115, 117-18, 121, 122, 124, 125, 126, 129-30, 131, 133, 141, 142, 144, 145, 149, 166, 171, 200(fn 33), 202(fn 54), 215(fn 140), 217 (fn 155); characterization, 67-71, 72, 202(fn 53), 204(fn 57); class of potential, 64, 65; extra-conventional, 127; interpersonal, 67, 68, 69, 70, 71, 72, 75, 128, 158; recurrent, 76; representation of the, 121, 122, 145, 163

situation convention(s), 6-7, 66, 69, 70, 71, 72, 73, 74, 75, 80, 81, 82, 83, 85, 87, 88, 90, 91, 92, 93, 94-95, 96, 97, 98, 99, 101, 102, 111, 113, 119, 120, 121, 122, 123-24, 126, 127, 128-29, 130, 131, 132, 133, 134, 135, 137, 138, 139, 140, 141, 142, 143, 144, 145, 147, 150, 155, 156, 159, 160, 162, 166, 167-68, 169, 171, 172, 177, 179, 181, 182, 204(fn 60), 206(fn 69, 72), 208 (fn 87), 209(fn 94), 210(fn 106), 216(fn 148, 149), 216-17(fn 151), 217(fn 155), 218(fn 163), 220(fn 170, 171), 221(fn 172, 173), 222 (fn 177), 223(fn 184), 224(fn 186, 187, 188), 227(fn 202), 229 (fn 211), 230(fn 214), 232(fn 224); attribution of, 139, 141, 148, 216(fn 148); boundaries

of, 126; context(s) of, 137, 138; contextual, 226(fn 197); contextualization, 224(fn 188); conventional, 217(fn 155); conventional meaning computation, 140; current, transformation of, 159-60; as definition of the situation, 69; epiphenomenal, 120, 150, 216(fn 150); frame, 140, 141, 154; goal, 155 (external structuring of, 126; internal structuring of, 127); Grice's conversational maxims, 166; and habitualization, 69-70; and illocutionary systems, 99, 119; indexical presuppositions, 123; indicators of representations in, 169; and institutionalized convention, 70; and language, 83; linguistic, 131, 142, 143, 144, 146, 149, 153, 183, 184, 229(fn 213), 231(fn 221) (and appropriate semantic structures, 146; and incomplete meaning, 143; representational principles of, 144); and linguistic acts, 134; and linguistic systems, 131; and locution, 130-31; of maximal communicative cooperation, 166; and meaning, 80; as objects, 94-95, 128, 143, 168; posterior, 130, 220(fn 171); presuppositions, 123 (of meaning, 123); prior, 145, 146, 154, 155, 219(fn 165), 220 (fn 171) (contextual, 165); representation, 140, 145 (of a situation, 121); representational structures, 152; and society, 90; transformation(s) of, 101, 105, 131, 142, 143, 180, 209-10(fn 96) (by locution, 101); usefulness of, 95-96; utterance, 105

situation image, 5, 43, 45, 46, 47, 48, 49, 50, 51, 52, 53, 54, 55, 56, 57, 58, 59, 62, 64, 66, 67,

68, 69, 73, 74, 75, 76, 77, 79, 80, 81, 82, 83, 84, 85, 89, 92, 94, 103, 109, 110, 111, 112, 113-14, 115, 116, 120, 121, 125, 126, 130, 132, 134, 137, 138, 139, 141, 142, 144, 145, 146, 147, 148, 149, 152, 155, 169-70, 173, 179, 180, 181, 183, 184, 198(fn 17), 198-99(fn 19), 199(fn 24), 201 (fn 43), 203(fn 56), 205(fn 61, 63), 205(fn 67), 206(fn 76), 213 (fn 127, 128), 215(fn 138, 143), 216(fn 144, 148), 217(fn 152), 220(fn 171), 221(fn 172), 224 (fn 185), 228 (fn 210); and action systems, 62, 103; attribution, 140; beginning for differentiation, 148; characterization, 214(fn 135); and communication significance, 114; component, 147 (of convention, 73); constituent, 180, 181, 182, 203(fn 55); context specifications, 117; and convention, 75; and effective communication, 113; and egocentrism, 74; and environmental redundancies, 53-54; explicit, 47, 48, 49, 50, 51, 57, 198(fn 19); and goals, 110; implicit, 47, 51, 198(fn 19); of the individual, 67; and interaction, 48-49; and interactive potentialities, 71; interactively compatible, 203(fn 56), 206(fn 68); interactively equivalent, 203 (fn 56); and internal structuring, 125; and interpersonal situations, 67; modification of, 116; and object schemes, 58; potential, 132, 149; potential for error, 112; products, 139; relation to world image,

74; relevancy structures, 54; representation of, 179; and schemes, 56; and situation convention, 94; structure(s), 145, 148; and trajectories, 76; transformation of, 144, 169-70; and world image, 112
social development, 182
social-institutional perspective, 28-29
social reality, 78, 86, 87; transformation of, 86
society, and language, 90
sophists, 101
sociolinguistics, 86, 202(fn 48), 206(fn 73)
sociology, 184; phenomenological, 13
space(s), 117, 200(fn 29), 201(fn 38); of available actions, 156; of possible (or available) illocutions, 159; of possible (or available) representations, 159; representations of, 60; transformation of, 118
specification(s), 146-47, 149, 151, 155, 181, 184, 211-12(fn 116), 216 (fn 144, 147), 227(fn 199), 231 (fn 222), 232(fn 228); of aspects of a conventional meaning transformation, 163; context, 116-17; by differentiated incomplete meanings, 151; in terms of form, 147; lexical, 231(fn 222); by relational position, 147
speech, 12
speech act(s), 13, 156, 173, 174, 181, 194, 217(fn 157); and productive decomposition, 181
squishes, 231(fn 222)
state (of the machine), 185-89; change of, 186
state of the system, 45, 46, 55, 113, 141, 148, 198(fn 16)
state transitions, 186, 188, 198(fn 16); structures, 188, 189

state transition diagram, 186, 187, 189
stoics, 10, 11
string, 187; of inputs, 187
structural types, 147
structures-of-the-whole, 40
subject of the characterization, 126
subject(s) of communication or of significance, 117, 122, 126, 146, 147-48, 149, 150, 179, 216(fn 145)
subjects, specification of, 148, 149, 150
subject-predicate differentiation, 170
subject-predicate structure(s), 118
subroutine, 150, 178, 190, 209 (fn 88) (servomechanism, 178)
sufficient speaker homogeneity, 211(fn 116)
supra-individual(ness), 72, 73, 81, 88, 132, 140, 153, 208 (fn 87)
symbolic play, 87
symbolic interactionism, 202 (fn 48)
syntax, 36, 86, 105, 106, 107, 108, 168, 170, 179

task context, 156
task definition, 183, 184
tense, 164
terms, 168
time, 117, 201(fn 38)
thought, 87
trajectory(ies), 65, 76, 199(fn 28), 214(fn 136), 228(fn 210); ability to compute, 99; computation of, 50; influence of object schemes, 58; loco-motor and perceptual, 200 (fn 29); situation, 48, 49, 51-

52; situational, 50; and situation images, 51-52; temporal, 49, 76, 99, 143, 211(fn 106); transforma-tional, 50, 130, 199(fn 28)
transformation(s), 101, 109, 111, 118, 123, 124, 125, 126, 130, 131, 141, 144, 145, 146, 148, 149, 151, 155, 161, 170, 200(fn 33); con-ventionalized, 129; decomposition of, 152; of functional focus, 148; interactive, 94, 125, 128, 172; institutionalized, 130; linguistic, 152 (stages of, 142); locutionary, 130; on possible world truth con-ditions, 164; representational, 156; subdivided, 155
transformation models (see "com-munication")
transformational, 48, 76, 79, 118, 152, 161, 199(fn 20); power, 133
transmission models (see "communi-cation")
transmission perspective, 35, 36, 37, 38, 39, 87, 159, 161, 168, 179
tree structure, 154
turn-taking, 170, 174, 176, 178
turing machine, 151, 221(fn 175)
typification, 70, 71, 72, 76, 219 (fn 164), 224(fn 186); minimal action, 135; and situation conven-tions, 70
typified, 70, 83, 91, 126, 150

understood (communication), 79, 80, 83
understood convention, 81
understood meaning(s), 80, 82, 83, 84, 85, 171; audience, 208(fn 87)
understood significance, 79, 80, 83, 84, 114, 115
unintended meanings, 84-85, 208 (fn 87)
update(s), 227(fn 199)

utterance(s), 80, 82, 83, 84, 85, 87, 89, 105, 107, 108, 119, 121, 122, 123, 124, 129, 131, 133, 134, 135, 137, 138, 139, 153, 155, 156, 159, 160, 161, 162, 164, 166, 170, 172, 179, 194, 195, 196, 207(fn 78), 208 (fn 87), 217(fn 155), 218(fn 160), 230(fn 214), 232(fn 225); acceptability of, 105; computation of complete, 132; construction of complete, 152-53; context of an, 164; context-dependent transformational conventional meaning of, 161; conventional, 138; conventional indirect, 130; conventional meaning of the, 138; decomposed conventional meaning of the, 135; and decomposition, 122; decomposition of, 121-22; decomposition of minimal occasion meanings of, 122; decontextualized, 160; and felt meanings, 231(fn 219); fulfilled, 82, 84, 85, 208(fn 87); as illocutionary act, 89; incomplete, 132; in-context, 197(fn 10); indirect, 124, 129, 217(fn 157), 219(fn 166) (conventional, 130); linguistic, 87, 134, 135, 152, 154, 155, 159, 183; linguistic, composition of, 134, 135 (computation of, 154, 155; differentiation of, 159; and goal meaning, 154; locution, 152; presuppositions, 135; transformation of, 159); and locution, 128, 129; locutionary, 133; as locutionary act, 89; and meaning, 122-23; perception of, 123; potential implicatures of an, 164-65; potential presuppositions of an, 164-65; and pragmatics, 108; presuppositions, definition of, 123; type, 83, 89, 90-91, 105, 128-29, 159; understood, 83, 84

utterer, 80, 81, 84, 85, 196

values, interactive model of, 26
verbal scheme, 173

words, development of, 38
world image, 5, 43, 45, 47, 48, 50, 51, 52, 53, 54, 55, 56, 58, 59, 62, 64, 66, 67, 72, 77, 78, 87, 109, 110, 111, 112, 126, 138, 146, 147, 148, 149, 152, 155, 183, 198(fn 17), 199(fn 24), 200 (fn 29), 202(fn 45, 51, 52), 203 (fn 56), 205(fn 63), 214(fn 135), 224(fn 190), 228(fn 209, 210), 231(fn 221); and action systems, 54; characterizations, 214(fn 135); construction of, 59; and control structures, 52; and environmental redundancies, 53-54; and goal-directed systems, 108-9; and goals of interaction, 52; and indices, 49; of the individual, 67; and interaction, 48; and object schemes, 58; potential, 132; potential for error, 112; as representational, 112; scheme, 147; servomechanism structure of the, 202(fn 44); and situation image, 110; and transformational procedure, 147

zero-sum games, 191

ABOUT THE AUTHOR

MARK H. BICKHARD is Associate Professor of Educational Psychology at The University of Texas at Austin, where he has been on the faculty since 1972. His interests focus on formal models of psychological processes, ranging from knowing, learning, emotions, and consciousness, to developmental stages, personality and psychotherapy, and microsociology.

Dr. Bickhard's publications have appeared in Human Development, Genetic Psychology Monographs, and the Journal of Individual Psychology.

Dr. Bickhard holds a B.S. in Mathematics, an M.S. in Statistics, and a Ph.D. in Human Development, all from the University of Chicago.